"A book that will infuse you with hope . . ."

"Don Hawkins is God's agent of hope; not the world's kind of hope, but real hope, biblical hope."

— Woodrow Kroll

"One of the most indelible principles of Christian living is that for Christ we should never give up. I know of no man who in his life and in his writings illustrates this better than Don Hawkins."

— Frank Minirth, M.D.

"*Never Give Up* provides a massive dose of hope designed to turn despair into perseverance."

— Josh McDowell

"Don Hawkins has a unique ability to share deep but down-home truths that all of us can grasp. His years of doing talk radio have clearly taught him the needs of the Christian of the '90s. Don's experience and ability meet in his latest book, *Never Give Up*. You will find this book easy to read, gripping and life-changing."

— Dawson McAllister

NEVER GIVE UP

DON HAWKINS

To Elizabeth

[signature]

Isaiah 40:31

First printing, June 1992

19,000 printed to date—1995
(1155-082—5M—75)
ISBN 0-8474-1704-2

Unless otherwise noted, all Scripture quotations are the author's paraphrase.

Printed in the United States of America.

Acknowledgments

To my wife Kathy, life and ministry partner, best friend, who is the living epitome of what this book is all about ... to you, dear, I dedicate this effort of encouragement—for you have truly encouraged me.

To Karen, Donna, and Brent, who have also faced adversity and not given up ... to my parents .... to Kathy's parents—none of whom gave up on me—a special word of appreciation.

To the board of *Encouragement Communications*—the *Life Perspectives* radio program ... to Jerry Bostick, Paul Klassen, Don Sapaugh, Pam Moize, and, of course, to Kathy—how can I adequately thank you for your encouragement and perseverance?

To Ruth Franks, skilled typist, word processor, cheerful of spirit, thank you—the many hours of typing and retyping those hundreds of manuscript pages will not go unnoticed.

To our friends at the *Here's Life* family, my genuine appreciation. And my thanks to Les Stobbe, friend for many years, to Dan Benson, diligent editor, to Ron Durham, who did the copy-editing, to Anne, Karla, Marilee, Priscilla, and others of the staff who have assisted on this project.

To all who, over many years, have encouraged me regarding this project, I offer a heartfelt thanks.

Foreword

By ROBERT S. MCGEE

**Founder and President,
Rapha Hospital Treatment Centers**

*H*ope is absolutely essential to life. Our spiritual, emotional, and relational health is dependent on a sense of hope, and is a result of our hopefulness. The will to persevere is often an outgrowth of hope. Yet, true hope is too often elusive for many of us.

All of us experience losses, and most of us can readily identify times in our lives when we felt hopeless. Perhaps death, disease, divorce, distance, or debt have suddenly or gradually thrown us into despair. We feel threatened, and out of control; we feel that *nothing* can get us through.

But often we have a very different problem. We have our hope fixed on the wrong person, status, or thing. "If I could only get that job," we might believe, "then I'd really be happy." "If he loved me . . . ." "If I could only look as good as he . . . ." "If I could please him . . . ." These—and countless other "if only's"—are rooted in objects or people who cannot meet our needs. They are false hopes, but we cling to the belief that they will give us what we desperately want. And we are bitterly disappointed when they don't. Then we experience the other extreme: forlorn hopelessness. If we harbor false hopes, these losses often lead to bitterness, not hope.

Then there is the age-old problem of simply running out of hope—of not persevering in hope, of allowing circumstances to dull the hope that once burned more brightly.

The Scriptures have much to say both about maintaining our hope, and about our true source of hope, Jesus Christ Himself. Certainly our salvation, eternal life, forgiveness of sins, and many other wonderful truths are sources of our hope; but ultimately these emanate from Him. He is the One who is supremely trustworthy in every circumstance and in every relationship in our lives.

In *Never Give Up,* Don Hawkins speaks out of the vast resources of his experiences as a pastor, speaker, and radio interviewer. He is a "real person" who doesn't gloss over the hard reality of life. But in seeing the realities, he looks to the Lord for true comfort and wisdom. In this insightful book, he gives us case stories from our contemporaries as well as from men and women in the Scriptures.

This book does not offer slick answers that comfort for the moment but later lead to heartbreaking despair. Don is willing to wrestle with the complications and difficulties of life . . . and to find Christ in the middle of it all.

I trust you will gain valuable insight and encouragement as you read *Never Give Up.*

"Find rest, O my soul, in God alone; my hope comes from him" (Psalm 62:5).

Contents

Introduction

$\mathcal{J}$t was the final day of the conference. Tomorrow morning we would board a plane to return to the United States. The dark clouds that rolled in across the German landscape from the north matched the mood of the missionary sitting across from me. "I've never been so depressed in all my life," he stated. "I've never felt this way before. I don't understand it. Things have gotten harder and harder. I'm ready to give up on the ministry. In fact, at this point I'm not even sure that I'm a Christian."

The occasion was a cool summer afternoon between sessions of a conference for missionaries north of Frankfurt, Germany. I had been invited to speak on the subject of burnout.

I responded to the husky young man who sat across from me wringing his hands. "Tell me, what's going on?" I asked. "What's happening in your life?"

"Don," he replied, "Everybody thinks I have it all together—even my wife. The missionaries I work with all seem to look up to me. They'd be shattered if I gave up.

"But I really don't. I'm just a shell of the person I used to be. I don't spend time in the Word anymore. I'm just going through the motions in terms of ministry. I'm shooting from the hip when I preach or teach. Financially, we're at the point of going under—and my wife doesn't even realize it!"

Emotion stretched his voice as he continued to express his personal pain. "To be honest, I've even thought of suicide at times. In fact, the idea of suicide is about the only thing that's seemed to give me any hope lately. I can't figure out why I'm continuing with this charade of ministry. I'm confused. I'm ready to quit. I've had it with myself, and with the people around me. To be honest, I've even had it with God."

As I listened to this respected missionary pour out the agony of his heart, I was struck with his pain and despair. "What can I say to this man, Lord?" I asked within myself.

Almost without thinking, I asked, calling him by name, "Why are you here? Why do you think God put you on this earth in the first place?"

My missionary friend—I'll call him John, which is not his real name—looked at me for a moment, then turned to examine the clouds and the German landscape.

He pulled his jacket up around him and said, "Quite frankly, I haven't thought much about that question for a long time. To be honest with you, I'm not sure I want to think much about it right now."

I replied, "I can certainly understand that. But let me encourage you to take a look at a passage that's helped me when I've been confused about why I'm here. You see, each of us probably feels confused about that at times."

WHY ARE WE HERE?

Together we opened a Bible to the Gospel of Mark. I suggested that he start with chapter 12, which describes some of the events just before Christ was crucified on the cross, and to begin reading at verse 28:

And one of the scribes came, and having heard them reasoning together, and perceiving that he had answered them well, asked him, Which is the first commandment of all? And Jesus answered him, "The first of all the commandments is: Hear, O Israel; The Lord our God is one Lord: And thou shalt love the Lord thy God with all thy heart, and with all thy soul, and with all thy mind, and with all thy strength: this is the first commandment."

Pausing, John looked up at me. With a sigh in his voice, he said, "I guess that's it. 'Love God with all your heart.'"

"Interesting, isn't it, John?"

"Yeah, and he didn't even say serve God or become a missionary."

"So do you think whole-hearted love for God is it?"

"There's something else here," John replied. He read on:

And the second is this, "Thou shalt love thy neighbor as thyself." After this, there is no other commandment greater than these.

At this point I summarized, "John, I'm convinced these verses contain the key to understanding why God put us here in the first place. They've helped me in some hard times, and they've helped people I know and have ministered to as well.

"John, I can identify with this young scribe. I think there are implications in what Jesus said to him for me. I really believe my major responsibility. . . ."

With intensity in his voice, John interrupted, "I don't want to think about responsibility. To be honest about it, I'm bitter with God. I don't know why He's let me go through some of the things we've experienced.

"Besides, I'm tired of people. Our fellow missionaries, my family. I don't feel like loving them—and I'm sure they couldn't care much about me, like this. In short, I've just flat given up."

I knew I didn't have any pat answers or magical formulas. I told John as much.

"John," I suggested, "Let me ask you to do two things before you give up on everything. First, take a concordance and look up all the passages in the New Testament that contain the words 'don't faint' or 'don't give up.' Spend some time studying those passages, and thinking about what they may mean to you.

"Second, look at what the Bible has to say about hope—not just the hope of the rapture, but hope in general. I'm convinced a lot of people—including Job, David, Jeremiah, and even Paul—felt like giving up hope. I think you could identify with them.

"I know you're close to giving up, too, John. But I certainly hope you won't."

I looked for John the next morning at breakfast, and as we left for the airport, but I didn't see him.

Back in Germany

Two years later, I returned to the same conference ground in the mountains north of Frankfurt, after a visit with missionary friends and a trip to what remained of the Berlin Wall. As I strolled across the conference ground, the sky was blue and the air was warm. But the sunny weather couldn't match the smile on John's face as we spotted each other across the courtyard.

After stowing my luggage away in my room, I came back down to the courtyard, sat down with John, and said, "Tell me what's going on. Are things better? Are they that different?"

John's reply was a bit surprising. "Well, yes and no."

I was puzzled. The smile on John's face, the sparkle in his eye, even his tone of voice, were in stark contrast to his mood at our previous conversation.

So I said, "Come on, John, what's going on? What's the difference?"

Grinning at me, he replied, "Do you remember those passages you encouraged me to study? The ones on not giving up? And the ones on hope?"

"Well, as a matter of fact," I responded, "I sure do."

John said, "They must have worked for you, too. They sure worked for me! Let me tell you, finances got even worse. In fact, right now, the dollar is at its all-time low against the German mark. Two of our best supporting churches have dropped us."

As I murmured appropriate words of Christian sympathy, my friend said, "Wait a minute, I'm not through. The engine in our vehicle blew up. I've been in the hospital twice over the past two years. And our young son had surgery that almost took his life."

"But you didn't give up hope, did you?"

Smiling, John replied, "No, my hope has actually been renewed."

IT HAPPENS TO THE BEST

You don't have to be a missionary, or be involved in vocational ministry to lose hope. Nor do you have to be a spiritual weakling. Losing hope can happen to the best and strongest among us.

Losing hope can impact us in every realm of life. In 1 Thessalonians 5:23, the apostle Paul refers to our whole being: "spirit, soul, and body." A loss of hope can affect each of these critical areas. Spiritually, it can leave you feeling bitter, and isolated from God. Emotionally, a loss of hope can leave you feeling lonely, empty, angry, and worried. Physically, a loss of hope can lead to disease, and even to death.

The Bible has so much to say on the subject of hope—in fact, it's often referred to as a book of hope.

Yet so frequently even those of us who know the Bible come to the place of losing hope—and at that point many of us simply give up. That's why hope must be persistent—and that's why my focus in this book is on *persistent* hope.

My purpose in writing this book is threefold: first, to help you *understand* hope. How did Job maintain hope in the face of incredible adversity? What technique did David utilize to regenerate hope when his life was filled with despair? How did hope rescue Jeremiah from the depths of despondency, as his country literally fell apart before his eyes? In what way did the truth of the Blessed Hope revolutionize the life and ministry of the apostle Paul when he faced opposition and incredible hardship?

Second, this book is written to help you *feel* hope, going beyond just understanding it. A number of modern-day women and men, like my friend John, have felt the depths of despair. Many have utilized God's re-sources and regained hope. Others have not. Their stories, told within the framework of biblical principles on hope, can help you relate emotionally both to hopelessness and hope itself.

Third, this book is written to motivate you to *choose* hope. Like so many other important ingredients in the Christian life, hope is, after all, a choice. You may be drowning, unable to swim, going under for the third time, and a friend on shore can toss you a life-saving buoy. However, you must choose between seizing the buoy, or sinking beneath the waves. It is my prayer that God will use this book to motivate you to make that choice of hope.

God wants all of us to fulfill those two purposes John and I examined in Mark 12—to love God whole-heartedly, and to love people unconditionally.

Without the essential ingredient of persistent hope, we can do neither. If we simply give up, it will not happen! With hope, however, it can. Whether you are a missionary like John, a pastor, a Christian worker, a Sunday School teacher, a businessman, a student, an executive, a housewife, or a factory worker; whatever your status in life, whatever your vocation, whatever your level of spiritual maturity, *Never Give Up* is designed to focus your attention on the only source of hope, Jesus Christ, and on His Word, which can help those who have lost hope regain it—and prevent those who haven't lost hope from doing so.

What causes us to give up? For that matter, what is <u>hope</u>—this quality that seems to be such an essential vaccine against giving up on life?

1

The Essence
of Hope

*H*ave you ever felt like giving up? Have physical pain, emotional conflicts, or spiritual difficulties ever left you feeling like just throwing in the towel? Has a project ever bogged down to the point where you were just ready to go ahead and pull the plug on it? Has a relationship soured to the extent that you were ready to terminate it—and perhaps even to terminate the other person as well? Has a ministry in which you were involved ever faced such obstacles you were ready to write it off?

If there is one thing that almost twenty years of pastoral ministry, plus a decade of Christian radio, have taught me, it's the certainty that one of Satan's most effective tools in derailing us is simply to plant the seeds of quitting in our hearts and minds, then sit back and watch them grow until they bring our growth, fellowship, and service for Christ to a screeching halt.

There was a time in my life when I thought I would never feel like quitting. I've always been a determined individual—some people, perhaps more realistically, refer to me as stubborn. Yet there have been times—particularly in recent years—when I've felt strongly like giving up. There were a number of reasons, many factors and definite stressors. But during this time, two realities gripped me. First, I was not exempt from feeling strongly tempted to give up. At times I desperately wanted just to go ahead and quit. To have failed to admit that I was susceptible to the temptation would have been sheer denial. But the second realization was equally strong: God did not want me to give up.

At times I felt like the Mississippi hunter described by Christian comedian Jerry Clower. While chasing raccoons one moonlight night, the hunter tangled with a wildcat in a tree, some thirty feet from the ground. "Go ahead and shoot up here!" the desperate hunter exclaimed to his companion as he struggled with the cat.

"I can't," came the reply. "I might hit you."

"Go ahead and shoot up here anyway!" cried the hunter as he wrestled with the wildcat. "One of us has got to have some relief!"

In the fast-paced world in which we live, how many of God's children do you suppose harbor feelings of secret exhaustion, struggle with the effects of burnout, and perhaps even feel suicidal at times? How many extramarital affairs have grown out of giving up hope on the marriage relationship? How many Sunday School teachers, elders, deacons, or faithful church members have just faded into the woodwork because they gave up? How many missionaries or pastors may even now be sitting down to draft that letter of resignation?

THE ANATOMY OF QUITTING

What causes us to give up? What is the missing ingredient when we feel the urge to quit? Austrian psychiatrist Victor Franckl was imprisoned by the Nazis in Europe. Franckl noted that some prisoners succumbed to the torture of prison camp and died sooner than others. In contrast, despite the horrors of imprisonment, others not only survived, but maintained an attitude of purpose in life. Franckl identified this as hope. Prisoners who lacked purpose lacked hope, and the will to survive.

In his book *Man's Search for Meaning*, Franckl, who succeeded Sigmund Freud at Vienna, identified hope as the ingredient which, when missing, produced "a deadly effect on man." As a result of his experiences in the Nazi concentration camp, Franckl contended that when people no longer have a motive for living, no future to look toward, they often give up and die. From his experience he wrote, "Any attempt to restore a man's inner strength in the camp, had first to succeed in showing him some future goal."[1]

Dr. Karl Menninger was perhaps the most highly respected secular psychiatrist in America. From his years of medical practice, observing patients, and training young doctors, Menninger pointed to the "prevalent mood of optimistic expectation about the future which we can perhaps call hope" as a key factor in the patient's recovery.[2] Dr. Menninger spoke of the hope factor as the "essential constituent of both treatment and teaching." Menninger described hope as "a kind of relentless and indefatigable pursuit of resolution and freedom. I would see in hope another aspect of the life instinct, the creative drive which wars against dissolution and destructiveness."[3]

Christian psychologist Dr. Gary Collins spends an entire chapter in his volume *Beyond Easy Believism* describing the importance of what he describes as realistic hope.[4] Collins defines hope as "the desire for some thing or some goal which we want but which is not completely within our power to obtain." He relates this basic definition to the routine of life: "The student hopes to pass an examination. The patient hopes to recover. The airline passenger hopes that the plane will not crash. Each of these experiences involves an element of uncertainty often mixed with anxiety, fearfulness or some expectation of what might happen." As Collins notes, "When people lose hope in their country, in their fellow human being, and in themselves, they begin to fall apart psychologically and sometimes spiritually."[5]

THE ANATOMY OF HOPE

What exactly *is* hope, this quality which seems to be the essential vaccine against giving up in life? The dictionary defines the verb "to hope" as: "to desire, with expectation of fulfillment. . . ." The noun "hope" is defined as: "desire accompanied by expectation of fulfillment; confident expectation of that which is desired . . . a cause of hopeful expectation."[6]

Most of us have a pretty good grasp of the ways we use the word hope today. We can relate to the anticipation of a bride-to-be who, upon receiving a trunk, renames it her "hope chest" and begins filling it with goods to become part of the new home. We can understand the feeling of a football team that goes into its two-minute drill, quarterback in shotgun formation, receivers spread across the field, moving to the offensive line without a huddle, anticipating that it will win the contest despite being down by a touchdown and a field goal, with a single time-out left.

We can all relate to the hope of Harry Truman, who, when confronted with banner headlines proclaiming "Dewey Wins!," still held out in the anticipation that he would become President of the United States; and sure enough, he did!

No doubt about it. Hope is an essential ingredient in life. From a theological perspective, Martin Luther is said to have declared that everything that is done in the world is done by hope; and Samuel Johnson claimed that "where there is no hope, there can be no endeavor."[7]

Throughout our lives we come face-to-face with hope—hope regarding finances, hope in relationships, hope in academic pursuits, hope in raising children, hope in overcoming illness—in short, hope of things getting better tomorrow—or at least the day after.

Focus on the Future

That's what hope is: *a positive expectation regarding the future.* And in that sense, biblical hope doesn't differ a great deal from human hope. Both are focused on the future. Both anticipate something positive occurring. Both provide motivation to persevere—in what may be a less than ideal present.

Menninger points to the importance of balance in hope, noting that "excess of hope is presumption and leads to disaster. Deficiency of hope is despair and leads to decay."[8]

Certainly there are times when, humanly speaking, it's time to give up hope. That was obviously the view expressed in a letter to "60 Minutes" and read on the April 1, 1990, edition of the program. An opinionated viewer wrote, in response to the reversal of the verdict of a convicted murderer: "Reversing guilt is one thing, but dead is dead, and no one has figured out a way to reverse that."

What a clear-cut example of where human hope and biblical hope part company! It was precisely this view-point that was being espoused in the first century city of Corinth, where critics of the apostle Paul's Christian teaching had concluded that "dead men stay dead—forever."[9] Yet the apostle argues strongly from the evidence of eye-witnesses—including himself—that the resurrection of Christ provides clear evidence that dead men live again. Apart from the eyewitnesses, we would conclude that Christ had not been raised from the dead. Our Christian faith is of no value. We have been duped into believing a lie. The present is marked by continued bondage to sin, and the future holds only a hopeless end.

Focus on a Fact

In sharp contrast to this hopeless end, the essence of Christianity is an endless hope—a hope based firmly on the fact that Jesus Christ rose from the dead.

It is often easy in the society in which we live to fail to reckon with the fact that much of our present is shaped by decisive events from the past. For example, I grew up in the South. Had not General Lee surrendered to General Grant at the conclusion of the Civil War, I might be living in a different country from my friends who grew up north of the Mason-Dixon Line. To take it a step further, had there been no Declaration of Independence and subsequent successful pursuit of the Revolutionary War, we might all have been raised under the British Crown! Significant past events have left their mark on our present.

We frequently talk about the shadow of the cross of Christ over history. Perhaps in some ways it would be equally accurate to talk about the shadow of the empty tomb. Both were central to Paul's proclamation of good news (1 Corinthians

15:3, 4). It is the resurrection to which Paul points in 1 Corinthians 15 as the ultimate evidence of victory over that final enemy we face—death—and as the motivation for remaining steadfast and unmovable, abounding in perseverance despite the difficulties of the present.

In essence, the Bible is a book of hope. The concept is woven throughout both the Old and New Testaments, as we will discover in the next chapter. Hope is cited by the apostle Paul in the magnificent conclusion to 1 Corinthians 13 as one of the three abiding cardinal virtues, the greatest of which is love. In fact, it seems upon careful examination of Paul's statement that his reference is not simply to hope in general (or for that matter to faith in general), but to the hope of the believer—a concept we will spend some time examining in a later chapter.

It has been well expressed that "There is a sense in which, whereas faith refers to the past and reposes on the cross of Christ, and love belongs to the present, hope looks ahead."[10] As Nigel Turner notes, hope "is centered in what God will do with us and with the world in days to come. Christian hope is always out in the front looking at something good which lies ahead. The Christian believer has hope for the life beyond."[11]

PEOPLE OF HOPE TODAY

It has been my privilege to see, during years of ministry, many people who were flesh and blood examples of men and women of hope. Some of them I have mentioned earlier; some I will introduce now. Others you will meet later in the pages of this book. All will spend eternity with Paul, Peter, and the author of Hebrews as our ultimate hope is fulfilled. These heroes of hope include:

- *Cleon,* who was diagnosed with two kinds of cancer—either of which would normally be terminal—but did not let the frightening reality of his medical condition hinder his continued missionary service or confound his hope and trust in God.

- *Melissa,* whose husband left her, his ministry training, and their children, to seek fame and fortune in the corporate world, but whose hope for his return was fulfilled after many years.

- *Marty,* a friend who faithfully served God for many years while waiting for the marriage partner God finally sent her way, and finally married when she was in her late thirties.

- *Nettie* and *Maxine,* who were both married to alcoholic, unsaved husbands. Both saw their hope of spending eternity with their spouses fulfilled just days before they became widows.

- *Melanie,* who had lost all hope in life after suffering sexual abuse in an alcoholic and dysfunctional home— but who was able to cling to faith and regain hope both in this life and in the future.

As I think of the many people I know who have evidenced hope by not giving up, I feel somewhat like the author of Hebrews must have felt as he came near the end of what we commonly refer to as Hebrews 11. Time would not permit to tell all the exciting stories of hope—that confident expectation that motivates us in godly fashion from the present into the future.

HOPE AND ITS CLOSE RELATIVES

A good counselor would not seek to understand nor help a counselee without finding out more about other family members. And it would be rare for a bridegroom to marry without getting to know the rest of the bride's family. When we defined hope we saw that the term has several close relatives. It will help us to develop at least a working acquaintance with these close verbal relatives of hope. They include:

Trust

We've already seen how Paul linked hope with trusting in Christ and trusting God. It's also interesting to note other things in which Paul trusted. He trusted that he would see the Roman Christians as he traveled (Romans 15:4). He trusted (hoped) that the Corinthians would understand what he had written to them regarding church discipline (2 Corinthians

1:15), and he hoped that he and the other apostles would continue to be those toward whom the Christians in Corinth would look for spiritual answers (5:11, 13:6). Paul even hoped Timothy would be sent to his friends at Philippi (Philippians 2:19), and that he himself would at some point be released from imprisonment (2:24). The apostle John used the term for hope or trust similarly (2 John 12, 3 John 14).

To exercise hope is to anticipate, and to trust. This is the essence of our responsibility toward God—to hope in Him, to exercise trust in Him. But as basic as this is, two biblical examples show just how difficult it is for us humans to exercise such trusting hope.

Case number one is Martha, a woman who would have been right at home in the twentieth century. Conscientious, hardworking, Martha was a "take charge" kind of lady—and she experienced significant difficulty with trust. From the New Testament record of her life, it seems that it was hard for Martha to trust people. For one thing, the house in which Martha lived with her sister and her brother was apparently in her name—"Martha received him [Christ] into *her* house" (Luke 10:38).

Also, it seems that it was hard for Martha to trust the judgement of others. She frequently gave people instructions—including the Lord! On three occasions, Martha rushed in where angels literally fear to tread. She gave the Lord unsolicited advice! Once she suggested that her sister stop wasting time listening to Him, and come help her with kitchen responsibilities (Luke 10:38-42). Again, she suggested that Christ should have arrived earlier in response to her brother's sickness. Then she actually tried to stop the Lord from having Lazarus' tomb opened (John 11:39)!

Most of all, it was hard for Martha to trust God. Her assertion to Jesus, "I know that he [Lazarus] shall rise again in the resurrection at the last day" (John 11:24) constituted a confession of trust. But the Lord used the word *pisteuo* (believe), rather than *elpizo* (hope) as He was gently attempting to point out to Martha that there was hope that her brother would live again that day, if she trusted Him (vs. 25).

Unfortunately, Martha didn't get the point—primarily because she didn't fully understand and trust Who Jesus was. Hope involves trust.

This same struggle can be seen in the entire band of Christians gathered in Jerusalem on one occasion during the early history of the church. James the apostle had been beheaded by King Herod, who had also imprisoned Peter. Herod's plans for Peter were no secret; he, too, was to lose his life after Passover.

The night before Peter was to die, the church gathered for an all-night prayer vigil. Sometime during the night, a knock was heard at the door. A young lady named Rhoda responded. Recognizing Peter's voice, she rushed into the group exclaiming, "It's Peter! It's Peter!"

To which the church, supposedly exercising their faith by praying, replied, in essence, "Don't disturb us. Can't you see we're busy praying for Peter? He's in prison. That can't possibly be Peter."

Perhaps in some sense they were exercising faith—but theirs was a faith void of trusting hope. You could hardly call their response anticipatory trust.

How frequently we identify with these early Christians. Struggling to raise our children, trying to deal with financial problems, attempting to plan for the future, we somehow have a vague hope that things will work out. But we haven't learned the kind of anticipatory trust that says, "Since God has worked out the answer to the greatest problem I have—sin—I can trust him to work out whatever future uncertainties I'm facing." (By the way, this is comparatively easy to write or speak about—and much more difficult to put into practice in daily life.)

Waiting

Waiting is an integral component of hope. This was the lesson Martha needed to learn as she expressed in frustration to the Savior, "Lord if you had been here, my brother would not have died." To Martha, Jesus was not in enough of a hurry. And, like Martha, we today become exasperated by waiting. We literally can't even stand to wait in a checkout line at the supermarket, to be placed on hold on the telephone, or to be tied up in rush hour traffic.

Some time ago a friend who is a professional Christian counselor encouraged me to take a weekend and do absolutely nothing. It took three suggestions on his part for me to finally agree. It wasn't that I didn't understand what he was getting at. It's just that for me, as it may be for you, it's difficult to do nothing, to wait. Yet intrinsic in the concept of hoping is a willingness to wait. Whether for renewed strength, for clear direction, for vindication, or simply for what the next day brings, waiting is a key part of living in hope. Such waiting is the antithesis of anxiety. Remember the words of Jesus: "Be not therefore anxious for the morrow, for the morrow will be anxious for itself. Sufficient unto the day is the evil thereof" (Matthew 6:34, ASV).

Endurance

In chapter 3 we will look at several significant statements in the New Testament that warn us not to give up. One of life's acid tests is the test of endurance. As a baseball fan, I noted the dramatic start by the Texas Rangers during the 1989 baseball season. Many of my friends and colleagues in the Dallas/Fort Worth Metroplex were convinced in early May that it was indeed "the year of the Rangers." Several months later, as August slipped into September, the Rangers had faded into the second half of the division, while the Oakland A's, who would ultimately become world champions, were disappearing into the distance. The Rangers just didn't have the endurance necessary to successfully complete the race for a pennant.

One of the most important concepts of Scripture is that of steadfastness, or patience. The word frequently translated patience, *hupomeno,* actually comes from two Greek words which, when taken together, mean "to remain under." Whenever I think of this word I'm reminded of a young man with whom I worked as a lifeguard in a Christian camp for several summers when we were teenagers. His name was Jimmy, and he was an incredible swimmer. One day he challenged several of us to join him in swimming across the lake on which the camp is located—underwater! Only one person in our group of self-acclaimed accomplished swimmers was able to make it all the way across the lake. Jimmy alone had the endurance of lung and the strength of arm and leg to meet the challenge. Steadfast hope involves utilizing God's resources to enable us to run with endurance the race set before us, with our eyes fixed on Jesus—our ultimate goal (Hebrews 12:1, 2).

Contentment

It seems absolutely foreign to the concept of hope in the New Testament to gripe, complain, grumble, or murmur about present circumstances. The word for content or contentment only appears six times in the New Testament. For one whose hope is set on God, contentment is possible in whatever circumstances, as Paul testifies from prison (Philippians 4:11). In one of the few mathematical formulas in Scripture, Paul reminds Timothy that godliness plus contentment equals great gain (1 Timothy 6:6); thus in this life we are to be content for God to supply our basic needs (vs. 8). An attitude of "This is enough for me" is an essential reflection of anticipatory trust in the Lord who promised, "I will never leave you or forsake you" (Hebrews 3:5).

Confidence

Four New Testament words reflect this concept. Paul uses *peitho* to indicate how strongly persuaded he is that the God who has begun the good work in the Philippians will continue to perform it until the day of Christ. The author of Hebrews challenges us to hold our *hupostasis*, or foundation, steadfastly until the end (Hebrews 3:14). Earlier he employs the third term, *parresia* (3:6), a word often translated boldness. And Paul asserts his confidence in the Corinthian believers in all his *tharreo*—courageous confidence in all things (2 Corinthians 7:16).

The apostle Peter, presenting the hope of eternal life on the day of Pentecost, drew on David's confident assertion, "Because I have set the Lord continually before me, I shall not be shaken. My confidence rejoices. My flesh shall rest securely in hope" (Psalms 16:9). Three thousand souls responded to this good news (Acts 2:26) as they personally placed their confident hope in the Lord.

THE POSITIVE POWER OF HOPE

One of the most confident, hopeful individuals I've met is an unusual man with a somewhat unusual name—Hilary. The president of a successful company and author of several best-selling books, Hilary is one of America's most respected businessmen. One evening I listened to Hilary describe, as he put it, "the shoes I've walked in."

"I was broke," he said. "I was despondent. I was without direction. During one five-year stretch I tried seventeen different businesses, most of which were unsuccessful. People might have termed me a wandering generality."

With a young wife and a newborn baby to care for, Hilary wasn't able to pay the $64 maternity cost. He had to go out and sell two sets of the cookware he was selling just to get his first baby out of the hospital!

A self-proclaimed failure, Hilary described his financial circumstances as "so broke that if it cost only fifty cents to go around the world, I couldn't get out of sight." But two things happened to reverse his feelings of hopelessness and infuse him with persistent hope.

See You at the Top!

First, Hilary met an individual named P. C. Merrell, who told him, "If you just believed in yourself and went to work on a regular schedule, incredible things would begin to happen." P. C. Merrell so motivated Hilary to believe in himself and his ability to sell, that in one year he went from an abject failure without confidence to finish number two out of 7,000 salesmen. The following year he finished at the top, setting records that stand to this day, over forty years later.

During the weekend of July 4th, 1972, Hilary and his wife invited two ladies to spend the holiday weekend with them at their home in Dallas. They were a friend named Ann Anderson and a lady named "Sister Jesse," whom they had met at a convention in Nashville, Tennessee. As a result of that weekend he spent listening to these two unlikely people, Hilary came to trust Christ personally. In his own words he says, "As a result of that weekend's experiences, I sold out lock, stock, and barrel to Jesus Christ."

Later, Hilary would write to his children, "The only thing we have today that is truly free is our salvation. It doesn't cost us anything. All we have to do is trust Jesus Christ as Lord and Savior..... And yet our salvation was not free. God paid a terrible price for it. He sent His only begotten son to earth as the supreme sacrifice for us. ... How grateful I am that each one of you has come to know Christ on a personal basis, and will spend eternity along with your mother and me, with Him. Love, Dad."[12]

Through these influences, Hilary was motivated to write two books that bear his more familiar name. The first, published in 1974, described the hope he regained in business. The second book explained the eternal and confident hope he obtained by becoming a Christian. Those books—*See You At The Top* and *Confessions of a Happy Christian*—are among a number authored by a man who is far better known as Zig Ziglar—a man whose unashamed and confident hope has been placed in the Lord Jesus Christ—and who consequently has become a living example of persistent hope—a man who never gives up.

2

Bible Definitions of Hope

I've had the opportunity to visit several foreign countries. Signs along highways, in airports, and even menu items, can be extremely confusing. However, I've discovered that looking at the root meaning behind certain key terms can add a great deal to our understanding and experience. For example, driving on the German *Autobahn* was much easier when I realized that the signs that said *Ausfahrt* actually meant exit. In England it made life much easier to know that the *loo* was the restroom. And of course, in Mexico, knowing the difference between *caballos* and *damas* is crucial in knowing which restroom facilities to use!

All this illustrates why it should be helpful to examine briefly specific terms the Bible uses to describe hope.

HOPE IN THE OLD TESTAMENT

The writers of the Old Testament did not have only one word that is translated hope, as is the case with the word *elpis* in the New Testament. Rather, the Spirit led them to utilize a veritable tapestry of terminology to give us insight into this important concept which can have such a profound effect on our lives.

Some years ago I asked a student to dig into the concept of hope in the Old Testament, to find out how many words were used. In response I received a paper detailing no less than ten Old Testament terms translated hope at some point or another. The *International Standard Bible Encyclopedia* notes that in the King James Version, "hope" (the noun and the verb) stands for some fifteen Hebrew words, nearly all of which in other places are given other translations.[1]

The extensive use of these terms shows that the lack of a specific word for hope does not indicate that the Hebrews undervalued this virtue. The life of almost every central individual in the Old Testament was marked to some degree by hope. Abraham, the father of Israel, hoped for years for a son. Undoubtedly Joseph, during his years of imprisonment in Egypt, hoped for liberation. Ultimately, he experienced a future that perhaps went beyond even his greatest hope. Who knows the full extent of Moses' hope during the forty years he spent tending sheep on the backside of the desert? Yet his hope ultimately came to fruition as he led Israel out of Egypt toward the promised land.

We could further chronicle this concept throughout the Old Testament history, from the hope of Caleb and Joshua for victory to David's hope for freedom from Saul's persecution, to the hope of the prophets for the nation to turn back to godliness, and the hope of such individuals as Daniel and Nehemiah for a return of Israel to her promised land.

An examination of the words translated *hope, trust,* and *wait* in Strong's and Young's concordances yields a fascinating array of verbal variety utilized by the Spirit through the writers of the Old Testament to help us understand what it means to persistently hope, wait, and trust.

Batach—Confidence

This word, with its noun form *betach*, is one of the most common words in the Old Testament. Fifty of its 181 occurrences are found in the Psalms.[2] Frequently translated *to trust*, its root idea is to be confident, take refuge, be bold, trust without anxious care. Interestingly, the Septuagint, the Greek version of the Old Testament, never translates *batach* with the word *pisteuo* (to believe), but with *elpizo* (to hope).

The three biblical narratives describing the challenge King Hezekiah faced from the Assyrian Rabshakeh are literally peppered with the word *batach*—it occurs twenty-three times in 2 Kings 18-19, Isaiah 36-37, and 2 Chronicles 32. If ever there were a situation where hope, boldness, and confident trust were demanded, Hezekiah faced it. Neither he nor his nation had any future, humanly speaking. Yet, as Scripture accurately records, and as the poet Lord Byron celebrates in "The Destruction of Sennacherib" it was precisely when circumstances seemed hopeless that God ultimately vindicated the hope of Israel and her king.

Chasah—Taking Shelter

A close verbal relative of *batach,* this word literally means to take shelter, as from a rainstorm (Job 24:8, Isaiah 4:6). The psalmist describes God as our rock of refuge (Psalms 52:7; 94:22). Like an eagle protecting its young under massive wings, God provides shelter for those who trust in Him (Ruth 2:12; Psalms 17:8, 36:7; Nahum 1:7). *Chasah* contrasts the insecurity and helplessness of even the strongest of men with the reliability of God; no one else is as trustworthy a refuge.

Hchul—'Painful Hoping'

The basic meaning of this word is to travail, to be in anguish, to be pained, or to fear. According to Hebrew scholars, its basic meaning is twofold: to whirl around in circular movements as, for example, writhing in pain or dancing for joy; or simply the emotion or sensation of pain.

This word is used of contractions of labor preceding childbirth (Isaiah 45:10), and of the anguish of those facing God's judgement (Isaiah 23:5, Jeremiah 5:3). This "painful hoping" is paralleled with quiet waiting by the prophet Jeremiah (Lamentations 3:26).

Ya'ash—Hope's Opposite

This term basically means to desist or quit. It describes those who are so desperate and despairing that they are without hope (Isaiah 57:10; Jeremiah 2:25, 18:12).

Yachal, Tohelet—Waiting

These frequently-used words describe the simple concept of waiting—something we all do in a variety of settings every day, and something extremely common in the culture of biblical days. For example, Noah waited seven days after the dove he sent out from the ark returned with an olive leaf (Genesis 8:12). These terms are frequently used of an expectation or hope which, when linked with faith or trust, results in patient endurance. Sometimes such hope is misplaced—for example, the prophet Ezekiel accuses the people of hoping for a positive fulfillment of the predictions of false prophets (Ezekiel 13:6)—predictions that were never fulfilled.

In contrast, the psalmist calls on Israel to "hope in the Lord" (Psalms 130:7, 131:3); He affirms God's word as the ultimate source of enduring hope (119:49, 81, 114; 130:5). This is not "pie in the sky"—Hebrew scholars describe such hope as "not a pacifying of the imagination which drowns out troubles, nor is it uncertain, but rather *yachal* is the solid ground of expectation for the righteous. As such it is directed toward God."[3]

The psalmist David uses this term at one of the lowest points of his life. Having found it necessary to flee Jerusalem, his beloved city and capital because of the rebellion of his son Absalom, David reminds himself, "Hope in God, for I shall yet praise Him for the help of his presence" (Psalms 42:5; see also 42:11, 43:5). Job employs the same word at the darkest hour of his life, crying out, "Though He slay me, I will hope in Him" (Job 13:15). Solomon uses *tohelet* twice in Proverbs to contrast the long-term hope of the righteous with the bleak expectation of the unjust (Proverbs. 10:28, 11:7).

Kasal—'Gut-level Trust'

The root of this word refers to that which is thick, or sluggish. In fact, *kasal* is commonly translated loins or viscera. Perhaps the idea of a "gut feeling" or "gut-level trust" comes from this term. Ironically, trust based on emotions can be foolish, and the root *kasel* is frequently translated foolish.

Such foolish trust is labeled evil in Ecclesiastes 7:25, in reference to the person whose way of life is focused simply on the present, without thought to the eternal. Positively, *kasal* is used in Job 8:14 and Proverbs 3:26 of confidence or trust in God.

Qavah, Miqveh, Tiqvah—the Woven Cord

The original concept from which these words are derived is of a woven line, cord, or cloth. It suggests that items which are woven together and stretched out can be trusted—in fact, *tiqvah* is used twice in Joshua 2 of the scarlet cord that Rahab of Jericho was to stretch from her window to show her hope and trust in Israel and in Israel's God.

The prophet Isaiah employs this term to suggest the ultimate source of renewed strength for those whose strength and hope is gone (Isaiah 40:31), and of waiting for God's completed judgement and eventual restoration and blessing of Israel (8:17).

Job uses the term to express his feeling that his hope had been uprooted like a tree (Job 19:10), and his life ended without hope (7:6). From Solomon's perspective, the righteous person who seeks wisdom from God has a positive future expectation, in contrast to the wicked, who has none (Proverbs 10:28; 24:14, 20). Ultimately, such hope for the future is rooted in the character and promises of God (Jeremiah 29:11). We can confidently "stretch out and trust," waiting upon Him (Psalms 62:5).

Sabar, Saber—Hope Based on Examination

The root meaning here is to probe, as in to examine, view, or inspect. The word could be translated "preview," as in Nehemiah's inspection of the walls of Jerusalem (Nehemiah 2:15, 16). The psalmist speaks of hopefully examining God's salvation (Psalms 119:166), of consequent obedience to His commandments, and of trusting anticipation of God's provision for daily needs (145:15). However, the Persians seeking to overthrow Mordecai and Esther's people, the Jews, watched and waited in vain for their demise (Esther 9:1).

Other terms for hope in the Old Testament include *tsapah*, to lean forward, peer, observe, or wait (as in Job 15:22); *chakah*, to pierce, or carve (Isaiah 30:18; Psalm 106:13); and *arnad*, to raise up, stand fast, abide, or endure; and to wait on or attend (Nehemiah 12:44; 1 Chronicles 6:32, 33).

From this wide range of terms employed by the writers of the Old Testament, several connections emerge. Hope is an expectation based on the future. Its basis is trust, and we are to trust in the God who is our refuge, rather than in men or ourselves. Since hope involves something in the future, we are to wait with patient endurance and confidence.

Sometimes such waiting is painful, and we may feel like quitting. These times test our patience, and our ability to cling to hope. Yet God's presence, refuge, and strength are available in the present to those who hope. And His positive purpose for us gives us every reason to confidently take refuge in Him, to scrutinize the hope He has made known in His Word, and to stretch out in trust toward Him, enduring life's present difficulties in light of the positive future He has provided.

HOPE IN ACTION TODAY

Perhaps at this point you feel like a person walking through a museum, examining old paintings by the masters, Renoir, Matisse, Rubens, or Van Gogh. You admire their beauty, but wonder about their practical relevance for today. Perhaps you think of persistent hope in the same way. It's fine for David, Abraham, Jeremiah, and Job—but they didn't live in an era of fax machines, satellite uplinks, twelve-lane freeways, and jumbo jets. However, I've discovered incredible numbers of people for whom persistent hope works just as well in the twentieth century as it did in the days of the patriarchs and the prophets.

Waiting for Love

My friend Scott was a Christian businessman committed to serving God faithfully. He worked hard, and advanced in his career. But his main expectation and hope was to find the right life partner. And he waited for just the right person—in fact, he waited many years.

After dating many girls over a seven-year period, Scott was convinced that he still hadn't met the right person. Finally, just after a significant career change, he met Jill at his new company.

Still his waiting wasn't over. The company had a policy against members of the same organization seeing each other socially. After what seemed an interminable wait, Scott decided it was time to ask Jill out to dinner. He did—but his waiting still wasn't over. Most men would have given up, but not Scott. It was almost a year before the two of them finally exchanged marriage vows. Scott's experience had taught him the importance of patient waiting, personal persistence, and trusting in Someone other than ourselves to bring hope to fruition.

Persistence in Service

Arthur Wiens and his wife Erma went through a similar experience. Arthur had served in Italy during World War II, then returned as a missionary in 1950. Three months later, Erma came as a missionary to Italy. As Arthur describes it, "The Lord brought us together in Florence. There were ten missionaries to Italy at that time, and God guided us to the same house. I was doing evangelism on the second floor, and she was knocking on doors on the third floor." Arthur and Erma met, became friends, and married. In 1953, they moved to Modena, the home of opera star Luciano Pavarotti.

It was during their second term that government officials sent terse instructions—they were to leave the country immediately. Following the suggestion of the American Consulate in Florence, the Wiens filed a letter of official protest with Italian officials. Back and forth the correspondence went—for two-and-a-half years!

Then another order arrived—leave the country within two weeks! When an official insisted that he sign an agreement ordering him to leave, Arthur replied, "God has called me here. I cannot sign." A night of intense prayer was followed by an appeal to Ambassador Claire Booth Luce at the American Embassy in Rome, but the order to leave the country stood. As Arthur put it, "By the end of the month we had to be out. We arranged to sell our car, closed our meeting place, got rid of our furniture. Then on Sunday, December 26, we said farewell to our believers in Christ.

"We came back home late that night, and there was a letter from the American State Department. We were to contact the American Embassy again." Finally, only hours from the time when they were to be forced to leave Italy, probably never to return, Arthur and Erma were told they could stay— but only until they again received notification to leave. Months passed before they finally learned that the decision had been made that they could stay. During that time, Arthur would tell the small group of believers, "Maybe it's my last meeting." But they persisted. They hoped. They prayed. They did everything they could do to satisfy the authorities— and they left the results in God's hands.

As a result, Arthur and Erma were able to establish the first evangelical Christian radio witness in their country of service. Many years later I had the opportunity of sharing the celebration that marked their fortieth anniversary of service to Italy—the longest term of any missionary serving in any country in Europe under their mission. For Arthur and Erma, persistent hope paid off.

Hope for a Change

Jim's sister Dorothy had no interest in spiritual things. A professed atheist, she even refused to discuss spiritual matters. Decades passed with no apparent crack in her armor. But Jim never gave up hoping that one day Dorothy would trust the Savior he had come to know as a young man.

Finally, years after most people would have given up hope, Jim and his son went to visit Dorothy in the hospital where she lay dying of cancer. Even at this point, when things seemed hopeless, Jim exercised faith. He stepped out of the room to pray while his son shared the gospel with Jim's sister once more. Jim's trust, persistence and confidence were rewarded when his son slipped out of the hospital room, smiling, and announced, "Aunt Dorothy just trusted Christ!"

HOPE IN THE NEW TESTAMENT

Elpizo (the verb) and *elpis* (the noun) are the Greek words translated "hope" in the New Testament. Originally, they did not have the kind of meaning the biblical record eventually gives them. They were terms marked by reserve, fear, and anxiety. Numerous uses by extra-biblical Greek writers indicate that *elpis* reflected either anxiety or cautious optimism about what is to be. At best, *elpis* spoke of a rosy look into a sad tomorrow.[4]

Euripedes once wrote, "Upon me and upon my children's children may *elpis* never come." Plato observed that everyone entertains opinions about the future which may be characterized as "expectations" *(elpis)*. These he divides into two categories: "That which precedes pain has the special name of 'fear,' and that which precedes pleasure we call 'confidence.'"[5] Plato's classifications provided a basis for two kinds of *elpis* in secular Greek—a nervous or anxious kind of hoping against hope, or an optimistic anticipation of good. As Sophocles put it, "Hope brings profit to some, emptiness to others, and no one knows how it will turn out."[6]

Plato tended to classify *elpis* in some instances as a mere assumption, or even presumption.[7] The historical narrative of Herodotus reflects a strong optimism when Maeandrius' brother thought it likely *(elpizo)* that Maeandrius would die. The same word is used in the tragedy of Sophocles, reflecting the despair of Teucer as he anticipated that a catastrophe would result from Ajax's going abroad.

What a contrast with the way the New Testament writers used *elpis*. Clearly, as noted in the *Theological Dictionary of the New Testament*, "The New Testament concept of hope is essentially determined by the Old Testament"[8]—not by its Greek background.

Of the Old Testament words already surveyed, *batach* is the most common to be translated by *elpizo* in the

Septuagint (Greek) version. The word appears some seventy-five times, generally referring to the idea of trust in God, His name, His loyal love, His Word, or His salvation. Perhaps the most representative rendering appears in Psalm 39:4, "Blessed is the man who makes the Lord his hope"; or Psalm 70:5, "You are my confident hope from my youth." *Elpis* is used only once in a negative context (Isaiah 28:19), where it carries the idea of fear.

Although the term is not as commonly used in the New Testament in the way in which we frequently use the English word hope, one such incident occurs in the Sermon on the Mount, when Jesus speaks of lending money to those from whom you hope or anticipate to receive it again (Luke 6:34). In a similar use, Herod hopes to see Jesus perform a miracle (Luke 23:8), and Paul hopes for a positive response by the Corinthians to an appeal for funds (2 Corinthians 8:5).

The term *elpis* literally springs into bloom in the record of the early church. In some sixty-one occurrences in the Acts and the Epistles, hope blankets these narrative like blue-bonnets covering a Texas field.

HOPE AND *THE* HOPE

The orderly mind might like to draw a careful distinction between the use of hope with the definite article ("the hope" of the believer, either of the rapture of the church or of the promised conclusion to which God will bring all things), and the general use of hope without the definite article. There is a sense, however, in which these two concepts tend to merge in the New Testament.

Hope in the New Testament is essentially a favorable and confident expectation involving the unseen or the future. It is so closely linked to the concept of trusting that we might term it "anticipatory trust." Hope, for example, involved *trusting in Christ* (Matthew 12:21; Luke 24:21; Romans 15:12); and *trusting in God* (2 Corinthians 1:10). Paul trusted the living God for future deliverance (1 Timothy 1:4), with hope thus serving as a motivation to continue present labors in God's service. Paul encouraged this same kind of hope in widows (1 Timothy 5:5); and Peter referred to it as anticipatory trust in

God on the part of the holy women of the Old Testament (1 Peter 3:5). Paul warned against hoping in uncertain riches (1 Timothy 6:17), in contrast to a confident and trustworthy hope in the living God.

Present Virtue, Future Reference

For the Christian, hope involves neither blind optimism, fear, nor doubt. The hope of the New Testament was not colored by the use of *elpizo* in the Greek literature of Plato, Sophocles, or other writers. As Turner observes, "For Christian believers, hope is a present virtue with future reference. It is their forward look at a distant goal."[9] Their highest hope is based on the joy of the appearing of the Lord Jesus Christ for His children (Titus 2:13; 1 John 3:3), the glory awaiting believers (Colossians 1:27), eternal life (Titus 2:13), and heaven itself (Colossians 1:5). The author of Hebrews describes hope as intrinsically related to faith, since faith provides the evidence of things hoped for (Hebrews 11:1). Such hope lies outside the realm of what is seen, yet is certainly no less real (Romans 8:24).

New Testament hope is a unique characteristic possessed by the believer, a gift not shared by those outside the family of Christ (Ephesians 2:12; 1 Thessalonians 4:13). Hope is a part of the calling shared by believers (Ephesians 1:18, 4:4), and is thus an intrinsic part of the gospel (Colossians 1:23)—when we believe the gospel, we place our hope in Christ (Ephesians 1:12). In terms of practical living, this hope is set before us as a prize awaiting the steadfast running of the race set before us (Hebrews 6:18, 12:13).

Such hope is at the core of the message proclaimed by the early church and its leaders. In the very first New Testament sermon preached by the apostles, Peter quoted the words of David, "My flesh shall rest in hope" (Acts 2:26). Paul, following Peter's advice to be ready to give an answer to those who challenged him (1 Peter 3:15), linked his mission with the hope of the resurrection in response to charges leveled against him (Acts 23:6, 26:6). The apostle was not hesitant to share with his former colleagues, the Pharisees, his new "hope for God"—the future resurrection (Acts 24:15), of which he wrote in detail in 1 Corinthians 15. For Paul, with his Jewish background, this was the ultimate hope of Israel (Acts 28:20).

What It's Like, What It Is

Peter, Paul and the author of Hebrews used several significant adjectives to describe hope. Paul initially identified it as *good* hope, given to us from God through the Lord Jesus Christ (2 Corinthians 2:16). He further described it as a *blessed* hope, providing a happy anticipation of the Savior's return (Titus. 2:13).

Peter described it as a *living* hope, founded on the empty tomb which the writer himself had witnessed as evidence of the resurrection of Christ from the dead. The author of Hebrews, who understood so clearly the details of the Old Testament priesthood, described the Christian hope as a *better* hope, centered in a new priesthood and a new and living way (Hebrews 7:19).

If we look, then, at what hope is like, it is good, it is blessed, it is living, it is better. If we look at what hope does, it provides the essence of our salvation (Romans 8:24). It produces endurance under testing as we await the return of Christ (1 Thessalonians 1:3). Hope provides an anchor for the soul amid the storms of life (Hebrews 6:18, 19). And it purifies believers even though they must, for awhile, live in a wicked world (1 John 3:3).

The construction of New Testament Greek shows that hope takes three directions, as indicated by three prepositions which follow its use. (1) Hope "unto" *(eis)*, means to hope *in,* as "hoped in God" (1 Peter 3:5). (2) Believers hope "on" *(epi)* Christ: "On Him shall the Gentiles hope" (Romans 15:12)—in other words, Christ is the ground or foundation upon which hope rests. And (3) we hope "in" *(en)* Him, as "We have hoped in Christ" (1 Corinthians 15:19). According to Vine, this structure indicates an emphasis on "the character of those who hope more than the action."[10] In other words they are "hoping in Christ" kinds of people—just like those we met in chapter 1.

Like the rescuers' message to the trapped miners, Jesus assures us, 'there is hope!'—if we never give in.

3

Jesus: Never Give Up Hope

*O*f all the stories told about Sir Winston Churchill, the legendary leader of England during World War II, perhaps none has had more impact than the account of his commencement address at Harrow, an exclusive prep school from which he had graduated. The war was just underway, and things weren't going very well for England.

After a long, flowery introduction, Sir Winston stood before the graduating class and the rest of the commencement crowd. Following stirring applause, and a lengthy silence, the crusty leader uttered these words:

> Never give in. Never give in. Never, never, never, never —in nothing great or small, large or petty, never give in, except to convictions of honor and good sense.

With that, Churchill turned and walked back to his seat. Few addresses—commencement or otherwise—have rivalled those brief words of reminder for their impact or their implications for life and ministry. We, too, must never give in, never give up.

That same message is prominent in the teachings of Jesus. Noted Bible scholar W. E. Vine defines two closely related New Testament terms often translated faint or give up. The first of these is the word *ekluo,* which means "to loose, re-ease (from *ek,* out; and *luo,* to loose); to unloose, as a boat string, to relax, and so to enfeeble. It is used in the passive voice with the significance to be faint, grow weary. . . ."[1]

Jesus used this term in referring to the multitude of over 4,000 people who had listened to His teaching for three days without stopping to eat. The Master refused to send them home "fasting, lest they faint [from *luo*] in the way" (Matthew 15:32, Mark 8:3.) The famous Greek physician Hippocrates used the term in a similar manner, referring to "a physical weakness."[2] It is an ideal way for Jesus to tenderly describe people who might lose heart, or give up.

IS THERE HOPE?

When I was a boy growing up on the west side of Birmingham, Alabama, my first job involved operating a Gulf service station on the old Bankhead Highway. The man for whom I worked was one of those unusual people who held two jobs. Mr. Haygood, a slim yet rugged man with dark, bushy hair and a soft-spoken voice, had been a miner all his life. By day he worked the coal mines of western Jefferson and eastern Walker County in northern Alabama. Then every afternoon when his shift was completed he came back to the service station which he had hired me to run during the day for the princely sum of $2 per diem, plus flats and wash jobs. From him I had the opportunity to learn both hard work and management skills. It was a great opportunity for a fifteen-year-old.

Often, late in the afternoon when business slowed down, Mr. Haygood would take two Hires root beers from the cold drink container and hand one to me. Then we would lean back against the front of the building in a couple of cane-back chairs. And as we watched the traffic whiz by on Highway 78, he would tell me stories about working in the mines.

Trapped in a Mine

One story in particular captivated my attention. A group of miners had been trapped in a cave-in. Volatile coal dust had exploded as a result of a spark several hundred feet below the ground, and this band of about a dozen men had been sealed off from the rest of the world. Although rescue efforts started almost immediately, the men who were trapped—several of whom had been injured in the explosion and subsequent collapse—had no idea what efforts might be taking place to reach them. Families were notified, and hundreds of people gathered near the mouth of the cave.

Rescue efforts continued throughout the night and into the next day—with no results. There was simply too much debris in the original shaft. Things looked hopeless. In fact, those directing the rescue weren't even sure which of several branch shafts off the main mine tunnel the workers might have been trapped in.

Dim Lamps, Dim Hope

Meanwhile, inside the little pocket where the dozen miners had been trapped, the batteries that operated their headlamps began to grow dim. What little food they had carried with them had long since been consumed, and their water was almost gone. At the point of giving up any hope of rescue, their spirits were even lower than their subterranean location. In desperation, one of the men came up with an idea.

Even though there was no light inside the mine, they remembered a metal conduit carrying electrical cords that ran across the top. Who could tell whether it had been severed in the crash, or whether sound vibrations might carry through? In the faint light of the one remaining head-lamp, one of the men climbed atop several boulders, and from a precarious perch used his hammer to begin tapping out a series of dots and dashes. His friends scoffed at him, "What's the use? You might as well give up. There's no hope for us."

However, one of his fellow-workers disagreed. "We can't just give up. We can't. Keep it up."

When the original miner grew tired, the co-worker who had encouraged him offered to take his place. Even though he didn't know Morse Code, he quickly picked up the ser-ies of dots and dashes that expressed their message with the following question:

"IS—THERE—HOPE? . . . IS—THERE—HOPE?"

Meanwhile, the rescue crew was literally at the point of

giving up. They had utilized both machine and hand tools, all without success. Attempts to sink a shaft parallel to the original mine shaft had been stymied by several layers of rock, which could only be moved by blasting—and the men knew that to set off even one charge of dynamite would probably remove forever any faint hope of finding their fellow workers alive.

As the rescuers prepared to pull back out of the mine, conceding defeat, one of the men—almost on impulse—leaned over and placed his ear to a piece of jumbled conduit sticking out of the debris.

"Listen!" he cried out to the others. "Everybody quiet!"

At first his fellow workers scoffed. Finally he persuaded them to listen. "I'm sure I hear something," he insisted, "I think it's a message. Does anybody here know Morse Code?"

One of the men volunteered that he did. He was rushed forward, and placed his ear to the tangled mass of conduit.

"Give me a pencil and paper!" he exclaimed. "I think it's them!"

Quickly he scribbled down the combination of dots and dashes being transmitted from the trapped miners.

"'IS—THERE—HOPE?' That's what they're asking," he said, "Is there hope?"

Immediately he took his hammer from his belt and began tapping out a reply. The response he transmitted differed from their question only in the word arrangement, for he tapped out: "THERE—IS—HOPE . . . THERE—IS—HOPE."

It was years later that I realized that the point of this story can be summarized quite simply in four words from the title of this chapter: *Never give up hope!*

One of the fascinating elements of the story involves the time lapse. It was several hours (and it must have seemed like days!) from the time the message of hope was transmitted and received, and the time when the miners were finally rescued. During that interval their limited supply of water ran out, and their batteries failed. They were plunged into absolute darkness; soon they lapsed into complete silence. Even though they knew there was good reason to anticipate being rescued, they continued to toy mentally with the prospect of giving up.

Finally a beam of light appeared in one corner of their dark prison. That pencil-thin beam of light reminded them of the message they had heard earlier, and they took heart.

Never give up!

BIBLICAL RAYS OF HOPE

There are several similar, strategically-placed messages in Scripture, reflecting differing circumstances but serving as divinely-inspired points of light for those of us who feel trapped in dark circumstances today. We read it in phrases variously translated, "Do not faint," or "Do not give up."

Grab Hold!

When I think of such admonitions, I'm reminded of the years I spent serving as a lifeguard at summer camp. One summer in particular it seems we had an epidemic of near-drownings. Now, any medical professional with half an ounce of sense will tell you that there's no such thing as an epidemic of near-drownings, but they certainly seemed contagious to those of us serving in that camp!

Several times during one particularly rigorous week I was faced with the prospect of either jumping into the water to pull someone out, or taking the recommended approach of tossing a lifebuoy attached to a rope. If the struggling individual were near enough, a lengthy pole extended in the person's direction would serve. When struggling people had the strength and presence of mind to grab hold of the buoy, the rope, or the pole, the lifeguard was able to pull them to shore. But when they would panic and relax their grip, we would have to enter the water to rescue them.

Now it's obvious that a drowning victim doesn't save himself or herself. That's why during all the time I served as a lifeguard, I never attempted to explain "swimming principles," or give swimming lessons to a person who was close to drowning. On the other hand, I saw clearly an important principle illustrated by this term in Scripture—that it's easier to bring rescue and hope to someone who hasn't completely given up!

Don't Cave In!

A second word used by Jesus in this connection, and discussed by W. E. Vine, is *enkakeo* or *ekkakeo*. A. T. Robertson, another respected Greek scholar, describes this word as "to give in to evil (from *en*, "in" and *kakos*, "bad"), to turn coward, lose heart, behave badly."[3]

This verb takes me back to a passage in Proverbs, and to my youth. Solomon advised, "My son, if sinners entice thee, consent thou not . . . My son, walk not thou in the way with them; refrain thy foot from their path" (Proverbs 1:1, 15).

Growing up in a Christian home I was frequently warned by godly parents of the dangers of peer pressure and the importance of having the courage and backbone to say No when given the opportunity to participate in evil activities. In fact, the activities in question did not necessarily have to be evil. Sometimes the enticement was simply to give up what needed to be done to pursue what was more enjoyable.

For example, late one evening during my first year in college, several friends invited me to join them for a late night round of bowling. I carefully weighed the options, thought about the amount of study I needed to put in for the next day's exam—and consented. Not only did my grade the next day suffer; we were all in trouble because we failed to get back to our dorm in time for curfew. Two facets of the term *ekkakeo* can be seen in this incident from my college career—I caved in, and it turned out badly!

Let's look at the way Jesus used these terms as "beacons of hope," then examine their relevance through the lens of some of God's servants from today.

JESUS: HOPE AMID URGENT NEED

Throughout his brief years of ministry, Jesus was constantly confronted with urgent needs. He was sensitive to the fact that physical needs could bring people to the point of fainting (Matthew 5:32, Mark 8:3). He was aware of urgent emotional and spiritual needs of people who were so harassed and helpless they were at the point of giving up because of their need for direction and support (Matthew 9:36).

But the classic use of the phrase "never give up" is in what we might identify as a "hinge verse"—"And he spoke a parable unto them to this end, that men ought always to pray, and not to faint" (Luke 18:1).

The setting is near the end of Jesus' ministry. In fact, Luke specifically notes that the discussion takes place as the Savior is enroute to face His crucifixion in Jerusalem (Luke 17:11). He has been face-to-face with many urgent needs—the spiritual needs of weak-faithed apostles (17:1-10), the physical plight of hopeless lepers (vss. 11-19), denial-fed harassment by the Pharisees (vss. 20, 21). Concerned that His diciples be prepared for troubled times ahead (vss. 22-37), Christ shares an important lesson from life—a parable designed to say, *Never give up.*

The particulars of the parable unfold in Luke 18:2-5. A wicked judge is confronted by a persistent widow who repeatedly asks for justice. The Savior's point, spelled out in verses 6-8, is that, though circumstances preceding His return will bring great adversity, God's people must never conclude that He will not hear and care for them. The point of the question in verse 8 is to underscore the point of the parable, explained in verse 1. When is it time to stop trusting? When is it time to give up? The answer, obviously, is *never*.

Of course Christ knows His frail followers. He understands that in a matter of days Peter, their acknowledged leader, will himself be at the point of giving up, and seeing his faith eclipsed (Luke 22:31, 32). So Jesus seeks to prepare them—and us—for the temptation to cave in under pressure.

Although the first application of the passage is that we should patiently wait and even endure suffering while praying for the vindication of God, the principle is a broad one. Certainly the book of Revelation reminds us how tribulation saints must patiently wait for God's vindication of their martyrdom (6:9-7)—and ultimately receive it (10:6, 7). When life seems unjust, when circumstances—and even companions—call upon us to collapse, to cave in, to give up, here are the two cardinal truths to which we must hold:

Always pray.

Never give up.

LARRY AND KERAL

On the evening of October 26, 1988, Larry and Keral, a young missionary couple serving in Marseilles, France, were near the end of a busy day. Keral went to bed about ten, her usual time. Larry, a night owl, continued to work in his upstairs office on a recently acquired computer.

About 3 a.m., Keral was suddenly awakened from a deep sleep to hear Larry crying out, "Keral, quick! I have to have help! I think I'm having a heart attack! This isn't a joke—you've got to do something quick!"

Jumping out of bed, Keral rushed to the phone, only to remember that she was in France. "What does a person do in France in an emergency? I had never thought about it before," she explained to me later. Finally, she called the French pastor with whom they worked, apologized for waking him, then asked what to do. She waited for what seemed like forever while he struggled to find his glasses. Then he gave her these letters to dial: "SOS MEDECINS" (meaning, in English, "SOS Doctors").

Quickly Keral dialed the number, then explained Larry's symptoms to the physician who answered.

"How old is your husband?" the doctor asked,

"Thirty-five," Keral replied.

The doctor pointed out that, in his opinion, even though Larry had the classic symptoms of a heart attack, he was too young to have one—so that could be ruled out. He added, "Take your husband's temperature."

'We Need Help!'

Keral replied, "I don't think that's necessary. This isn't a case of the flu. We need help right away!" But the doctor became indignant, insisting that she take Larry's temperature.

When she finally agreed to do so, Keral found Larry's temperature was an even 96 degrees, although he was sweating profusely. Calling the emergency medical number again, Keral found herself talking to a different doctor, starting over at ground zero. Later, when asked why she just didn't get in the car and take Larry to the hospital, Keral explained that the car was broken down. And, as she had been told, "You didn't just take someone to the emergency room in France." The doctor had to see the patient first, then admit them to the emergency room.

Finally the second doctor agreed to see Larry. "I guess I will come to the house," he said. After hanging up the phone, Keral checked on Larry, then anxiously went to the living room to watch the street for the doctor.

As she sat there silently in the early morning hours, thoughts raced through Keral's mind. "This must be a dream. This is weird. I must be crazy. Here I am in a foreign country. My husband is lying in the bedroom in trauma, perhaps dying, and I'm just sitting here doing nothing." But instead of giving up, Keral prayed—and she waited. At intervals she would call to the back of the house to see if Larry was still alive. Each time he replied weakly, "I'm doing the best I can."

After about an hour, Larry suggested calling his family in the U.S. to ask them to pray. As Keral told this story to me later, she said, "At this point we knew God was our only answer."

Another half hour dragged by after the call to the States. Finally, more than an hour after the initial call to the doctor, a car pulled up in front of the house.

'There's Nothing Wrong'

By this time, some of Larry's symptoms had subsided. The doctor listened to his heart, examined him, then said, "There's nothing wrong with this man."

Larry had four attacks that first week. Each time Keral called the doctors. Each time it took forty-five minutes or longer for a doctor to arrive. One doctor, a younger cardiologist, brought a battered little black box to attempt an electrocardiogram. Keral described her feelings upon seeing this equipment. "I felt like I had stepped back into time about forty years. The doctor couldn't get the machine to work, and kept pounding on it with his hand—that certainly didn't build my confidence."

Three weeks after the first attack, Larry was finally hospitalized. They still didn't know what was wrong with him—they just knew it was serious. In fact, according to Keral, Larry thought at this point he would never return to the house, to their home, alive.

The admitting process at the hospital took two hours. Finally, Larry was undressed and in bed. A few minutes later, a nurse came in to tell the old man in the next bed it was time for him to go to surgery. Although the man protested violently, he was nonetheless wheeled away forcibly. This frightened Larry greatly, since he had been having blackout spells. He became even more concerned when, two hours later, the old man was returned with a large surgical scar on his temple.

'Doesn't God Care?'

Larry's hospitalization was a tiring experience for both of them. "Our three-year-old daughter stayed with two different friends during the day," Keral said. I was becoming exhausted, worn down, and extremely frustrated. One night I came home feeling at the end of my rope. I asked, 'Where is God? Doesn't He hear my prayers? Doesn't He even care?'"

After nine days, Larry was in no better health; but he was released to go home. The next week, visiting the doctor's office, he was informed that he had a rare virus called Bornholm's Disease. This particular disorder was a virus that had not been seen in Europe for forty years, and for which supposedly there was no treatment. The virus would simply have to run its course.

The following Sunday Larry attempted for the first time in weeks to attend church services. After Sunday services at the fellowship lunch, he experienced an attack that was, if possible, even more severe than the preceding episodes. Unable to see the doctor until the following day, he was then told he had suffered food poisoning from the meal at the church.

But after two weeks of persistent attacks, sharp chest pains, extreme chest pressure, aching left arm, rapid heartbeat, sudden weakness, losing consciousness, shaking, and sweating, Larry and Keral finally heard the doctors admit what they had suspected all along—the medical professionals were stumped! Keral describes her feelings: "I became completely disheartened. We had spent six weeks with this debilitating illness, only to find out that the medical profession hadn't a clue as to what Larry had. Now what?"

Desperate conversations with missionary executives in the United States and with their French Field Director gave Larry and Keral a consensus that an immediate trip back to the States was in order. But how? Larry's doctors said he was too weak to make it back to the States alive on a commercial flight. They recommended a medical evacuation. The authorities told Keral this procedure would take forty-eight hours to arrange, and would cost $10,000. As Keral observed, "There was no way! I didn't have $10,000, and I felt like forty-eight hours was too long to wait. Larry was sinking fast. He was losing a pound a day in weight."

The mission reserved places for Larry and Keral, plus their three-year-old daughter, for a Friday morning flight from Marseilles to Zurich, Switzerland, then back to the States. While Keral was pouring herself into making all the arrangements for the return trip home, Larry experienced another attack—the worst yet. The doctors said there was no way he could return to the States; he would have to go back to the French hospital. "I just couldn't bear it," Keral said. "This was too much for me. I felt like we were so close to getting home and getting help. I went to bed exhausted, feeling hopeless."

No Tickets

But the next morning a strange thing happened. Larry awakened before Keral, with more strength than he'd had for a week. The couple dressed, took their daughter, and rushed to the airport. But the tickets weren't there—they had been sent to a travel agency by mistake! Their flight left at 7 a.m., and the travel agency wouldn't open until 9:30 a.m. The only solution was to repurchase the tickets on the spot in order to get to Zurich, then reclaim the remaining portion of the fare in Zurich during the layover.

After arriving in Zurich, Keral waited with their daughter while Larry went over to the ticket counter to try to make arrangements to be reimbursed for the remaining portion of their tickets. Although physically weak, he walked back and forth from counter to counter, trying to settle a misunderstanding between airlines. As Keral repeatedly glanced at her watch and at the wall clock in the terminal, she realized it was almost too late for them to make the flight.

Snowstorm from Heaven

Then, as Keral described it, "A very beautiful thing happened. Big snowflakes began to fall. Thank God. He sent a snowstorm—and our plane couldn't leave!"

For two hours, as the snow fell, Larry argued with the officials about the tickets. Finally, the tickets were approved, the baggage checked, and they were able to board the flight for New York. At this point the snow stopped, the runways were cleared, and the plane was able to take off.

Arriving in New York, Larry and Keral discovered they had missed their connecting flight to St. Louis because of the delay in Zurich. During the wait for a connection at Kennedy Airport, Larry experienced yet another attack. At this point, he was almost unconscious, and Keral was at the end of her rope. Somehow the couple was able to board the flight to St. Louis, where they were to connect with their flight to Wichita, Kansas—their final destination.

Incredibly, their departure gate at Lindbergh Airport in St. Louis was right next to their gate of arrival. There were only six passengers on the entire flight to Wichita, so Larry, Keral, and their daughter Jeannette were all able to lie down across three seats and rest.

Finally, safely home, Larry was able to obtain the skilled,

specialized medical help he needed and eventually regained his health.

What was the key to Larry and Keral's being able to stand up under all this strain? They had followed the instructions Jesus gave His disciples in Luke 18:1. They continually prayed, and they never gave up.

When they told me their story at a missionary conference where I was ministering, what impressed me most was the discovery Keral made the day after they arrived in the States.

Larry's sister, who lives in Oklahoma, told him that a number of missionaries in a retirement home near her house had met to pray on a Thursday night for missionaries who were still on the field. During this prayer time, they chose a name from a box with about 400 missionaries' names in it. Then they prayed around the clock for twenty-four hours for the one family selected.

That night, they had chosen Larry and Keral. With the time difference, they began praying Thursday night in Oklahoma—but it was Friday morning in France, just about the time Larry and Keral were getting up to leave for their flight. The group had prayed twenty-four hours. The flight took twenty-two hours. "I'm convinced that their prayers were what God used to get us home!" Karel says.

What kind of impossible circumstances are you facing? A mountain of financial obligations, a chasm of irreconcilable relational differences, impossible work responsibilities, unforeseen health difficulties? Whatever the circumstances, it's so easy to consider, then to follow, the course of giving up. But whatever the urgent need you are facing, remember Jesus' urgent counsel: "Always pray. Never give up."

Even with conflicts within and fears without,
Paul could say, 'I press on' because his
faith was rooted in a risen Christ.

4

Paul and Hebrews:
Hope in the Hard Times

*D*uring my ministry to Larry and Keral and their colleagues, I had the privilege of teaching what I consider to be one of the most neglected books in Scripture—2 Corinthians. I had been asked to speak on the subject, "a philosophy of ministry." Now, I'm not a philosopher—most people who know me would agree with that—but my experience in ministry has convinced me that the apostle Paul is the best source for any philosophy of ministry, and that 2 Corinthians contains perhaps the most complete description of both his philosophy and practice of ministry.

Significantly, during an extended discussion of the glorious ministry of the gospel which had been entrusted to him, Paul twice used the phrase "We faint not." As he wrote to Corinth, a church in which he had ministered, and yet a place from which he faced an attack on his credibility and ministry, Paul was under great personal stress. Later in the book he would explain that, "without were conflicts, within were fears" (2 Corinthians 7:5) His name, Paul, meant "little"— and some of his foes in Corinth were accusing him of being a spiritual lightweight—a wimp. Writing in response to these attacks on his ministry, Paul notes that the ministry itself is difficult, perhaps even impossible. "Who is able to achieve these things?" he asks (2:16).

Yet Paul was convinced that God had placed him in ministry (3:5, 6). And in view of his having received this call to serve from his Creator and Redeemer, the apostle concludes, "We must never give up" (4:1). From this passage, which is permeated with practical principles for effective ministry, we might summarize Paul's view like this: Ministry is glorious—but it's still extremely hard.

PAUL: DON'T GIVE IN

Paul viewed ministry as a treasure given him by God—yet a treasure to be exercised in a physical body which could accurately be described as "just a jar of clay" (4:7). Surrounded by adversity (4:8), Paul was nonetheless not ready to give in to the pressure. He frequently couldn't figure out what to do, but he didn't despair. Pursued by his foes, he had not been abandoned by God. Tripped up from time to time, he was nonetheless not permanently sidelined. His hope for the future was rooted in a confident, present faith in a risen, living Christ (4:13, 14). In view of this, Paul viewed adversity as an opportunity to experience God's grace and bring Him glory (4:15). He was able to repeat his earlier resolution: "For this cause we do not give up."

Countering Satan's Strategy

Why did Paul feel it necessary to repeat this strong statement? From my personal experience in ministry, and from talking with literally hundreds of pastors, missionaries and others involved in vocational forms of service, plus people from all walks of life involved in ministry, I'm convinced that one of Satan's major strategies is to convince us to just go ahead and give up. Paul is simply countering this strategy.

In high school I was convinced I needed to go out for football. Since these were the glory years of Joe Namath, Bear Bryant, and national championships for the Alabama Crimson Tide, I decided to try out for quarterback. I'll never forget those first horrible days of summer practice. They called them "two-a-days." Our coach, a burly man with the unlikely first name of Rudolph, tortured us unmercifully. We ran, ran, and ran some more. We did exercises that must have been invented by Simon LeGree and refined by Adolf Hitler. Finally, lying on our backs at the point of passing out, doing leg lift after leg lift with heavy football cleats on our feet, we we would hear our coach encourage us with these words: *"Think about the good things in life."*

Even though I was exhausted, it was all I could do to keep from laughing. "I think I see his point," I thought. "He's trying to get us to quit." At the end of practice that first day I discovered he had succeeded—a number of our teammates turned in their equipment.

I never became a football star; in fact I was never very good. But just by refusing to quit I was able to move up several notches, and finally get the opportunity to earn significant playing time—partially because a number of players either quit or were disqualified because they did not maintain the necessary grades.

Ministry is a lot like football. Certain elements are absolutely exhilarating—I'll never forget the first pass completion I threw, despite the fact that we only gained five yards. Other aspects are difficult almost beyond description. The bottom line is, we must never give up.

Two Ways to Keep On Keeping On

How can we manage to avoid quitting? Paul's concluding words in 2 Corinthians 4 isolate two important factors. First, he took life one day at a time. As he put it, "Although our outward man is perishing, yet the inward man is renewed day by day." That's how Paul could look at his difficulties as "light affliction which is but for a moment (working) for us a far more exceeding and eternal wait of glory." Paul followed the instruction of Jesus, who reminded His listeners in the Sermon on the Mount, "Do not be anxious about tomorrow, for tomorrow will take care of itself. Each day has enough trouble of its own" (Matthew 6:34). That's why the apostle could confidently leave his friends, the elders in Ephesus, and head to Jerusalem "not knowing the things that shall befall me there" (Acts 20:22). Unmoved by the uncertainty he faced, Paul remained committed to finishing "My course with joy, and the ministry which I have received of the Lord Jesus, to testify to the gospel of the grace of God" (vs. 24).

The second factor in Paul's commitment not to give up took his experience a step further. He not only lived day by day, but he lived in light of eternity. As he expressed it in 2 Corinthians 4:18,

> While we look not at the things which are seen but at the things which are not seen; for the things which are seen are temporal, the things which are not seen are eternal.

The word translated "look" in verse 18 is not the usual word with this meaning—rather, it is the Greek term *skopos*, from which we get our word "scope." This word is often used to describe two important tools—the telescope and the microscope. The microscope enables the biologist to focus on items which are far too small to examine with the naked eye. The telescope enables the astronomer to examine objects in the heavens which are far too distant to be closely examined, or perhaps even seen, unaided.

Every hunter who has pursued deer, elk, or similar big game has probably at one time or another made use of a "scope." On a hunting trip to Colorado several years ago, I remember aiming at a large bull elk across a canyon. I had him in the crosshairs of the scope. But I made the mistake of removing my eye from the scope, then trying to focus on him again. When I took my eyes off the scope, all I could see was the vegetation on the mountain across the way. Of course the elk escaped.

Some years later, on a combination ministry-and-hunting trip to Alaska, I had a caribou in the crosshairs of a scope mounted on a 30.06 rifle. The delicious caribou steaks we later enjoyed in camp, and which we brought back with us to Texas, were testimony to the fact that I had learned a lesson—keep your eye in the scope.

In essence, that's the key to not giving up in the face of daily adversity in ministry and in life. We must keep our eye focused through God's biblical "scope"—focused on eternity.

It may seem paradoxical to read the words "We look . . . . at things not seen." Yet that's precisely what happens when we use a telescope or microscope. Later Paul elaborates on this concept, describing it as "walking by faith, not by sight" (5:7). Throughout these verses, Paul's point is evident—for those who have placed faith in Christ, as the old song says, "This world is not my home, I'm just a-passin' through."

Our focus must remain on "the house not made with hands, eternal in the heavens" which will be ours when we are reunited with the Lord. Whether we join him by death or are caught up with other believers to "meet the Lord in the clouds" (1 Thessalonians 4:17), that's our hope. We shall see more of this element of hope in a later chapter.

Don't Faint!

It was this attitude of not giving up in his ministry, even in the face of adversity, that motivated Paul to write to the Ephesians, "I desire that you not faint at my tribulations for you, which is your glory" (Ephesians 3:13). In the context of the ministry committed to him, Paul expresses not only his personal commitment not to give up himself, but his encouragement to his colleagues who would read the Ephesian letter not to allow his adversity to discourage them.

His words to them remind me of a high school football game in which I was playing quarterback. It must have been about midway through the second quarter with the score tied when I took the snap, pivoted to the right, and handed the ball to our halfback, a young man named Cecil. Diving into the line, he was sandwiched between two defensive players. His leg was bent at an awkward angle. The bone snapped with a crack like a shot—I can remember to this day the sound of the breaking bone and his subsequent cry of pain. It took several minutes for him to be taken off the field, and our team was demoralized by his adversity. I think we wound up losing the game by about 30 points.

This is exactly what Paul doesn't want to happen to his colleagues at Ephesus—so he prays they will be strengthened within (Ephesians 3:14-16), given insight into their loving relationship with Christ (vss. 17-19), and reminded of God's ability "to do exceedingly abundantly above all that we ask or think according to the power that works in us," for His glory (vss. 20-21). In summary, Paul suggests that to walk worthy of our calling means not giving up in adversity.

Paul broadens this principle in Galatians 6:9, against the backdrop of his discussion of the fruits of the Spirit. Based on the grace of God, the apostle encourages healthy ministry to one another, fulfilling the law of Christ (6:1-6). Our willingness to invest in the lives of others, as Paul did, will lead to a harvest of spiritual blessing. The basic principle is that as we sow, so shall we reap (vs. 7). Furthermore, we can sow to the flesh, with corruptible results, or sow to the Spirit, with eternal results (vs. 8). Paul then applies this axiom to his Galatian readers: "And let us not be weary in well-doing, for in due season we shall reap, if we faint not."

The reminder is both practical and pointed. Weariness from the busyness of life can cause us to fail to seize ministry opportunities, both to believers and to the lost. When we grow wearied and come to the point of giving up, those opportunities are lost. Paul reminds us of the harvest of blessing, both temporally and spiritually, when we "faint not."

HEBREWS, HOPE, AND DISCIPLINE

Preparing this chapter on the biblical reminders to "never give up" surfaced yet another memory from high school days —hearing those dreaded words of the man who was both my football coach and physical education teacher: "Run the bank." Surely not even Simon LeGree could have come up with a more effective disciplinary tool.

The stands at our football stadium were on the sloping sides of a ravine. Circling the field was a path, known by everyone who had ever experienced the wrath of the coach as simply "the bank." When you "ran the bank," you circled behind and above the home stands, then dropped steeply down below the level of the football field into the ravine, only to climb back out of the ravine on the opposite side, circle above the visitors' stands, then repeat the process at the other end of the field.

It was a grueling ordeal—I often think that today it would be considered cruel and unusual punishment! But it was our coach's favorite disciplinary tool because it not only had a great deterrent effect to either goofing off in class or not putting 100 percent into football practice; it also built stamina and conditioning. In other words, in spite of the fact that those of us who had to run it didn't admit it, "running the bank" actually had a positive and beneficial purpose.

So it is with God's discipline as described by the author of Hebrews. Writing to first century Christians who faced incredible persecution while running the race of life, and who were sorely tempted to quit, he encourages them twice in Hebrews 12: "Do not faint" (vss. 3-5).

Although Bible scholars seldom agree on the identity of the author of Hebrews, I'm convinced on the basis of Hebrews 2:3 that the author was a disciple of Paul and other apostles . . . someone who had heard the Lord firsthand. Like Timothy, he was fulfilling the mandate to take the truths he had heard from men such as Paul and pass them on to faithful followers, who could use them to encourage others as well (see 2 Timothy 2:2).

Run the Race!

After painting a vivid mural of the life of faith (Hebrews 11), the author points out that his preceding material is not simply a work of art to be enjoyed, but a motivating tool to encourage his readers (and us) to keep running with steadfast endurance the race marked out before us. Our focus must remain on Jesus, who pioneered and perfects our faith. When readers felt they had more than they could handle, they were to compare their adversities with what He suffered. Such comparison could prevent their becoming worn out and fainting, or giving up (vs. 3).

For many years I felt that my life had not included a great deal of adversity. I saw others going through difficulty and remembered to thank God that, although some adversity came my way, it didn't seem to be more than I could handle by His grace. Then over a period of time, several extremely adverse events occurred in succession. For the first time, I began to learn how to empathize with those who felt they had more burdens than they could bear. I found myself wondering, "Where is God in all this? Doesn't He know how much I'm able to stand? Doesn't He realize how painful this is for my family, how difficult this is for me? After all, I've been trying to serve Him faithfully. I've been involved in ministry. I've helped other people for His sake."

Hebrews 12:3 provided me with a needed jolt back to reality. No matter what I've suffered, and no matter why, it will never compare with the intense suffering the Savior experienced in my place. As Hebrews 12:4 puts it, "We have not yet resisted to blood, striving against sin." Sometimes the race of life becomes a horrible ordeal—financial reverses, illness, shattered relationships, broken dreams. We may become weary to the point of exhaustion, but we must choose to never give up.

The Battle Within

That's precisely the point made by the author of Hebrews —the battle is in our mind. As coaching legend Vince Lombardi used to tell his Green Bay Packers, "Weariness is just a state of mind. You're only as tired as you think." The key is mental discipline.

Part of the mental discipline encouraged by the author of Hebrews involves remembering the purpose of God's chastening or discipline:

> And you have forgotten the exhortation which speaks to you as to sons; my son, despise not the chastening of the Lord, nor faint when you are rebuked of Him. For whom the Lord loves, he chastens (Hebrews 12:5, 6a).

None of us likes discipline. When I was growing up, I received what I considered to be my share of it. I've since discovered that psychological studies indicate that parents are often harder on the oldest child than they are on the rest of the family. I've always felt my personal experience bore this out!

Looking back on it, however, I'm convinced that God used my parents' firm yet loving discipline to shape me in many positive ways. My dad had served in the Marines during World War II. My mother worked in an Army factory. Both of them were highly disciplined, hardworking people. I frequently heard my parents quote the proverb—it's not in Scripture, but there are similar words there—"Spare the rod and spoil the child."

In fact, frequently I tell audiences at conferences where I'm speaking that my dad's Marine Corps belt hung on a hook on the wall behind the bathroom door with a sign above it that read, "I need Thee every hour"!

At the time, I never enjoyed the discipline of curfews or the consequences of misbehavior, even the discipline of my dad's Marine Corps belt or a switch wielded by my mother. But later I was able to recognize and acknowledge that these were all evidences of their genuine love and concern for me. My parents did discipline me—and thereby proved that they cared about me.

So it is with God. The author of the book of Hebrews explains that part of the mental discipline necessary to keep from giving up comes from remembering God's loving purpose in discipline.

Dealing with Discipline

As we respond to God's discipline, this passage serves to provide several pointed reminders. First, we are not to despise, or treat as a light matter, God's discipline in our lives. Second, we are never to give up when we face His rebuke. Third, we are to endure the chastening He allows to come into our lives (vs. 7). After all, His discipline is for our profit, to enable us to partake more fully of His holiness (vs. 10). Rooted in Proverbs 3:11, 12, these words of encouragement underscore the importance of accepting discipline as a part of God's training, remembering that every believer is to share in it.

The word for discipline in Hebrews 12:7 is *paideia*—the same word used by Paul in Ephesians 6:4, where he refers to the training process children undergo in the home. In other words, as the Hebrew writer says, discipline is a part of the heritage of every legitimate child of God.

Part of that disciplinary process in my life was an attempt to teach me proper table manners. Frequently I found this a very difficult lesson to learn. After all, I felt that if God had intended for us to use proper silverware, he would have put forks at the end of one hand and spoons at the other! Furthermore, as a child I considered it much easier to eat most things with my hands—I found I could shovel it in much quicker. Patient parental discipline, coupled with appropriate consequences, finally broke me of most of my bad habits of those early years. I often put my parents to the test, and they frequently countered with appropriate disciplinary consequences. As a result, I learned—sometimes painfully—but always beneficially!

THE HIGH COST OF GIVING UP

Mike (not his real name) was one of the most gifted pastors I believe I have ever met. As an outstanding teenager in his church youth group, he committed his life to Christ and to ministry service in a summer camp, then went on to train for the ministry. In spite of handsome good looks, Mike was initially shy; yet he worked hard to overcome his shyness. He became a gifted communicator, both in the pulpit and in person. When I spoke in a conference in Mike's first church, everyone seemed to love and respect him and his family. His ministry seemingly had unlimited potential.

Some time later I discovered Mike was struggling with two areas in his life. One was a temptation to illicit relationships with the opposite sex; the other, a stubborn insistence on doing things his own way. As I learned later, Mike seemed to repent after his first affair, and was able to keep both his family and his ministry.

Yet there were consequences, and Mike by his own admission struggled with these. As he acknowledged, his relationship with his own father had not been based on loving discipline. Rather, his dad had constantly criticized him, even when he did well. Mike tended to project that attitude onto his Heavenly Father, and had difficulty accepting even loving discipline. Even though several friends encouraged him to view the consequences in his life as evidences of a loving Father's compassionate discipline, Mike could not bring himself to view them in that light. His second extramarital affair cost him his pastoral ministry; his third brought about the breakup of his marriage.

Today, Mike is involved in a business far removed from any kind of ministry. Successful by some human standards, he is nonetheless, according to those who know him well, miserable. He freely acknowledges that God is disciplining him, but refuses to view that discipline as loving. Instead he has given up the prospect of ministry, or even walking in fellowship with the Lord. Mike has failed to realize the truth of Hebrews 12:11:

> Now no chastening for the present seems to be joyous but grievous; nevertheless afterward it yieldeth the peaceable fruit of righteousness unto them who are exercised by it.

But Mike's response has been to ignore the biblical warning against a lack of discipline (Hebrews 12:12, 13). He seems to have closed his heart to its call to holiness (vs. 14), and its warning against bitterness (vs. 15). He is still learning the hard way that failing to respond positively to discipline can lead not only to personal ruin but can spread its devastating consequences to many others.

THE REWARDS OF DISCIPLINE

Harold, like Mike, began to succumb to sexual temptations while in ministry. Like Mike, he suffered consequences—his marriage was shattered and his ministry lost. Unlike Mike, however, Harold refused to give up. He was shattered when he faced the consequences of his misconduct and the break in his fellowship with God. But he sought counsel, placed himself under the accountability of godly men, and began working through the personal issues in his life that had led to his failure.

When rebuked by God, Harold refused to faint or give up. Today, he plays a key behind-the-scenes role in a para-church organization, and is a highly involved minister faithfully serving the Lord and others.

OUR RESPONSE TO THE LIGHT

During his run for election in 1988, President George Bush called for a "Thousand Points of Light"—volunteers to step forward from the private sector to help make a difference in many areas of society in a darkening American scene.

The Scriptures of the New Testament have given us numerous points of light, designed to remind us not to give up in adversity. From the lips of the Lord, from the pen of Paul, from the author of Hebrews, we have seen underscored repeatedly the importance of never quitting, of not fainting in adversity, whether in difficult circumstances, under pressure in ministry, or when disciplined because of our personal misconduct. How crucial it is that we heed these warnings of Scripture and never give up hope!

Scripture faces frankly the fact of despair in life—then offers remedies available in the everyday walk of the Christian.

5

Portraits of Despair

I'll never forget the first time I felt despair. The setting was a familiar hospital waiting room—a room where I had shared encouragement with despairing, depressed, distraught church members on many occasions. Now it was my turn to feel their emotions.

I had just received the word firsthand from the doctor. My beautiful fifteen-year-old daughter Karen might not make it. Even if she did, there was a good chance of permanent brain damage. Three times during the past hour, Karen's heart had stopped. Three times she had been revived. The scene was grim.

Looking back, it's hard to describe the emotion I felt. I'd been discouraged, perhaps even depressed at times before—usually over such relatively trivial matters as a less than desirable grade, the breakup of a teenage romance, or watching one of my favorite sports teams lose an important game.

Sure, I had lost relatives—even close ones. In fact, the first funeral I had been called upon to conduct was for my father's dad. My Grandfather Hawkins and I had been quite close. I had learned a lot about discipline and hard work cutting his grass, helping in his garden, and carrying and shoveling coal for the furnace that heated the big white house in the Norwood section of Birmingham. I was a junior in college, preparing for ministry, when he died. I felt the loss keenly. It was tough, but God helped me to focus on providing encouragement for others in the family. And this, perhaps coupled with an element of denial of my own feelings, helped me through that difficult time.

But this thing with Karen was different. Young, enthusiastic, talented, Karen had everything to live for. Now the likelihood of her living was greatly diminished, while the possibility of her death—dare I use the word?—was both real and imminent. Never before had I felt firsthand the depression or despair with which I was gripped at that point.

Glancing in a nearby mirror, I was shocked at the person who looked back at me. His countenance reflected depression and despair. I immediately remembered similar portraits of despair, mental snapshots from my ministry. Young parents, faces strained with grief, standing beside the casket of an infant in a windswept cemetery. The shocked look on the face of a graying grandmother sitting next to me as the surgeon said, "I'm sorry . . . he didn't make it through the surgery." The tear-stained face of a young wife and mother whose husband had abandoned her and the family for another woman and another life. The puzzled grief of three children, ages seven through twelve, whose parents' seemingly happy, solid marriage had been suddenly shattered by divorce. Like me, they had all felt despair, depression, hopelessness.

AN EMOTIONAL CRIPPLER

I'm convinced that few things can cripple us emotionally the way despair can. Understanding despair—why it happens, where it comes from, and, most important of all, what to do about it—is what this chapter is all about. I purposely chose to make despair rather than depression my focus here. Despair, I believe, is broader than depression. Depression is, in essence, a feeling of profound sadness. Despair includes this —yet it goes a step further to include the underlying root of hopelessness.

The dictionary defines despair as "utter hopelessness and discouragement, the utter abandonment of hope that leaves the mind apathetic or numb."[1] A dictionary study surfaced four similar terms, all coming from the Latin root *de* (away from) plus *sperares* (hopes). The four words include despair, desperation (an energized state but without real meaning or effect); despondency (paralyzing despair combined with deep sorrow or chagrin), and hopelessness.

Despair and depression go hand-in-hand today. Sources too numerous to cite have described depression as the "common cold" of emotional disorders—in fact, it has been suggested in the *Journal* of the American Medical Association that depression has brought on more human suffering than any other single disease affecting mankind.[2] Dr. Karl Menninger cites numerous studies of mental patients, prisoners of war, and others faced with despairing circumstances who died as a result of what medical observers termed "give-up-itis . . . in a setting of serious demoralization, humiliation, despair and deprivation of human support and affection [they] . . . finally die."[3]

The Age of Sadness

How widespread is depression and despair? Widespread enough to prompt one Christian psychiatrist to call ours "an age of sadness. Depression—our most prevalent emotional disorder—has assumed such epidemic proportions that we have thirty-five million sufferers in this country."[4]

Depression, the clinically observable manifestation of underlying despair, affects approximately 20 percent of women and 10 percent of all men during their lifetimes.[5] Depression occurs twice as often in women as in men, perhaps because of childbirth, hormonal effects, and varying stresses. It can occur at any time from childhood to old age, but 50 percent of depressed patients experience depression for the first time between the ages of twenty and fifty, with a mean age of about forty.[6]

Modern psychiatry differentiates between the more common manifestations of depression and "bipolar" depression, commonly referred to as manic depressive disorder. Bipolar depression has a stronger, more definite genetic component, and includes moods of elation and euphoria interspersed with despair, helplessness, and other depressive symptoms.

Statistical surveys indicate that mood disorders are common to all races. They are found at all social levels (though some studies show a high incidence of some forms of depression among the upper socioeconomic classes), and more commonly among people who are divorced or separated, or who have no close interpersonal relationships.

A Brief History of Sadness

Depression has been recognized since antiquity, both in biblical and extrabiblical literature. Persistent depression permeated the later years of King Saul, who was one of seven suicides in Scripture. A number of other Bible figures expressed suicidal feelings, including Elijah and Jonah.

Depression is commonly recorded in historical literature outside the Bible. Homer's *Iliad* details the story of the suicide of Ajax. The term melancholia is first used to describe a mental or emotional disturbance by Hippocrates about 450 B.C. Both Hippocrates and later writers such as Cornelius Celsus (*De Medicina*, A.D. 100) and Galen of Pergamum (*On The Affected Parts*, A.D. 200) attributed melancholia to an excess of black bile, one of the four bodily fluids thought to affect personality.

Ironically, many modern methods of categorizing human personality still grow from the roots of these categories. It was not until 1586 that Timothy Bright, writing in England, divided melancholia into emotional disturbances caused by "humeral" (hormonal or chemical) imbalance, and those caused by psychological factors.[7] Modern clinicians also recognize that some depressions originate in the medical or physical realm, while others originate in the mental and emotional or even the spiritual realm.

Although the Bible is not a medical textbook, it is accurate when it touches on areas such as science, medicine, and the mind. Writing to a group of Christians he had briefly discipled in the city of Thessalonica, the apostle Paul expressed a strong desire for *wholeness*—spiritually and otherwise:

> May the God of peace Himself sanctify you wholly, and may the whole of each of you—spirit and soul and body—

be preserved blameless unto the coming of the Lord (1 Thessalonians 5:23; author's translation).

Significant for our consideration is Paul's phrase "the whole of each of you—spirit and soul and body." It is the apostle's desire that each of those believers experience thoroughly the process of sanctification—indicated by the verbs *hagiasai* and *taratheia*, and meaning to be set apart from their sinful society for God's use. He further desires that this process of sanctifying and preserving impact "every part of each of you."

Significantly, Paul refers first to the part of them he designates as spirit—the immaterial part of our makeup with which we relate to God. Next he refers to the soul, commonly considered to include the mind, emotions, and will—aspects of the inner person with which we relate to ourselves and others. Finally, he refers to the body—the outer dimension of personhood with which we relate to others and to the world about us.

Many theologians consider this passage to provide a definitive answer to the theological controversy over whether persons are composed of two parts—physical and immaterial—or three. However, it does not seem to me that Paul's point is to settle some dusty theological disagreement about the number of parts in our makeup. Rather, I'm convinced he is concerned about the totality of our being. He cares that each one of us become all God intends us to be in every facet of our being. As he expresses this desire, he simply identifies three crucial areas of human existence. Because we are whole persons, feelings of depression and despair can arise from, and affect, any of these areas.

CHRISTIANS AND DEPRESSION

Perhaps you've never been depressed. Maybe you, like many Christians, believe that the godly will never suffer from feelings of depression, or that to feel depressed is a sin—or, at the very least, a sure sign of the presence of sin.

Do Christians feel depressed? Listen to these words from a devotional penned by a respected pastor, Chuck Swindoll:

How much like the tide we are! When our spirits are high, we are flooded with optimism, hope and pleasant expectations, but when low, with our jagged barnacles of disappointment and discouragement exposed, we entertain feelings of raw disillusionment. We usually hide the plunging inner tide line from others, protecting ourselves with a thick coat of public image shined to a high gloss finish with the wax of superficiality ... embellished with a religious cliché or two. But all the while, at ebb tide within, cold winds blow across the empty, empty sand.[8]

Have you ever been there? Perhaps not. Perhaps you are one of those rare individuals—I've known a few, and they were godly—who never became depressed, who have never suffered from feelings of despair. But for most of us, even believers, feelings of depression and despair can be a very real part of existence.

I remember vividly a time when my eyes were opened to this fact. As a relatively naive seminarian, over the space of less than a week, I heard a church history professor describe how such spiritual greats as Martin Luther, Charles Spurgeon, and William Cowper experienced bouts with depression. A few days later, I was amazed to hear Dr. Howard Hendricks, one of the most dynamic and respected Bible teachers of the seminary faculty, share how feelings of depression and despair frequently gripped him after successful Bible conference ministries. Later, as I began to understand the dynamics of depression and despair, and as I came to know "Prof Hendricks" better, I realized how traumatic and painful experiences in early life could combine with current circumstances to trigger waves of depression and despair.

How Does Depression Feel?

Let's try for a few moments to put ourselves into the *experience* of the depressed, despairing person, rather than simply reshuffle a list of depressive symptoms such as those found in numerous sources like the DSM-III-R.[9]

Depressed is as good a word as any to describe how you feel. If you're like many people with whom I've talked, you feel as though you're under a thick cloud. Life looks bleak, dark, hopeless. It's almost as though you're seeing things in black-and-white rather than in color. Your mood is one of sadness and sorrow. Even though at times you may feel agitated and anxious, you're just *down* much of the time.

Perhaps like some people you experience frequent crying spells, or you may have a great deal of trouble expressing feelings with tears. You feel sorry for yourself, sad about circumstances, helpless to change things, and generally hopeless about the future. You find yourself becoming more and more forgetful. You search in vain for relief. You feel worthless. Your feelings of depression are generally worse in the morning, but the improvement you note later in the day is not permanent—by the next morning you know you'll feel just as down as you did today.

Mentally 'Stuck'

What's worse, your thinking is as bad as your feeling. Your thought patterns have become locked in a negative mode. It's as though the remote control for your television set has left you stuck on a channel that only transmits a poor, fuzzy, black-and-white picture. No matter how much you fiddle with the fine tuning, things don't improve—and you just can't seem to change the channel. You keep going over things from the past, replaying them in your mind—things over which you feel either angry toward others, or yourself. These thoughts of self-anger or self-hatred are liberally laced with feelings of guilt, self-blame, and self-denigration. Yet even the thinking process itself is slow. Your mind, like life, seems to be moving in "super slo-mo." Furthermore, it literally seems to hurt to think. Not only is life painful, so is the thinking process. You're plagued by indecisiveness, and perhaps even by irrational ideas.

Nowhere is your flawed thinking as evident as in the way you perceive yourself. You no longer seem to have any self-esteem or self-respect. You find yourself focusing on all the negative facets of yourself, maximizing these while minimizing or ignoring any positive thoughts or evidences. When you think of the future—and you try not to—you don't really see how you fit into it. Occasionally you may even find yourself having thoughts of suicide—fleeting at first, then more frequent. You feel terribly guilty for thinking this way—but the guilt feelings fail to banish the thoughts.

You wake up at night feeling lonely and sad—your mind races from one negative thought to another and back again in an obsessive negative spiral. You even *appear* depressed, physically. Perhaps those around you even notice, and comment. Your sleep patterns are disturbed. You have little or no appetite. Or, if you're like some people, you find yourself eating more and more to try to dull the pain.

Because of the change in your sleep patterns, you're more irritable and cross with those around you. You actually feel more physical pain, such as headaches or aches in other parts of the body. You've lost interest in anything pleasurable—the physical relationship with your spouse, that creative new project at work, the hobbies from which you have derived so much pleasure in the past. Unable to concentrate and susceptible to such physical difficulties as colds or flu, you may be tempted to "medicate" your sorrow with alcohol—a depressant which simply makes matters that much worse.

In short, you are depressed. You may not even realize it. You may try to deny it, even to those closest to you—those who've noticed the differences in your thinking and behavior. But there's no question—you're "down in the dumps," having to reach up to touch bottom.

Statistics indicate that approximately two-thirds of those who are depressed consider suicide, and that 10 to 15 percent actually take their lives.[10] Almost all of those who are depressed complain about reduced energy and decreased motivation, and four out of five acknowledge sleep difficulties, particularly early morning awakening. Two out of three admit to impairments in thinking.

In other words, if you (1) have lost interest to a significant degree in pleasurable activities, (2) don't feel much better, even temporarily, when something good or enjoyable happens, (3) generally feel more sad and depressed in the morning, (4) frequently awaken during the night, or an hour or two earlier in the morning, and cannot fall back to sleep,

(5) feel strongly agitated or, conversely, like life is "moving in slow motion," (6) have stopped eating and begun losing significant weight, (7) have begun to experience a number of the above symptoms for the first time in your life, (8) have had a previous depressive episode followed by a recovery, but now are experiencing the symptoms again—then you probably have what mental health professionals refer to as major or clinical depression.

DEGREES OF DEPRESSION

Since everyone's feelings fluctuate to some extent, it's clear that when we talk about depression and despair, we're looking at a continuum. That's one reason why diagnosing depression isn't always easy. And, while it's frightening to consider the possibility that perhaps one person in seven suffers from depression, most of this is mild rather than clinical in nature. Frequently such depression is situational, or what might be termed reactive or "exogenous"—you're reacting to something outside yourself.[11] Such depressions can cause plenty of sadness, and even bitterness and anger, but they don't always result in serious physical symptoms.

The Pink Slip

Gerald was a very godly man, quiet but cheerful, active in the church. He had worked contentedly for years as a foreman in a manufacturing plant. One evening at church, we noticed he didn't look like himself. He hardly spoke to me or anyone else. At the close of the service I made it a point to catch him at the door. "What happened, Gerald?" I asked.

"Nothing," he replied. "Not really anything."

To which I replied, "Are you sure?"

"Well, I guess there is something," he admitted. Speaking slowly rather than at his normal pace, Gerald told me how he and the other workers at his plant had received pink slips that morning. It seems the plant had been bought out by a foreign corporation and targeted for almost immediate closing. Caught in the shuffle, too young to retire, and fearful of changing careers after so many years in the same position, Gerald frankly admitted, as we slipped away to my office to talk, that he'd felt like he'd been kicked in the stomach. "I have four children to feed. I don't know what to do. Maybe I'm just in shock."

Gerald was actually suffering from mild depression. Depression at this level of intensity may be triggered by circumstances, or by factors such as diet, hormonal disorders, and allergies. Although there is no clear-cut line distinguishing symptoms of mild and moderate depression, most professionals agree that slow talking and moving, sleep difficulties, headache, and fatigue frequently indicate moderate depression. In fact, it might be accurate to say that most moderate depressions could be classified as "clinical" depression, since the symptoms indicate a change in the chemistry of the brain. Often moderate depressions respond to treatment by antidepressants. These drugs affect the brain's sensitivity to norepinephrine and serotonin, two important neurotransmitters utilized by the human brain to relay thoughts.

Negative Thoughts

Although she was able to function, Louisa was probably moderately depressed. My wife and I agreed, after a visit to her home in which both she and her husband talked at length about her symptoms, that Louisa probably needed professional treatment for her depression.

Ever since she could remember, Louisa had struggled with negative thoughts, especially about herself. She had met and married her husband while in Bible college. She felt a degree of satisfaction in their marriage, but expressed concern that "He really doesn't understand how I feel." I'm sure he couldn't completely understand her complex feelings.

Even though she denied that it bothered her, Louisa talked at some length about her disappointment about not completing her college education, and about being unable to have children. Although she had poured herself into other activities, including church, work, and hobbies such as gardening, she really seemed to be a rather unhappy person. She complained about a number of physical ailments and said she usually had trouble sleeping. Louisa was probably moderately depressed.

Tragic Losses

The extreme category of depression moves beyond the basic clinical symptoms to the point where the person's life is threatened, either by strong suicidal impulses or by losing touch with reality. Some studies indicate that the level of dopamine—one of the amino acids in the body—may be reduced by depression. Some authorities believe that this imbalance can literally cause a person to lose touch with reality—to experience delusional thinking or what is commonly called a "psychotic break."

That's what happened to Vivian. She and her husband had already suffered the loss of one child in a tragic accident. Then one Christmas morning their daughter locked herself in the bathroom with a pistol and took her life. Vivian's husband was convinced that she had suffered a "nervous breakdown."

Although this term is no longer in clinical use, it was true that Vivian had experienced so much mental and emotional trauma that she could no longer function. She was highly at risk for suicide, and a psychiatric examination confirmed that she had lost touch with reality. Thankfully her husband was willing to help Vivian get the help she needed. Immediate hospitalization, followed by treatment with appropriate medication, helped restore the chemical balance in her brain so that long-term therapy could deal with the delicate emotional and spiritual issues related to the losses Vivian had incurred.

Thankfully, Gerald, Louisa, and Vivian have all been able to recover from their depression and despair.

A BIBLICAL PERSPECTIVE

Not only is Scripture filled with examples of people who experienced feelings of depression and thoughts of despair, the vocabulary of Scripture itself contains a tapestry of terms that vividly describe what depression and despair are like.

Giving Up

The most basic Old Testament word translated despair, *yaash*, is from an Aramaic root conveying the idea of hopelessness or desperation. As used by David in 1 Samuel 27:1, it describes Saul's "giving up" his relentless pursuit of David and sparing his life.

Let's imagine for a moment we could enter a time machine and go back to become one of the ragged band of misfits who accompanied David as he spent each day fleeing from Saul. It's a pursuit Saul began shortly after David became part of the royal household, and it must have seemed it would never end. Yet on two occasions, God sovereignly placed King Saul at David's mercy. In a strong public statement of faith, affirming God's sovereignty, David requested of Saul, "As your life was much esteemed this day in my eyes, so let my life be esteemed in the eyes of the Lord, and let Him deliver me out of all tribulation" (1 Samuel 26:24).

Ironically, immediately following this dramatic evidence of God's power to protect David, he says in his heart, "One day Saul will kill me" (1 Samuel 27:1). There is further irony in the fact that David used the word despair of Saul's "giving up" his pursuit of David in the very verse in which he expresses his own personal feeling of despair and his intent to flee to Philistia.

The Despair of Vanity

An intensive form of this word is used by King Solomon in Ecclesiastes. While cataloging his various pursuits in search of meaning and happiness, Solomon describes how hard he has worked to lay up for his son who will come after him. Yet in the midst of these pursuits he pauses to reflect:

And who knows whether he shall be a wise man or a fool. Yet he will rule over all my labor in which I toiled and in which I have shown myself wise under the sun. This also is vanity. Therefore I turned my heart and *despaired* [author's emphasis] of all the labor in which I had toiled under the sun (Ecclesiastes 2:19, 20, NKJV).

Solomon's logic in turning from intense effort to despair is most understandable. Many a businessman has built a successful, thriving corporation, only to see it ruined by sons or daughters who lacked their father's wisdom and business acumen. Perhaps one notable example can be seen in the multibillion dollar oil empire developed by entrepreneur H. L. Hunt—an empire seriously shaken when his sons failed spectacularly in an attempt to corner the market on silver, losing billions in the process.

Coming Up Short

During the forty years while Israel wandered through the wilderness between the Red Sea and the land of Edom, Moses described the soul of the people as "much discouraged because of the way" (Numbers 21:4). The term he used, *qatsar*, literally means to shorten or to come up short. It is the precise term God used to tell Moses that His hand was not "shortened that it might not save" (Numbers 11:23).

Despite previous evidences of the power of their God, the Israelites had become intensely discouraged, even embittered toward God. As evidence of the despair of their hearts, they vented their bitterness toward both God and Moses: "Why have you brought us up out of Egypt to die in the wilderness, for there is no bread, neither is there any water, and our soul despises this manna" (vs. 5).

Other uses of *qatsar* in the emotional realm indicate such nuances of meaning as to grieve, trouble, discourage or vex. At times it indicates feebleness (Isaiah 37:27), at others impatience (Proverbs 14:17) or even shortness of life (Job 14:1).

The Despair of Frustration

During that same discouraging wilderness journey, Moses confronted the members of the tribes of Reuben and Gad over their hesitation in going to war in support of the other tribes (Numbers 32:6, 7). Twice he used the word *nuah*, another term sometimes translated despair, with the basic meaning of hinder, restrain, or frustrate.

Moses' use of this word suggests his concern that the men of Reuben and Gad might dissuade or neutralize the emotions (hearts) of their fellow Israelites. Today we might paraphrase him as saying, "You're breaking the hearts of your brothers in Israel." Moses also used this term to urge restraint or to forbid the performance of a vow (Numbers 30:6, 9, 12).

'Don't be Shattered!'

Another Old Testament term, *chatach*, also appears in the narrative of Israel's wilderness journey, but in a more positive setting. Shortly before his death, Moses reminds the new generation of what he had shared with their fathers:

> Behold the Lord thy God hath set the land before thee: go up and possess it, as the Lord God of thy fathers hath said unto thee; fear not, neither *be discouraged* (Deuteronomy 1:21; author's emphasis).

This strong word told the Israelites not to be shattered or dismayed. It can also mean to lie prostrate, to flatten, or to break. It is used of nations broken under divine judgement (Isaiah 7:8, 30:31), and of the destruction caused by weapons (Jeremiah 51:56). It is commonly used in the emotional realm, meaning to dismay or frighten because of external circumstances, such as a lack of rain (Jeremiah 14:14) or the intense dismay brought about by nightmares (Job 7:14).

Faintness of Heart

In this same message, Moses uses yet another word from the Old Testament vocabulary of despair. Recalling those who had warned Israel not to invade the promised land, Moses confessed that "Our brothers have *discouraged* our hearts" (Deuteronomy 1:28).

The term he uses here, *masas*, literally means to melt, to liquefy, to dissolve, or melt away. *Masas* was used of the melting away of manna (Exodus 16:21), Samson's removal of his physical bonds (Judges 15:14), the liquification of a snail (Psalms 58:9), and the wasting away of the wicked (Psalms 112:10). Its most common use was to describe faint-ness, despair, and fearfulness of hearts, or feelings of worthlessness, rejection, or intimidation. In fact, it would be accurate to translate Deuteronomy 1:28, "Our brothers have intimidated us."[12]

Despair and Torment

The final Old Testament word for despair is *shachach*, a word frequently used by David, who was perhaps able to feel both the height and depth of human emotion to a degree un-paralleled in the biblical record. Originating in the Canaanite language, the word means oppressed or tormented. It came to mean being bowed down, prostrated, or humbled by experi-ences or circumstances, as when a city and its walls were devastated (Isaiah 25:12, 26:5) or a person was totally humbled (Isaiah 2:11, 17; Job 9:13). It is used by Solomon of the physical and emotional weakening that precedes death (Ecclesiastes 12:4).

This word also appears in Psalms 42 and 43, written during a time when David was taunted by his enemies. He acknowledged how "cast down" he had felt, literally to the point where his soul was "disquieted," or, as it were, over-powered by noise within. Feeling isolated from God and overwhelmed by his enemies as though sinking under the billows of the sea, David longs to be back in the fellowship with his Creator. He tempers his despair by expressing his heartfelt hope that he "shall yet praise Him who is the health of my countenance, and my God" (Psalms 42:11). Later we shall look at these feelings in more detail. Suffice it to say at this point that David provides clear evidence that even those with a genuine heart for God can become depressed to the point of despair.

There is no question that depression and despair were common in the Old Testament. Words that convey thoughts of melting, breaking, crushing, intimidating, shortening—all these describe the variety of intense negative feeling experi-enced not only by individuals of that era, but of people today who feel despair.

DESPAIR IN THE NEW TESTAMENT

It's one thing to see Old Testament saints experience de-spair, but we might assume that such New Testament giants as Peter and Paul, or even Christ himself, never experienced this emotion. Nothing could be further from the truth.

Denial and Despair

No one played a more central role among the followers of Christ than did Peter. Frequently he served as spokesman for the group, verbalizing his commitment at crucial times (John 6:67-69). One of those instances was when the disciples were eating their final meal with the Lord. In response to a warning from Jesus, Peter responded that he was ready to go with Him both to prison and to death.

A short time later, after three instances of failure and denial, "Peter remembered the word of Jesus, which said unto him, Before the cock crow, thou shalt deny me thrice. And he went out, and wept bitterly" (Matthew 26:75). The Gospels indicate here the depth of depression and despair experienced even by this champion of Christ, at the point of his deepest personal failure.

Jesus and Depression

Failure and sin are not the only cause of depression in the New Testament. The New Scofield Bible translates Matthew 26:37 as follows:

> And He took with Him Peter and the two sons of Zebedee and began to be sorrowful and very depressed. Then sayeth He unto them, "My soul is exceedingly sorrowful even unto death . . . ."

Although Scripture clearly presents Jesus Christ as sinless and perfect, He was not immune from feelings of depression, despair, and sorrow, even to the point of death.

Jesus' depression provides not only strong encouragement for those of us who face feelings of despair, but also a three-step plan for combatting depression when we experience it. First, Jesus called on his friends for encouragement (Matthew 26:38). Second, he verbalized His feelings of despair to God in prayer (vs. 39). Finally, He faced the source of despair—His appointment at the cross—head on.

Paul and Depression

Just as Peter towers over the Gospel records, the apostle Paul casts his shadow over the history of the early church. Fearlessly, zealously serving Christ, tirelessly seeking to advance his Savior's cause, Paul might seem to us like one who never felt despair.

However, as the apostle bears his soul regarding the adversity he faced in ministry, he twice uses a compound word which means "to be utterly at a loss, to be in despair,"[13] and implies the inability to see any way out. In 2 Corinthians 1:8 Paul candidly admits, "We did experience utter despair, even of life itself." As he writes this letter, he asserts that his despair is real, but not total (2 Corinthians 4:8).

As I pored over the biblical data contained in this chapter, I was overwhelmed by one overriding thought—that godly individuals of both the Old and New Testaments were *honest* about their feelings of despair. David, Job, Peter, and Paul didn't try to hide their feelings. They expressed them, letting them be known either by their tears or their words.

What a contrast to the typical approach to depression and despair taken for so many years by those of us who have practiced what we might call "stiff-upper-lip Christianity." Depression has been viewed at best as a sign of spiritual weakness, if not a clear-cut evidence of the presence of sin. Like the Pharisee and the Levite confronted by a wounded traveler, our approach to depression has often been to ignore it, to pass by on the other side of the road.

How encouraging it has been to see a shift in this attitude on the part of Christians during recent years. Now there are many who, like the Good Samaritan, are willing to get involved in the lives of people who have been left devastated on the road of life by feelings of depression and despair. May we be motivated to face our own feelings honestly, and to seek to provide encouragement, help, and hope to those affected by depression and despair.

*Along with Job of old, countless people who
have faced disaster seek a way to make
a comeback. What can we say?*

6
Over the Brink
of Disaster

$\mathcal{V}$ic was a tall, tanned man with broad shoulders,
muscular arms, and a gravelly voice. He had been written up
several times in Texas newspapers, primarily because of his
early successes in the oil industry, then in real estate.

But Vic's world came crashing down around him shortly
after the decade of the Eighties began. It turned out he had
become involved, somewhat inadvertently he contended, with
several individuals who had been a big part of what became
the Texas Savings & Loan Scandal. In the process, Vic lost
millions—in fact, he lost more money in a matter of weeks
than most people will earn or spend in a lifetime.

But the worst of it was that Vic lost his sterling reputation
for character and honesty. His name and picture appeared in
the papers associating him with other people who had been
indicted for a variety of white collar crimes. Eventually Vic's
marriage collapsed, and his once robust health deteriorated
until he was but a shell of his former self. Is it too late for
Vic to hear the message of this book: *never give up?*

WHEN SMILES FADE

Lou was a slim, petite young mother with a quick smile
and an easy way with people. She had sandy hair, a light
dusting of freckles across her nose, and two notable dimples
in her cheeks. But circumstances in Lou's life had caused her

smile to all but disappear. Following the birth of her second child—within a year of the first—Lou had been hospitalized for a serious illness. Her husband, a young professional with extraordinarily promising career prospects—chose to leave her during the time she was hospitalized. Depositing the two babies with a member of her family, he disappeared for a time. When he resurfaced, he was living with another woman. It later turned out that his true love and allegiance were neither to Lou nor his new live-in girlfriend, but to crack cocaine.

Lines of strain etched the faces of Carl and Rhonda as they sat at a booth in a small barbecue shop in Central Texas sharing their story. Graduating from seminary at the same time I had, they had entered the pastoral ministry with high hopes. After being caught in the middle of two nasty church splits, suffering serious financial reverses, losing a close friend to a murderer, and, worst of all, receiving the news that their ten-year-old daughter suffered from terminal cancer, they were devastated, to the point of despair. As Carl so aptly put it, "We're not *on* the brink, Don—we're *over* the brink!"

It's not surprising that all of these people—Carl and Rhonda, Lou and Vic—have been compared to Job, the classic sufferer in the Old Testament, by those closest to their circumstances.

THE PATIENCE OF JOB

Perhaps the phrase was first uttered in a sermon preached to the early church in Jerusalem after a time of particular adversity. Whatever the case, it found its way into a letter written to Christians scattered and shattered by the multiple adversities under which they lived:

"You have heard of the patience of Job."

The words were penned by James, pastoral leader of the church in Jerusalem and half-brother of Jesus Christ. James was a man who had not come to faith easily. Perhaps it was the frustration of growing up in a home where you had to live with an older brother who was perfect. Many of us have lived with older brothers—or sisters—who thought they were perfect. And undoubtedly, even though Jesus was a gracious and loving brother, it must have grated against James' personality—and that of their other brother Jude—to be reminded constantly of their own shortcomings through the reflection of a perfect brother.

In any case, it was not until after Christ's resurrection that James came to faith. But his heart for the Lord and his personal growth quickly brought him to a position of leadership as a shepherd of the flock in Jerusalem. His letter, providing a wealth of practical exhortation for people tempted to give up, contains this pointed reference to Job, the Old Testament patriarch long recognized as the classic example of a person who could have easily given up—but didn't.

Perhaps this is why, to both pagan and faithful, to atheists and saints alike, Job is the name that comes to mind when the subject is devastating adversity.

Etched across the pages of the forty-two chapters of the book of Job is one word: *Why?* And it's a question asked by most of us today at one time or another. Why did life hand me such a raw deal? Why do horrible things happen to good people?

Why? Why? Why?

During the nineteen years I pastored a variety of people in the South, Southwest, and Midwest, I was frequently asked that question. There were times when I couldn't help but ask it myself—when talking to the young children of a mother who, facing despair over broken health and a broken marriage, had chosen to end her own life—and had left incredible suffering for her daughters. Or when standing beside the young couple who had just been told by a kindly obstetrician the horrible news that there was no way their infant son could survive. Or the time when a lady walked into my office, both eyes blackened, arms scraped and bruised, only to say, "He's really not such a bad husband—he only hits me when he's drinking."

Why?

It's not as though Job deserved a disaster of the magnitude

he suffered. Quite the contrary. He was a paragon of virtue, a man to whom we could point as a standard of moral and spiritual excellence for his day and for ours. Living early in history in a strange land, Job was identified by God as "a blameless and upright man, one who fears God and shuns evil" (Job 1:8. NKJV). The author of the book—perhaps Moses—identifies Job as a man of godly character, genuine faith, and personal holiness. He was not perfect, for as Solomon wisely observed, "There is not a just man upon earth who does good and sins not" (Ecclesiastes 7:20). Still, God and man alike identified Job as a person of excellent character.

Significantly, when his friends later accuse him of sin, their charge is hypocrisy—"the hypocrite's hope shall perish" (Job 8:6, 13.) Their charge: Job, you appear to be godly on the outside, but surely you must be hypocritically hiding some internal sin.

WHAT'S YOUR SIN?

One of the most serious sources of pain in the Body of Christ is the charge, frequently made by well-meaning Christians trying to help, that most if not all suffering originates from a specific personal sin. There is a place to confront sin; but how tragic it is that many in the Body of Christ feel somehow divinely driven to a mission of exposing the wickedness in the lives of others—when there may be no personal wickedness involved at all. It's happened to you. It's happened to me. It's happened to people to whom I minister. And it hurts, doesn't it?

You're already in pain. You don't understand why. Although you know you're not perfect, you've tried to follow godly principles in your life.

Then . . . someone comes to you, that well-meaning look in his or her eye, perhaps even with a hand on your shoulder, and the words are like a hot knife, gouging to the heart. *Poor you. What is your sin?*

Two incidents come to mind. Perhaps you can identify with one or the other.

Making the Sick Sicker

A young pastor went to visit a member of his church the night before she was about to undergo a serious operation. Sitting uninvited on the foot of her bed—a practice not recommended in the pastoral ministries courses in most seminaries—he addressed his parishioner straightforwardly:

"Let me help you—let's see if we can figure out what sin you've committed that caused you to have this problem."

The lady and her husband were astounded. Needless to say, that pastoral visit brought very little encouragement—and probably not a lot of insight either, since the young minister apparently wasn't aware of any specific sinful issue. Unfortunately, he operated under the assumption of Job's friends—"Whoever perished being innocent?" (Job 4:6-7).

Confronting Without the Facts

The second incident happened to me when I was involved in a busy time of ministry. I was interrupted with the message, "Zack needs to see you immediately. It's urgent."

Thinking that perhaps this brother, who was also involved in a ministry, and whom I knew casually, might be seeking encouragement, I immediately excused myself. Zack was waiting for me outside. We went to a private room and closed the door.

Almost immediately he turned to me, an intense look in his eyes. "I'm here to confront you. I've been waiting for an opportunity to do this for quite some time."

As I listened, a look of surprise on my face, he proceeded to unload on me his complaint. From his perspective, I had failed to share some important information with the congregation to whom I had ministered.

Now, there have been times when I have been confronted in love—and felt encouraged and supported in the process. Unfortunately, this was not one of those times.

The problem wasn't necessarily the confronting brother's tone of voice. In this case, it was actually his content.

When he finally paused, I simply asked him two questions.

"Were you present at the service in question?" When he shook his head negatively, I continued, "Have you listened to a tape of the service?"

When I explained to him what I had shared with the congregation on that occasion, it was his turn to reflect surprise. In his haste to confront me, he had actually gone beyond the facts, and confronted me on a charge that was in error.

We talked together for some time, and it finally turned out I had offended this brother in another matter. I admitted to that wrong, asked his forgiveness, and in turn he asked me to forgive him for not checking the facts. We left the room, our fellowship restored. However, I took the incident as a vivid reminder of the importance of not always assuming that things are as they look.

In Job's case, his condition indicated to his friends that he was suffering the consequences of some secret yet serious sin. However, nothing could have been further from the truth.

A Scheming Board

My friends Carl and Rhonda weren't perfect—but they didn't deserve to be forced out of the church he had pastored faithfully for over a decade. Carl had shouldered an exhausting work load, often putting in sixteen-hour work days, assuming the burden of shepherding a flock of over 400. He didn't add to the staff because he didn't want to burden his congregation. (He admitted later that this probably wasn't his wisest move—but certainly his motives seemed right.)

Then, in a series of behind-the-scenes-moves initiated without the knowledge of the congregation, three board members successfully carried out a power play that finally forced Carl to resign. Later one of the men actually told Carl, "We knew you weren't in the wrong. We didn't want you to resign. We just wanted you to change."

Later, Carl's suspicions were confirmed. His board's agenda for the church was simply different from his. They wanted it to go in another direction. And although Carl had sought counsel and direction from them, they simply decided to get rid of him—and they did. It was the first in a series of disasters that would eventually leave Carl and Rhonda shaken and, as he put it, "over the brink."

CARL AND RHONDA—AND JOB

With unexpected suddenness, everything that was solid and secure in Job's life came unglued—and he hadn't a clue as to why. First, he suffered a financial reverse as great as that of any victim of the Great Depression. He had been the wealthiest of men—7,000 sheep, 3,000 camels, 500 pair of oxen, donkeys, household possessions—Job had that rare combination of incredible wealth and indelible integrity. But in a moment's time, they were gone, his wealth decimated and his integrity tested.

All these catastrophes that came upon Job struck in a single day. Perhaps it was the Black Friday of his era. One messenger bearing bad news was followed by another with worse, and another with the ultimate bad news—the sons and daughters for whom he had prayed daily, and into whom he and his wife had sought to instill godly character—all had been killed in what was apparently a massive tornado.

How many losses can one person handle at one time? Job's must have pushed the limit.

His initial response is admirable, even though he doesn't have a clue about the controversy taking place in heaven between God and Satan. My mentor, Dr. Alden Gannett, who has taught God's Word for more than fifty years, observes in his excellent book on Job, *How to Keep Your Eyes On God When They're Full of Tears*:

> Job never learns this while alive. The Lord chose never to reveal to Job that he was to be the showcase of a man of integrity in the dark hour of testing.[1]

A Special Kind of Pain

It's one thing to lose your income or your assets. It's another to face the loss of those who are the closest to you. That's exactly what Carl and Rhonda faced, shortly after the disaster that occurred in their church. The family had taken time for a much needed vacation to get away from the stresses and conflicts of ministry. One morning, during a stop for breakfast at a roadside restaurant, Rhonda hugged her daughter—and felt a strange lump near her collarbone.

It wasn't long until a cancer specialist delivered an ominous report—osteogenic sarcoma—a rare yet deadly form of cancer. Carl and Rhonda were in shock as they listened to the doctor: "The greatest danger occurs when these bone tumors metastasize or spread to the lungs." Further testing made it clear that this had already happened in Jessica's small body. This confirmed their worst fears—the cancer was spreading rapidly. Jessica's only hope was the intense, extended rigor of chemotherapy and radiation treatment.

Then Things Got Worse

At this point Carl, Rhonda, and Job may have felt like the man who once said, "Things were really bad. A friend suggested, 'Cheer up, things could get worse.' So I cheered up. Sure enough, things got worse."

Things did get worse for Job, again as an outgrowth of a conversation between God and Satan—another conversation of which Job was unaware. Already he had lost his entire wealth—measured, as was the custom of that day, in livestock—all his children, and most of his servants. But Satan now attacked Job's own person. Painful, festering sores developed over his entire body. Perhaps it was smallpox, possibly he had elephantiasis or the skin disease pemphigus-foliaceus.[2] Certainly it was miserably painful.

Imagine if you will that you were experiencing the multiplied agonies Job suffered. Open, inflamed sores, intense itching, degeneration of the skin on your face, loss of appetite, intense emotional depression, depleted physical strength, difficulty breathing, weight loss, peeling, blackened skin, and persistent fever. And to top it all, continual pain—days of pain and restlessness: "My heart was in turmoil and did not rest. The days of pain came upon me," he wrote.

Most of us learn early in life about the reality of pain. Some pain is brief but intense—the kind of pain we experience when the dentist is drilling and strikes a nerve he hasn't deadened, or when a bone in the wrist is broken. Then there is the chronic, never-ending pain that eats away at the fabric of our being, like that of severe arthritis, or the pain associated with a ruptured disc in the back, or the pain of cancer.

It appears we're all different in how we perceive pain, the degree to which we feel it, and even how we handle it. But what we have in common is that intense or persistent pain can push us to the point of giving up.

This is especially true if the pain includes both physical and emotional components. Some time ago a young man preparing for ministry asked me, "Which kind of pain is worse —physical or emotional?"

Pausing to consider, I replied, "Both, I think."

I've thought about that question often since that encounter. How do you compare, for example, the never ending pain of cancer with the hopeless emotional pain suffered by the victim of physical, emotional, or sexual abuse. Who is to say that the victim of a traffic accident suffers more from the physical injuries incurred or from the emotional grief from knowing that the spouse sitting next to him or her was killed?

Job didn't have the advantage of modern pain management clinics, or the latest research on treatment at such facilities as Johns Hopkins Hospital or the Mayo Clinic. He just hurt—did he ever hurt! And to compound his pain, Job had a "systems failure"—not his autoimmune system or his cardiovascular system; Job's emotional support system failed.

Support System Failure

First there was Job's wife. She could have offered comforting words to relieve his pain, even though she, too, suffered the hurt and loss. Yet in her pain she refused to reach out to encourage her husband. In fact, her suggestion —"Curse God"—actually recommended the very thing Satan had predicted Job would do in response to the adversity he suffered. "Forget your integrity. Curse God. In effect He's deserted you."

While we can understand Job's wife's pain, we could have wished for less bitterness and lack of spiritual discernment. Her advice was simply to give up, and it compounded Job's dilemma while intensifying his pain. No wonder one Bible teacher suggested that Job might have felt better if Satan had taken his wife and left some of his children alive. But of course that's not what happened.

Then Job's friends arrived. Have you ever had friends like these? Hearing of Job's calamity, they met together and decided to pay him a visit to share encouragement. Their motive was certainly appropriate. But the method they used could hardly be called encouraging.

Some time ago a ministry friend relayed to me a series of bitter experiences he had undergone as a result of conflict with some of his colleagues when he faced adversity. Their approach had been, as he put it, to "kick me as I was going down." Then they were quick to point out to others their opinion concerning the personal and ministry failures they perceived to have brought about his downfall. He concluded his observations by noting, "With friends like these, who needs enemies?"

Sitting with Job in silence for seven days, identifying with his suffering, was just fine. Arriving at the place where Job was seated—in a garbage dump outside the city where he had once served as a civic leader—they threw dust on their heads after the custom of their day. They even waited for him, as was appropriate, to express his emotions first.

But once Job verbalizes his pain, expressing his desire to die, once he acknowledges his inner fear that a disaster such as this might occur (Job 3:25), they begin to unload their perspective on him in great detail—that he is being punished for some hidden, wicked matter. In doing so, they water and cultivate the seed of doubt sown in his heart by Mrs. Job.

Like many of us facing disaster today, Job simply cannot see any light at the end of the tunnel. And his friends offered no hope, since his experience didn't fit their perception of God, circumstances, or theology.

Christmas with Job's Friends

In the agony of their multiple adversities, Carl and Rhonda experienced a visit from a "friend" not unlike Job's. He stayed only an evening instead of weeks. But as Rhonda explained, "It hurt just about as badly."

One of the leaders of the church—in fact, one of the men who had been instrumental in forcing Carl's resignation—came to visit unexpectedly, just four days before Christmas. It was soon apparent from his comments that his primary purpose wasn't to dispense Christmas cheer, although that's what he had claimed.

"I think he was trying to convince us to let go of it [the church]," Rhonda observed, her voice halting. "He kept suggesting we just needed to let go of it. And then he went home to his happy Christmas. But he left us emotional wrecks."

Another person from the church, a lady they had known for years, came calling to provide encouragement. "But she wound up spending the entire time telling us all her problems," Carl said. "We would love to have helped her, but it was sort of like we had just been run over by a truck, as if we were lying there in the highway, and she was the ambulance driver. But instead of putting us in the ambulance or giving us help, she just kept telling us how badly *she* hurt."

Carl and Rhonda, summed up that Christmas as "Two weeks of severance pay, followed by five-and-a-half months in limbo." Forced to store their household possessions, they and their four young children moved out of the parsonage the week before Christmas. With no place to go, they moved in with Rhonda's sister and her husband—ten people crowded together in a small frame home. "It was the toughest Christmas we've ever been through," they said.

Tears came to my eyes as I listened to them describe the emotional pain they had suffered—pain most of us can identify with, because it is pain often inflicted in the name of encouragement. A few glib words—"Trust the Lord, He'll work it out…God is good…He'll never put more on us than we can handle." The words roll so easily off our lips, but the hurt remains.

Perhaps you're wondering, Just what is the right thing to say when trying to encourage someone who hurts?

Responding to Others' Pain

Actually there is no single "right" thing to say. Sometimes the best thing to say is nothing. At other times, a simple comment such as "I know you hurt, and I care" can help.

And, although some of us may not believe it, it is possible to affirm an individual who has done wrong without commending wrong behavior.

One thing *not* to do is to tell the sufferer, "You shouldn't feel that way," or "You shouldn't say those things." Once the prophet Elijah, at the point of despair, ventilated his feelings with the words:

> I have been very jealous for the Lord God of hosts. For the children of Israel have forsaken your covenant, thrown down your altars, and slain your prophets with the sword; and I alone am left, and they seek my life to take it away. (1 Kings 19:10).

But God didn't respond by saying, "Elijah, don't say that. You shouldn't feel that way." He did gently correct Elijah's misconceptions (vs. 18), but only after encouraging him to fully express or ventilate his feelings (vss. 13, 14).

Significantly, God also extends to Job a great deal of freedom to express his pain, his hurt, and his frustration. Using terms like darkness, deep shadow, and stifling likeness, in chapter 3, Job describes himself as like a man who could see no light at the end of the tunnel—or perhaps a man for whom the light at the end of the tunnel turns out to be the headlight from an onrushing freight train!

So Job, in the face of multiple disasters, has every reason to give up. Surely he wondered, Isn't God big enough to do something about my hurts? Isn't He good enough to know this isn't fair? Doesn't He care?

As Carl and Rhonda sat with me in the barbecue stand that cloudy afternoon, they admitted to having many of the same feelings. In fact, they went on to explain how, following their months in limbo, Carl had accepted another pastorate, one they considered an exciting challenge. However, soon after beginning that ministry, they discovered what looked like a great opportunity was instead a church infected by conflict, apathy, and what eventually turned out to be a lack of respect for their ministry. "After the conflict we'd just been through, we didn't know what to do. We had expected God to give us something a little easier. But it was as though we had gone from the frying pan into the fire."

So it was with Job. But like my friends Carl and Rhonda, Job refused to give up.

HOPE FROM THE ASHES

No one knows for sure who wrote the Book of Job. Opinions range from Moses to Solomon to Hezekiah to an anonymous author who wrote after the Babylonian exile. Due to the minute and accurate detail of the conversation, it's possible the book was written by an eyewitness. It could have been Elihu, the younger man who came along later—or it could have been Job himself. I'm inclined to suspect that during the 140 or so years Job lived after his disaster and recovery he may have taken the time to record the details which eventually became a part of Scripture.

No matter who wrote the book, it's obvious that Job is a man of persistent hope. Sixteen times he uses one of several words translated *hope,* seven times *trust,* and four times he employs a word translated *wait.* One of Job's favorite words, *yachal,* is translated all three ways.

The Power of Honest Confession

Yet when we examine Job's complaint in chapter 3, or listen to his cry in 6:11—"What is my strength that I should hope?"—it is evident that his quota of hope, humanly speaking, has been used up. In all likelihood, if you or I had written the book we would not have revealed this fact. We would have been more likely to portray his hope slowly, steadily building to a glorious climax in response to some flash of divine insight or revelation near the end of the book.

Ironically, that's not what happens.

In the first place, Job experiences numerous ups and downs during his dialogue with his three friends. One moment he exclaims to God, "You have granted me life and favor, and your care has preserved my spirit" (10:12). A few words later, he cries out, "Oh that I had died in childbirth, unseen by anyone" (10:18). Later, just after expressing confidence in the Lord with the words, "Though He slay me, yet will I trust Him" (13:15), he cries out in agony, "Why do you hide your face and consider me an enemy?" (13:24).

Haven't we all experienced those emotional ups and downs? How true to life is the experience of this flesh and blood patriarch who lived so many centuries ago!

So how did he recover?

First, Job admitted that his hope and perseverance were depleted. His honesty is refreshing. Unlike many pious Christians today, Job was willing to say, "Where is God when the going gets tough?"

Creth Davis was a Dallas businessman investing his life in serving others when he died an untimely death in a plane crash while returning from a meeting with Dr. James Dobson and other leaders involved in the *Focus on the Family* radio ministry. Shortly before his death, Creth preached a message at his home church entitled, "Where is God when the going gets tough?" His widow gave me a printed copy of that message. In it, Creth refers to three common illusions we sometimes fall prey to. He said we make think that:

+ The presence of trouble means the absence of God;

+ If we follow the Lord, life will be easy;

+ Christians will not really ever hurt.

Certainly Job did not suffer from those illusions after he finally admitted he had lost hope. He had been hurt deeply. Although he had followed God scrupulously, he had nonetheless suffered great disaster. Yet initially he was affected by the first illusion—he felt God was somehow missing. In fact, at times he held God personally responsible for the loss of his hope (Job 14:10).

But God was big enough, kind enough, and gracious enough to allow Job his feeling of hopelessness. When the patriarch cried out, "Where is my hope? Who will see it?" (17:15), God did not respond like Job's friend Bildad by rebuking his painful statements. Instead, He allowed Job to feel his hurt, to ventilate his emotions.

Life Is Difficult

Facing rather than denying his hopelessness brought Job to a second important conclusion. That conclusion, stated simply, is that life is difficult. Using a word for hope that really means shelter, Job speaks of the pain and difficulty that are part of life. Earlier he had expressed this truth by saying, "Man is born unto trouble as the sparks fly upward." Job 24 reads like a description of the last part of the Twentieth Century—violent crime, white collar crime, hopeless poverty, homelessness, financial reverses, physical pain, and moral bankruptcy.

Psychiatrist M. Scott Peck expressed it so simply yet clearly in the opening words of *The Road Less Traveled*:

"Life is difficult."

So what turned Job's life around? Two factors are evident from the book that bears his name. One is extremely obvious, the other almost hidden, yet equally significant.

Refocusing on God

First, Job refocused his attention on God rather than on himself. His very first response to disaster was to worship. His words were, "The Lord gave and the Lord has taken away. Blessed be the name of the Lord" (2:24). This statement has long been held before God's people as the ideal response to adversity.

But Job didn't stay there. Acknowledging his fears, he plunged into the depths and blackness of despair that was focused on himself.

Ultimately, however, in the process of struggling, Job's hope begins to return, to redevelop. Weakly at first, ever so slowly, it rebuilds. After a time he can say, "Though He slay me, yet will I trust Him. I will defend my ways before Him" (13:15). In essence Job is saying, "I'll trust Him no matter what—but why does life have to be so bad?"

Later, at his emotional lowest, feeling deserted by God

and his friends, Job calls for a permanent record of his life to be inscribed in stone. It's as though the embers of his faith and hope suddenly burst into flame as he cries out:

> I know that my redeemer lives, and He shall stand at last on the earth; after my skin is destroyed, this I know, that in my flesh I shall see God, whom I shall see for myself, and my eyes shall behold, and not another. How my heart yearns within me! (Job 19:25-27, NKJV).

Here Job acknowledges God to be his "kinsman redeemer," his vindicator, his defense attorney. In essence, he is expressing hope beyond the grave. He doesn't know what's happening. He hasn't a clue as to what the future holds. Yet he can rise above the dashing waves of the present to focus on the light-house of the future, confident of the One in whose hands the future rests.

Twice in these words Job restates his point so his hearers —and those of us who read his dialogue—can't miss it: "I, even I will see Him."

Job continues to struggle even after reaching this mountain top, battling personal bitterness. "Even today my complaint is bitter," he says in 23:1—the fourth of five references to his personal bitterness. Finally, however, he comes to acknowledge not only his confidence in God's person, but his faith in God's program:

> But He knows the way that I take. He has tested me, I shall come forth as gold (23:10).

JOB'S THREE GOLD NUGGETS

In these three statements of Job 23:10, we come as close to an answer to the question Why? as can be found in the book of Job.

First, Job acknowledges that God knows him and is with him. Although he has felt isolated from God—and he will probably feel that way again—at this point of insight he affirms God's complete knowledge of his circumstances. It's easy for us to affirm God's watchcare and presence when things are going well. It's much more difficult when we face a disaster of the magnitude of Job's.

Second, the patriarch acknowledges God's sovereign hand in the circumstances—"He has tested me." Though he questions the fairness of his experience at many other points, here Job simply acknowledges God's sovereignty. Although He didn't initiate the hurt—Satan in his cruelty did—God, who was big enough to prevent it but loving enough to know what was best, allowed just the right amount of His hedge of protection around Job to be removed.

What an incredibly difficult truth to acknowledge! For Vic, who lost his financial resources and his reputation, that was the toughest thing of all to swallow. As he put it, "I committed the sin of stupidity—I became involved with people who were more clever than I, and who were dishonest. The thing that hurt most of all was the way people at church looked at me sideways—sort of like 'we know what kind of person you really are.'

"But I realized God had a hand in what happened. There were some areas God wanted to strengthen in me, some character flaws I probably would not have dealt with otherwise. He put me to the test—and as I look at it now, He knew what He was doing."

Job's third and concluding statement puts his entire experience into perspective—"I shall come forth as gold." Now Job's focus is not on the pain, nor even the fairness of the circumstances. He finally sees things from God's point of view. He looked toward the future, and the end product.

Over the years, I've had a couple of close friends who were dentists. Alhough different in personalities, both were friendly, likable, enjoyable people—but both could cheerfully concede that few people enjoyed visiting them—at least on a professional basis. In fact, most of us would probably rate a trip to the dentist right up there with an IRS audit or a dead battery in a rainstorm.

At times, both my dentist friends have hurt me. They haven't intended to, but they did so—for a good cause. They would drill and scrape, poke and prick, all in the interest of replacing decayed tooth material with, in many instances, a compound consisting of a high percentage of gold.

That's exactly what Job finally saw God doing in his life. Putting him to the test. Allowing the heat to come. Turning up the pain. All with the purpose of installing gold character!

Did Job like it? No. Did he see a valid purpose? Yes. Can we adopt Job's attitude? We must if we are to triumph over disaster and avoid giving up hope.

Refocusing on Others

A final observation about Job in his recovery comes from an obscure statement in the final words of the book. "And the Lord turned the captivity of Job when he prayed for his friends" (42:10). In dialogue after dialogue, Job has focused on himself, his own pain, his personal misery. Now, after repenting before the awesome sovereignty of God (42:6), Job moves from focusing on himself and his pain to refocusing on others. Now he is able to reach out in love and intercession on behalf of his friends—the very friends who had inflicted so much pain on him.

A similar focus played a significant part in the recovery of Carl and Rhonda. Shortly after their disastrous second episode of ministry rejection, some of their closest friends—who lived in the community where they had previously pastored— suffered a tragic loss. Earlier, Carl and Daryl had become their close friends. Daryl, a successful businessman, became suicidally depressed when he lost his business. Reaching out in love, Carl had provided great encouragement.

In the midst of their own pain and rejection, Carl and Rhonda received a phone call from Daryl. His eighteen-year-old son had been missing for almost two weeks. No one— including his friends—had seen a trace of him. He'd been attending school in Phoenix, but even his roommate didn't know what happened. Police were investigating.

Despite his personal pain, Carl had reached a decision— one with which Rhonda agreed. "I have to fly out to Phoenix. Daryl is flying there tonight. He's been depressed. If it turns out his son is dead, he'll certainly need encouragement."

Catching the next plane to Phoenix, Carl met his friend at Sky Harbor Airport late that same night. By eight the next morning, the two men were at police headquarters, where they received grim news. During the night, Daryl's son's body had been discovered. He had been shot several times, his car stolen, his body left in the nearby desert.

In the hours that followed, Daryl asked Carl to do something incredibly difficult. "I know it would be hard—especially after what happened. But would you go back home with me and conduct my son's funeral?"

Carl thought of the pain he had endured at that place where he had served as pastor—of the people who had rejected him and his ministry—people he would undoubtedly encounter at the funeral. He thought about the personal pain of his present, the difficulty he was facing.

But without hesitating, he agreed to go.

As he told me about it that afternoon in the booth at the barbecue stand, long after the dishes had been removed and the final glass of iced tea finished, Carl expressed feelings similar to those of Job.

"I've never understood fully what God was doing in our lives. I'm not sure I ever will. But I'm confident now—even more than I was in the middle of all this—that God knows what He's doing. He's certainly put us to the test. I can't even begin to tell you how hard it was to conduct that funeral—to be involved in ministering to people who'd been so much a part of the pain we experienced there.

"But God used it to strengthen us, to broaden us—and probably, most of all, to make us more like Him.

"And the best thing of all was when Daryl came up to tell me at the cemetery and said, 'Don't worry about my depression or feelings of suicide. I really think I'm over them. God's used this—and you—to help me. I had no idea how much we were loved.'

"We were tempted to give up plenty of times," Carl said. "We were over the brink. I'm glad we didn't give up."

*Death seems to pose the ultimate threat
to hope—until it meets its match
in the promise of resurrection*

7

Hope Beyond
Death

"Nothing's as certain as death and taxes."

How many times have we heard, or even voiced, that old cliché? Frankly, death affects us a lot more than taxes. For one thing, we typically think of taxes only around certain times, such as April 15, or when we receive an envelope in the mail with the return address marked **"Internal Revenue Service, Audit Division: Official Business."**

On the other hand, death rears its ugly head almost every day of our existence. The author of Hebrews tells us, "It is appointed unto man once to die." And human experience both before and since has borne out the universality of this truth.

Death commands our attention in the media—within the twenty-four hours before I wrote his chapter, television, radio, and newspapers carried detailed accounts of a tragedy in Evansville, Indiana. Five Kentucky Air National Guardsmen lost their lives when their C-130 Hercules transport plane crashed into a motel and restaurant near the Evansville airport. Eleven people on the ground—patrons of the restaurant and motel died suddenly, tragically, unexpectedly. None of them knew that morning that it would be the last day of their lives. But they died—and all of us who heard about it felt, at least to some degree, the impact of their deaths.

Sometimes the impact is more personal. Just the other night a teenager—she was probably about sixteen—phoned my radio call-in talk show to ask for help in getting over the death of a close friend. "He was killed in a plane crash almost a year ago," she explained. "I think I should be getting over my feelings. It's been almost a year, but I miss him so much."

DEATH NEXT DOOR

Her comments brought me back vividly to a summer evening in Alabama many years before. We had heard the ambulances racing down Republic Road past where we lived. It wasn't long before we heard that Michael, my next-door neighbor, three years younger but nevertheless a close friend, had been out riding his motorcycle. A carload of teenagers sped through a stop sign, leaving Michael and his motorcycle crushed.

I remember the shock. As a teenager this was my first up-close brush with death. "This can't really be," I thought. "Surely there must be some mistake. He's bound to make it."

Two days later we were standing outside when his mother returned home from the hospital. Tears stained her face as she told us, "Mike had lost a leg—but he had so much will to live. He hung on for so long, then he told me, 'Mom, I'm gonna make it.'"

Just minutes later, Michael passed into eternity.

That night I saw something I had never seen before. My dad, a rugged Marine, wept when he heard that Michael hadn't made it.

It is not by accident that the apostle Paul referred to death as the last enemy. Death is not only the enemy of life; it's probably the ultimate enemy of hope.

We go to great lengths to deny the reality of death. Shirley McLaine goes out on a limb to tell what she has been in previous lives—and to predict that she'll be back in another incarnation. Professional coaches leave complimentary tickets for Elvis at major sporting events, while his fans raise their ironic cry, "The King is dead—long live the King!"

Those of us who are old enough to remember will never forget what we were doing November 22, 1963—the day an assassin's bullet—or was it assassins?—cut down the President of the United States as he rode in an open motorcade in Dallas. I remember vividly—it was my birthday. A freshman in college, I was just about to leave campus for a weekend at home when a friend stopped me at the entrance to the administration building. Like millions of others, my initial reaction was stunned disbelief—denial. The young president was dead. "Camelot," the term coined to describe the thousand days of the Kennedy Presidency, was over, interrupted by untimely death.

THE DEVASTATION OF DEATH

Why is death so devastating? Why do we react to it with such revulsion that it has assumed the status of the ultimate enemy?

The Great Terminator

Death threatens to rob us of hope because it is, literally, "the livin' end" of life as we know it. Death terminates. In the genealogies of Genesis 5 the narrative reads like a broken record. "And he died . . . And he died . . . And he died . . . And he died . . . ." Even Methuselah, who lived well beyond nine centuries, finally had those three fateful words written about him. Enoch is the one exception—the exception that proves the rule, that "it is appointed unto man once to die."

A generation of young people grew up watching "sci-fi" thrillers with *Star Wars*, complete with technology that could explode a spaceship in living color. But the picture of an exploding spacecraft was also indelibly etched into the memories of many young people and adults across America who were glued to television sets in 1986. Christa McAuliffe—a Concord, New Hampshire, school teacher, had been selected as part of the Space Ambassador project of NASA.

An entire country seemed fascinated with the opportunity she had to fly into space. In a sense, she represented us all. She was like my friend Michael, the person next door. One minute she was smiling, giving us the thumbs-up sign as she climbed aboard the space shuttle—then, unbelievably, there was the explosion—almost like it had occurred in slow motion—and we knew the worst had happened.

The Painful Separator

Death not only terminates, it separates—as nothing else can. Over the years I served as a pastor, I conducted hundreds of funerals. There were funerals for cancer victims and accident victims, funerals for babies and senior citizens, funerals for the godly and funerals for the ungodly. Whatever the circumstances, whatever the life or spiritual condition of the person who died, one common denominator stands out from every funeral I've ever attended. Although friends and loved ones expressed it differently, there was always the recognition of the separation that had been brought about by death.

In my mind's eye I can replay scenes from numerous funerals. A wife crying hysterically. Her sister by her side, her weeping muted, repeating, "No, no, no." A man standing back—a brother, seemingly unaffected except for a noticeably quivering lower lip. The acquaintance walking past the open casket, carefully averting his eyes except for a quick glimpse at the individual he had known so well in life. A little girl looking up at her mother whispering quietly, "Don't cry, Mommy, don't cry."

These are all memories that verify the pain visited upon us by the separation brought about by death.

The Rude Interruptor

Something else I've learned about death is how it interrupts previous plans. Many of us like to plan our lives carefully. We utilize computer technology, write things down carefully in our DayTimers, our Performance Planners, or our Seven Star diaries. Then a death occurs, and we have to go back and change those plans. Sometimes it's the sudden interruption brought on by a collision with a drunken driver, or a myocardial infarction. Or it may simply be the climax of the lingering effects of terminal cancer, or the ravages of old age. Whatever the case, death always interrupts.

Death interrupted the life of Joyce Graves in shocking fashion. I had never met Joyce, but after meeting, conversing with and corresponding with her mother, I felt I'd come to know Joyce rather well.

I had met Joyce's mother Nell at a radio rally at which I spoke in Grand Rapids, Michigan. Here was this petite, cheerful, silver-haired lady whose activities included collecting Valentines and listening to my radio talk show. Following the rally, Nell Rose Graves and her husband told me about their daughter's untimely death, and how it had interrupted her life and theirs.

Born on a snowy Valentine's Day in 1957, almost ten years to the day after her parents were married, Joyce was well-named—she was a source of constant joy to her parents. A bright, outgoing young lady, she had trusted Jesus as her Savior at a very early age, participated in church and Bible memory associations, and eventually chose to attend Moody Bible Institute. Following her college education, Joyce had chosen to stay on at the Institute, working in the accounting department.

She had been a giving person. She gave cheerful encouragement to her fellow workers. Even the president of Moody, Dr. Joseph Stowell, acknowledged several enjoyable conversations with her about the Detroit Tigers baseball team—a subject of interest to them both.

It was in early April—just about time for the tulips to begin blooming in Holland, Michigan—when Nell Rose and Howard Graves' lives were interrupted by a phone call from the Chicago Police Department. A sudden, unexpected heart attack had ended Joyce's life.

Joyce's sister Polly and her husband Brian hadn't planned on interrupting their lives in Virginia to return home—but they did. According to her mother, Joyce had dated and loved a young man for over four years. One of her hopes was that he would finally ask her to marry him. He never did. After her death he shared his feelings of devastation and regret at those interrupted hopes and dreams.

RESPONDING TO DEATH

How do we respond to death? What emotional reactions does it stir within us? What behavior does it produce in reaction to its threat?

That Which We Greatly Fear

Before death arrives, we fear it. We certainly fear our own mortality. Perhaps worse, we fear the loss of those closest to us. It may have been the deaths of his seven sons and three daughters that Job had most in mind when he cried out in his sorrow, "The thing which I greatly feared has come upon me, and that which I was afraid of has come unto me" (Job 3:25).

Consider David, King of Israel and father of Absalom, who had killed his brother Amnon and later caused David to desert his capital in shame. As he stood near Mount Ephraim preparing for the possibility of direct conflict with Absalom, the fear of his son's death must have hung like a fog over David. His words to his lieutenants, Joab, Abishai, and Ittai were, "Please deal gently for my sake with the young man Absalom." Those orders, repeated to David's entire army, demonstrated his concern for Absalom's life.

On that tragic day in Israel, 20,000 men died in battle. But David's primary concern was for one—his son Absalom. As the king sat at the gates of the city, one question burned in his mind: "Is the young man Absalom safe?' Then came the word from the messenger of Joab, "May the enemies of my Lord the king and all who rise against you to do you harm be as that young man" (2 Samuel 18:32).

Dealing with Grief

His worst fear realized, David responded as we do when death strikes close to home—with intense grief. Greatly moved, the king went up to his chamber over the gate, and wept. And as he wept, he uttered words now etched both in the history of Israel and on the minds of grieving parents of wayward children of all ages: "Oh my son Absalom, my son, my son Absalom, would God that I had died for thee, oh Absalom my son, my son."

Grief. Tears. Weeping. These are the common attendants

of death, even more than the quiet music, solicitous funeral directors, and freshly cut flowers of our society.

The essence of grief is loss. Any loss can bring grief—no matter how small or how large. It can be the loss of a job, the break-up of a marriage, a child's leaving home, or even the loss of an item of equipment. During the writing of the previous chapter I lost the Dictaphone I have used for a number of years. Just today, after I had sadly decided to purchase a replacement, my wife located the missing equipment—and my grief over that loss was relieved.

Of course for most people the loss of *things* cannot be compared to the loss of people. The grieving we do over the loss of loved ones is in a class by itself. What is it like, typically—this mourning brought on by the loss of a loved one?

The process of grieving became a major focus among mental health professionals following the publication of a book in 1969 detailing the stages of grief, by Chicago psychiatrist, Dr. Elizabeth Kübler-Ross.[1] She and others who specialize in grief outlined specific stages through which the bereaved typically go.

Our first reaction is likely to be denial—"It can't be. There must be some mistake. Surely not him. I just saw him today. I just talked with her last night. She looked so good. He was doing so well."

When realism replaces denial, we should be prepared for intense emotions. These feelings commonly swing back and forth. There may be anger, perhaps turned inward—perhaps we feel guilty because we weren't there. Or somehow we think we could have magically prevented the person's death. Then anger can be turned outward—we're upset with the medical staff who, in our opinion, didn't do everything that could have been done. We may even be angry with the person who died. Although we don't always understand it, we may accuse them of unfairly abandoning us in death.

Finally, our anger may be focused upward, directed toward God. Surely He could have prevented it. We often feel such emotions as were expressed by Martha to Jesus, "Lord, if you had been here my brother would not have died." Actually, the anger may go back and forth, upward, inward, and outward, in random order and even rapid-fire succession.

At this point in our grief we may even try to bargain with God. Although such bargaining is futile, it's extremely common. "I'll do anything for you, Lord—just bring my loved one back. Let me somehow find out that it didn't really happen."

The resolution of our grief comes when we finally experience a genuine point of realism, usually involving the shedding of tears—a point where we can own and accept those painful, hopeless feelings of loss, anger, and hurt.

GRIEF-WORK OBSERVED

As helpful as clinical studies are in detailing what to expect in the grieving process, nothing can take the place of observing how specific people have handled the assault of death on their lives.

The Grief of a Mother

Shortly after I talked to Howard and Nell Rose Graves in Grand Rapids, she wrote me to grant permission to tell about their grief over Joyce in this book. In the letter she admitted,

"I would be less than honest if I failed to admit that her dad and I have been overwhelmed with personal grief and sorrow. We *have* been. And even as this is being written, the tears are flowing freely."

Howard and Nell Rose wept at the death of Joyce. My dad wept at the death of our next-door neighbor Michael. Most of us have wept when confronted with death. And somehow we felt guilty for it, as though somehow we *shouldn't* weep, and as though it is foolish and weak.

Somehow we've bought into the philosophy of pop music expressed by song writer Frankie Valli—We tell our children, "Big girls don't cry." Certainly big boys wouldn't dare.

I'll never forget a time several years ago when a ministry colleague of mine lost a child in a traffic mishap. Although my friend suffered serious, painful injuries and probably should not have left his hospital bed, he was encouraged by well-meaning, but, in my opinion, misinformed Christians to put in a public appearance, along with his wife, at a memorial service. Although some friends encouraged the two of them to feel free to weep and mourn, others—by implication, hint, or even direct statement—implied that somehow they would be more spiritual, more godly, if they didn't weep.

A single verse of Scripture explodes that entire viewpoint. Two simple words shatter the perspective that somehow Christians need to have a "stiff upper lip" or paste on a smile in the face of death. It's the simple statement in John 11:36 that so many of us memorized in childhood: *"Jesus wept."*

How incredible! The Son of God, the Creator of the universe, the One Who knew that, within minutes, He would restore Lazarus' physical life and reunite him with his sorrowing sisters—He wept.

Why?

The answer is found in the following observation noted by the apostle John, who was present to record the events firsthand. Years later, committing to paper his record of the life of the Savior, John noted the response of those who were present: "Behold how He loved him" (vs. 37).

Surprised by Joy, Shattered by Grief

Some time ago I watched a public television special called *Shadow Lands,* the story of C. S. Lewis. After viewing this drama, I felt I had become personally acquainted with the man who had become such a brilliant writer and spokesman for Christianity. The movie especially put me in touch with Lewis' grief at the loss of his beloved Joy Gresham.

Lewis had begun correspondence with Joy Gresham when she wrote him as an appreciative reader of his *Chronicles of Narnia.* He was taken by her effervescent personality and her open—even blunt—approach. It was the beginning of a relationship that found him, in the title of one of Lewis' books, "surprised by Joy."

Joy traveled to England from the U. S. to visit Lewis. They soon became so close that they began to speak of marriage. Sometime after this, the word cancer surfaced. Joy discovered that she had cancer of the leg, and of the breast.

Lewis had been shattered by the death of his mother when he was age ten. "It was the end of my world," he observed. "I remember my father in tears. I wanted my mother, I cried for her to come—she never came."

It was not until late in life and his companionship with Joy that Lewis felt again the fullness and warmth of a relationship that he would describe as "one of life's most precious gifts."

Sitting beside her in the hospital, her body wracked with the pain of cancer, he would cry out, "Don't leave me, Joy!" His marriage proposal reflected his fears—"Will you marry this foolish, frightened old man who needs you more than he knows how to say, and who loves you more than he knows how to say?"

Her reply was, "Okay. Just this once."

And they married. It was 1956.

Shortly thereafter, Joy expressed what everyone facing death has come to know. "There's nothing like dying to make you realize you're not in charge."

From winter to spring to winter they lived, they walked, they played Scrabble together, sensing the shadow of death looming larger. To a close friend Lewis admitted, "I must not hope too much. First you hope, then you fear, then you hope. It's the sheer helplessness that's such torture."

In a dialogue with God as he envisioned it, Lewis imagined himself saying, "You told me that all prayer gets results—but not always the results we want."

And God's supposed reply was, "I was wondering what you would say if you didn't get it."

At her deathbed Lewis confessed to Joy, "You've made me so happy. You're the truest person."

Shortly thereafter, in 1960, Joy died. Lewis himself died of heart and kidney failure three years later. His death, however, hardly caused a ripple—because he died on November 22, 1963, the same day John F. Kennedy was assassinated.

In the bleakness of winter following the death of his wife, feeling profoundly alone, Lewis poured out his hurt and anger in a conversation with his pastor. "I turned to God now that I really need him, and what do I find? A door slammed in my face, the sound of bolting and double-bolting, and after that . . . silence."

Later, he would describe his feelings in terms of a man sitting in the total darkness of a dungeon. He hears a sound, brief and far away—perhaps the sound of waves or the wind—and for a time he senses that there is another world out there. It's as though the cell door is not bolted after all. Joy Gresham brought Lewis such a moment; and then she was gone. It was enough to make him wonder if the door was ever really unbolted after all. "Or was it bolted on the inside by my own desperate need?" he asked.

THE VITAL DIFFERENCE

What made the difference for C. S. Lewis, as he felt the waves of grief and painful loneliness? It was the same thing that made the difference for Howard and Nell Rose Graves. It was the same truth that comforted Job in his hour of bitterest loss, the same encouragement David experienced following the death of the infant born to the King and Bathsheba.

Simply stated, that truth is that God has provided hope. For the Christian that hope is centered in Jesus Christ. We believe in His power over death, not only because He had the power to restore Lazarus to physical life, but because He uniquely, in space and time, arose from the dead. Two Scripture passages in particular affirm the basis of this faith.

But Now Has Christ Risen!

First Corinthians 15 is an incredibly powerful portion of God's Word. There Paul tells how, out of the worst of news, comes the greatest hope, the best news—the good news of the gospel: "He rose again the third day, according to the Scriptures" (1 Corinthians 15:4).

After all, if death is final and irreversible, where is the hope? Paul first makes it clear that there is no hope apart from resurrection. In fact, had Christ not risen, Paul's efforts to preach the Christian message were pointless, and those who believed it were simply engaging in futility. Christianity stands or falls on the truth of His resurrection:

> If Christ be not raised, your faith is vain. You are yet in your sins. Then those also who are fallen asleep in Christ are perished. If in this life only we have hope in Christ, we are of all men most miserable (vss. 17-19).

Thankfully, Paul doesn't stop at this dark point in his logic. Rather, like the brilliance of a many-thousand-watt spotlight piercing the darkness, like the sound of trumpets shattering silence, he thunders,

> But now has Christ risen from the dead and become the first fruits of them who slept. For since by man came death, by man came also the resurrection of the dead. For as in Adam all die, even so in Christ shall all be made alive . . . For He must reign till he has put all enemies under his feet. The last enemy that shall be destroyed is death (vss. 20-22, 25-26).

Apart from the resurrection, the life of Christ becomes just the history of another religious leader who failed. But Paul's record is clear. Over 500 eyewitnesses saw Jesus Christ physically alive after his death. Their unanimous corroborating testimony is clear: There is hope beyond the grave! Death is not the end. There is an infinite reality beyond this life.

The Dead in Christ Shall Rise!

Before he wrote to his Christian friends in Corinth, Paul sent another letter to a group of relatively new believers in Thessalonica. Some of these Christians, unaware of the implications of Christian truth about their loved ones who had died, feared they would never see them again. They needed their mistaken impressions corrected and their hearts encouraged regarding their dead Christian relatives and friends.

During his few weeks in Thessalonica, Paul had taught the Christian community the truth of the resurrection. Now he uses that cornerstone of faith as a foundation on which to build the truth about our being reunited with loved ones who have died in Christ:

For this we say to you by the word of the Lord, that we who are alive and remain until the coming of the Lord will by no means precede those who are asleep. For the Lord Himself will descend from heaven with a shout, with the voice of an archangel, and with the trumpet of God. And the dead in Christ will rise first. Then we who are alive and remain shall be caught up together with them in the clouds to meet the Lord in the air. And thus we shall always be with the Lord (1 Thessalonians 4:15-17, NKJV).

Imagine the looks on the faces of some of the Christians in Thessalonica as they listened to Paul's words read for the first time. Perhaps some nudged each other—"Those who are asleep? Who's he kidding? They're dead. They're gone." Yet the certainty with which Paul paints the portrait of the reunion must have ultimately changed the thinking—and the feelings—of these sorrowing Christians.

Grief with a Difference

Two observations from Paul's words have striking implications for us today. First, it is appropriate that we grieve. Second, the grief of the Christian is significantly different from that of the person who suffers such a loss apart from Christ. In other words, Christ doesn't keep His followers from grieving—but He makes a difference in how we grieve. And what a difference it is!

It was appropriate for Howard and Nell Rose Graves to grieve. And they did. They had been emotionally wounded, severely shocked, deeply pained, as had their daughter Polly. Like David at the loss of his infant child and his son Absalom, like Jesus at the tomb of his friend Lazarus, and like those Christians in the assembly in Thessalonica, they grieved—and so do we.

But their grief was as different from the world's grief as a top-of-the-line Mercedes Benz 500 SEL luxury sedan is from a 1958 Chevrolet Bellaire Sedan—without the engine! Both are automobiles—just as both Christians and non-Christians grieve. But the grief of the Christian is tempered with the absolute certainty that Christ's answer for death works.

Our Blessed Hope

The portrait Paul paints in 1 Thessalonians is commonly called the "blessed hope"—the snatching up of believers to "meet the Lord in the air" and to be reunited with those who died in Christ. The picture is completely consistent with Paul's words in 1 Corinthians 15. For the Corinthians, Paul designated this a "mystery"—not a Sherlock Holmes who-dunit, but something that never could have been known before, because it had just now been revealed from God. Taken together, these two portions of Scripture describe an incredible series of events, still future to us today—events that are compressed into an atom of time, a period more rapid than the blink of an eye.

First, the spirits of those who have died will be reunited with their restored bodies—bodies which bear resemblance to those in which we live today, yet are astonishingly different. They never grow tired, or hungry, or thirsty; they never hurt.

Then, with a sudden mighty sound, the Lord, with these believers, descends into the atmosphere of earth. Instantaneously, believers who are still living—and Paul expected to be one of these—find their old, worn physical bodies exchanged for glorified bodies which will never hurt or decay, just like those of "the dead in Christ."

The instant and joyous reunion that takes place is followed by an unending time together—with the Lord and with our loved ones.

What powerful motivation for serving God steadfastly, unshaken by the swirling winds of our grief and loss! And what reassurance and encouragement, removing the "stinger" of life—the fear of death.

REMOVING DEATH'S STING

When I was a child growing up in Alabama, we frequently encountered wasps, bees, and yellow-jackets. Their stings were seldom fatal—unless you were allergic to them—but they always proved painful. Early in life I learned the importance of "pulling the stinger" after being stung. When the stinger stayed in, the result was persistent pain, often followed by infection. If someone lovingly "pulled the stinger," the sting could heal much more quickly. The sting still hurt— but things got better in a hurry.

In essence, that's what Paul does with his words to the Thessalonians and the Corinthians. He pulls the stinger of death! He gives us a basis for encouraging each other—and he challenges us to a life of steadfast service, unshaken by pressures, abounding in fruit pleasing to God.

'We Chose to Be Better, Not Bitter'

That's precisely the impact hope beyond death had in the lives of Howard and Nell Rose Graves. As Nell Rose wrote,

"We knew we could go into isolation and have a pity party, licking our emotional wounds. Or we could go right on living our lives. We chose the latter.

"That morning [after receiving the terrible news], I had heard Warren Wiersbe of *Back to the Bible* say on the radio, 'In any difficult experience we face in life, it can do one of two things. It can make us bitter or it can make us better.' We decided before the Lord that night to bow before His sovereign will, for Joyce and for us, and that we would not be bitter. And Don, we have *not* been bitter. The Lord has surrounded us with scores of loving, caring friends, old and young, who have continued to meet our spiritual and emotional needs. Young women in her age group have told me they would be my substitute daughters, and they are."

The same truth sustained C. S. Lewis through the pain that followed the loss of his beloved "Joy." His writings such as *A Grief Observed,* published the year after her death, have provided great encouragement for many in their moment of grief—and beyond.

And it was the same truth that strengthened psychologist and broadcaster Dr. James Dobson following the death of his father December 4, 1977. Addressing those who attended the memorial service, Dr. Dobson candidly noted, "This is the most difficult moment of my life. The man whose body lies before me was not only my father and my friend, but he was also the source of great inspiration for me."

After paying appropriate tribute to the impact his father had on his own life and the lives of many others, James Dobson looked at his audience and posed the question, "So where do we go from here? I now understand that the death of my dad was not an isolated tragedy that happened to one unfortunate man and his family. In a real sense, this is the human condition which affects us all. Life will soon be over for everyone in this sanctuary . . . and for everyone whom we love."[2] As he concluded his remarks, Dr. Dobson made it clear that his faith in Christ—and the faith of his father—made the difference in the way he sorrowed.

For so many others—of biblical days and contemporary times, well-known people and men and women who lived in obscurity—the reality of death has brought us to that point of response. We grieve, we sorrow; but not as those who have no hope.

SELF-INFLICTED DEATH

One particular kind of sorrow and death is so painful that it deserves attention by itself. Suicide is the tenth leading cause of death among adults today, according to many studies, and perhaps the second leading cause of death among teenagers.

One of the first funerals I conducted was that of a member of the church I had been called to pastor just months before—a lady whose marital breakup, coupled with feelings of rejection from her children and difficulties with her employment, combined to produce intense feelings of despair. Apparently her helpless thoughts about those desperate circumstances drove her to the point that, early one Sunday morning, she started her car in her garage and took her life through carbon monoxide poisoning.

Perhaps you're wondering, as many have—can a person who takes his or her life, who commits suicide, actually be a Christian? Certainly there is no question that to take one's own life is to violate God's will and God's Word. Jesus reminded His disciples that Satan's mission is to steal, kill, and destroy—while His mission is to give life, and to give it more abundantly (John 10:10).

Yet Christians can come to the point, under great pressure—deceived by Satan, out of fellowship with the Lord—of taking their lives. The lady whose suicide occurred so early in my ministry was, in my opinion, a genuine believer. So was Nancy, a beautiful young lady with blue eyes, long blonde hair, and a heart for people—a close friend of my two daughters. Yet Nancy had never been able to come to grips fully with a series of terrible, traumatic things that happened to her earlier in life. Believing the pain too great to go on, she finally ended her earthly life.

Whenever we sense that someone is in a depression so severe that it leads to thoughts of suicide, it's important that we somehow face the issue with that person. Every mental health professional I've worked with over the last decade has agreed: You need not fear that you might plant the idea of suicide by bringing up the subject. You actually relieve pressure and provide the person with an opportunity to talk about it and perhaps seek help and encouragement.

At times when people have called my radio program while gripped by strong suicidal thinking, either a colleague or I would ask them for a "no suicide contract"—a simple promise not to do anything self-destructive, nor to act on any impulse to take the life God has given them—until they have first talked with a counselor about their situation.

As we shall see in a later chapter, it is possible for those who are suicidal to the point of despair to regain hope.

COPING, AND HELPING OTHERS COPE

How can we face the reality of death, and be of support to others who are confronted, either unexpectedly or gradually, with its reality?

First, it's important to adjust our thinking to remember that death isn't the end. My friend Larry Moyer, an evangelist and frequent guest on my radio show, likes to put it this way: "Life without Christ is a hopeless end. With Christ, life is an endless hope."

Consequently, I don't have to be uncomfortable talking about death. It's not a taboo subject for the Christian. This has become important to my wife and me as we have talked at length recently about our parents. All four are still living, but as the years have passed we've become increasingly aware that they—like us—are not immortal. Unless the Lord returns first, we will lose them. Sometimes we would like to pretend it isn't so—but we need to think carefully, accurately, and biblically about the reality of death.

Second, we need to accept permission, and grant permission to others to feel our emotions. We will feel hurt, angry, discouraged, lonely, afraid—all the emotions C. S. Lewis described and more. At times we'll probably feel overwhelmed by the emotional waves in our hearts.

Former surgeon general Dr. C. Everett Koop was noted for years as one of America's top pediatric surgeons. One day while on vacation, Dr. Koop received word that his son David had died. Expressing their emotions in writing, Dr. and Mrs. Koop wrote,

> Our family life will never be the same. But we are trusting the Lord to help us accept the empty place in our family circle, and to keep us constantly aware that David is in heaven—which is far better for him.[3]

In such words, our sad emotions are balanced with the objective truth.

Third, we must choose life. Sometimes the death of a loved one is so overwhelming that we'd just as soon give up ourselves. Sometimes this choice is overt, as in the case of teenagers who have taken their lives after learning of the suicide of a friend. In the community of Plano, Texas, near where I live, the local high school was wracked for a time with what seemed like waves of teenagers taking their lives.

Sometimes the choice to give up is not so overt. The person who has lost a loved one simply withdraws from support, and doesn't take care of physical and personal needs. Psychologist Dr. Gary Collins points out several studies that have shown that grief hinders the body's immune system so that viruses and other disease-causing organisms are more difficult to resist, especially during the first six months of mourning.[4] When we sorrow, as we face the reality of our grief and loss, it's important to take both active and passive steps to choose life.

REACHING OUT

Finally, death affords a unique opportunity to reach out to others. Grief can often isolate those who mourn. Others are there, but it's like "sort of an invisible blanket between the world and me," as Lewis observed. "Yet I want the others to be about me. I dread the moments when the house is empty. If only they would talk to one another and not to me."[5]

There are so many practical ways we can provide encouragement for those grieving the loss of a loved one—and a number of things we need to avoid.

First, and most obvious, make connection: a visit, a phone call, even a card—and encourage others to reach out as well.

Second, just be there. Don't worry about what to say. If you have to say something, a simple "I'm sorry" is better than a biblical Band-Aid or a pious platitude.

I remember one instance in which I had suffered a great personal loss. Several friends dropped by. They simply sat with me in silence for what seemed like hours. I was greatly encouraged. Don't be frightened by the silence—just be there for the grieving person, and be yourself.

It's important also to listen. Don't argue with the person who expresses anger over the loss. Don't try to straighten them out. Just let them share their feelings. Utilize the approach we observed earlier, when God simply listened as the prophet Elijah, in a moment of despair, cried out, "Oh God, take away my life" (1 Kings 19). There is no greater way to honor—and to encourage—a person than to listen.

An appropriate hug, a pat on the shoulder, the gentle but firm press of the hand—physical contact can encourage the grieving person as well.

Providing tangible help, even in seemingly small ways, can also be greatly encouraging. So many times during my years of ministry I've seen God's people come through with food, transportation, and a variety of other creative ways to be of help. Surely our Savior's words, "Blessed are the merciful, for they shall obtain mercy" can be applied to those who mercifully reach out to those who grieve.

Finally, don't be afraid to show your own emotion. In the midst of sharing the most comprehensive theological truths with the Christians at Rome, the apostle Paul reminded them, "Rejoice with those who rejoice . . . and mourn with those who mourn" (Romans 12:15). By doing so, you may be the instrument God chooses to use to infuse a deeply grieved relative or friend with hope beyond death.

King David faced the reality of death on many occasions— the death of his colleagues in battle, the death of his friend Jonathan, the death of the infant born to Bathsheba, the death of other children, including Absalom. Ultimately facing death himself, David looked beyond the grave to write:

> For You will not leave my soul in hell; neither will You permit Your Holy One to see corruption. You will show me the path of life. In Your presence is fullness of joy. At Your right hand there are pleasures forever more (Psalms 16:10-11).

For David, there was hope beyond death. And there is hope for us, as well.

Distractions, interruptions, delays—can such
facts of modern life be transformed
into 'waiting upon the Lord'?

8

Hoping When
Life Is on Hold

I've never enjoyed waiting. I've done my share of it—sometimes, I think, more than my share. I wish I had a dollar for every minute I've spent waiting "on hold" on the telephone over the past decade. I could probably retire—or at least take my wife on a vacation cruise.

You probably don't enjoy waiting, either. I can't think of many people I've met who really like to wait, although most of us are forced to at times by the circumstances of life.

Our fast-paced society is an age of fax machines, overnight delivery services, direct dial long distance telephone service, brief electronic summaries of the latest news, credit cards that let us buy now but pay later, microwaves to immediately heat our instant foods, superhighways to enable us to drive hundreds of miles without having to stop for cross traffic, jet aircraft to transport us even faster, and a host of other modern inventions.

Sometimes these very inventions actually serve to delay us. We can almost see God's sense of humor in allowing us to invent things to speed up life—then those very things force us to wait.

Yesterday, for example, the fax machine jammed. My daughter, who works in the office of our ministry, couldn't make it work properly. She called me in to help. We both spent half an hour working with our machine, then talking with two people at the insurance office to which we were attempting to fax an inventory of our radio equipment.

Finally, after we had determined that our machine had been un-jammed, we attempted to fax the inventory again. I dialed a half dozen times. So did Donna. We couldn't make the machine connect. Finally, one of the men at the insurance company called me back and said, "Try once more, Don. I finally figured out the problem. We had deactivated the receiving mechanism on our fax machine when we removed the paper jam." Finally, after more than thirty minutes and no little frustration, our "instant fax" went through!

THE FRUSTRATION OF DELAY

That experience reminded me of all the things in our society that frustrate us by delays. Just in the past few days I've experienced several. Those massive ten- and twelve-lane freeways built to carry traffic nonstop around and through the Dallas/Fort Worth Metroplex—the other day I spent two hours on a freeway here that bears the name of a former president. A couple of months ago I spent three hours on a freeway in Chicago that is named after another former president. And a few months before that I was delayed nearly four hours on a freeway in the Greater Los Angeles area—but it only bore the name of an outlying suburban community!

Is there a pattern here? A lesson for those of us who like to live life in the fast lane?

Then there's the game that could probably earn greater royalties than Nintendo if someone had thought to copyright it. I'm talking about Phone Tag—a game played at great length by leaders in business and industry, professionals, housewives, and others from all walks of life.

For the very few of you who may not know the rules of Phone Tag, you place a call to someone. Unable to access them directly, you leave a message (a) with their secretary, (b) on their voice mail, or (c) on their telephone answering recorder. When they return your call, (a) you're tied up on another call, (b) you've just stepped out of the office, (c) you are unavailable. Therefore, they follow the same procedure, leaving a message for you. Back and forth the messages go, like tennis balls during an extended volley—until finally, both of you are available at the same time and actually make connection. The process can take hours, even days. Last week I was playing the game with eleven different people at once!

Then there are interruptions that lead to delays. As I was writing the preceding paragraphs, the doorbell rang. It was the postman needing a signature on a registered letter. A simple enough process—I signed and he handed me the registered letter, plus another stack of mail. One return address in particular jumped out at me. Five words demanded my undivided attention:

INTERNAL REVENUE SERVICE: Official Business

With a somewhat elevated pulse rate, I set aside this chapter to examine the communiqué I had received from my friends at IRS. It turned out they weren't interested in auditing my personal tax returns—simply needed an additional three pages of information regarding our ministry organization. For them it was probably a fairly small, simple request. The only problem I perceived is that they wanted this information within the next ten days—a period of time coinciding with my writing deadline.

Distraction, interruption, delay. All translate into waiting. (By the way, I have two telephones in my office. As I was writing the above paragraph, both rang—at once!)

Hurry Up and Wait

Just last week I was flying home from a broadcaster's meeting in Washington, D.C. I had allowed what I thought was a sufficient amount of time to pack my carry-on bag and check out. (I have a strong personal conviction against checking luggage with the airlines—nothing personal against them, you understand, just a few experiences with lost luggage.)

I attempted to check out of the hotel with the sophisticated "computerized check-out," which allows you to bypass standing in the hotel cashier's line—after all, I had used it successfully before. This time, however, I discovered it wasn't in operation. No problem—I had allowed enough time to stand in line. As usual, I exercised my unique ability to select the longest line possible—perhaps you have that ability as well—but finally, I reached the cashier.

After settling up with the hotel, I rushed to the entrance, grabbed a cab, and we headed into afternoon rush hour traffic just in time to miss being able to take the quickest route to the airport. It seems that the District of Columbia has the custom of closing Rock Creek Parkway to inbound traffic during the afternoon rush hour—a policy that makes a lot of sense in the big picture, but left me a little pressed for time since it usually provides the quickest, most direct route to National Airport from my hotel.

After a close-up look at numerous embassies, government office buildings, the White House, the Washington Monument, the Capitol, the Lincoln Memorial, the Jefferson Memorial, the Potomac, the Pentagon, and many other scenes I normally would have enjoyed, I finally arrived at the American Airlines entrance to National Airport, paid the cab driver, then rushed inside just in time to catch my flight.

Guess what. The flight had been delayed. Rain and fog in Dallas had left the flight running more than an hour late. No problem, except I needed to be in Dallas in time for my wife, who was picking me up, to drive me from the airport to the studio at our home so I could prepare for a live 10 p.m. radio broadcast. I would have preferred to be poised on the runway at National, taking off at the scheduled time. Instead, God saw fit for me to be spending that time doing something He frequently finds profitable for me to do—waiting.

A PEOPLE IN WAITING

My copy of *Strong's Concordance* contains 158 entries for a variety of Old and New Testament words translated wait, waited, or waiting. Even when you weed out the references to things like "lying in wait," there are still a significant number of references to this concept. Then there are the men and women of Scripture whose waiting experiences have been chronicled:

Noah and his sons and their families waited for decades while building the ark—and finally saw something that had never occurred in human history—a flood!

Abraham and Sarah waited over a quarter-century for the birth of a promised son—and they were physically too old to have him to start with.

Joseph waited in a Palestinian pit, then in an Egyptian prison, not knowing what his future held.

Moses invested forty years in a barren Arabian desert with only the companionship of the sheep he tended.

David was anointed to be king while he was an adolescent, but spent years in hiding, fleeing for his life from King Saul before he ever became king.

Daniel waited seventy years for the fulfillment of the prophecy God gave him about the restoration of his people to their promised land.

Isaiah, Jeremiah, Hosea and Micah, Habakkuk and Zephaniah—all were prophets who both wrote about waiting on the Lord and practiced their advice.

Nehemiah waited out his detractors and persevered during the rebuilding of the city of Jerusalem.

Simeon and Anna, two senior citizens of Jerusalem, waited for years for "the consolation of Israel," and finally saw their hope rewarded in the form of a Baby they met in the temple.

A paralyzed man waited beside the pool of Bethesda in Jerusalem, only to have his waiting rewarded by a Savior who gave him strength to take up his bed and walk.

Martha and Mary waited in vain for Jesus to arrive in time to heal their brother before he died—but their waiting was rewarded when Lazarus was restored to life.

A small band of frustrated, disillusioned disciples fearfully waited behind locked doors, hoping against hope that Jesus' promised resurrection had indeed occurred.

A larger band of disciples later waited in an upper room for promised power to preach the message of Jesus to multitudes gathered in Jerusalem for the feast of Pentecost.

Simon Peter waited in Herod's prison, certain that he would be beheaded like James the brother of John, unaware that he was about to be miraculously delivered by an angel from God.

The apostle Paul waited in a variety of circumstances—for deliverance from prison in Philippi, for action on his appeal to Caesar, and throughout his life for the coming of the Savior he loved.

Pretty impressive, isn't it, this emphasis on waiting? In fact, one of the Old Testament words we met earlier, *miqveh,* is as often translated *wait* as *hope.* I was fascinated to discover a use of a similar word from the same root. The root refers to a woven or braided line or cord, which can be stretched out. A similar word, *tiqveh,* is used by the two Israelite spies when they instructed Rahab, the prostitute, to stretch out a "line of scarlet thread" from her window in the wall of the city of Jericho (Joshua 2:18).

After the spies had left to return to the camp of Israel, Rahab gathered her family, tied the line in the window as insructed, then waited while the Israelites prepared to assault Jericho. Her waiting continued. It went on for six days as the Israelites marched silently around the walls of her fortified city. She continued to wait the seventh day as, hour after hour, the marching continued. Finally, her waiting was rewarded when the same two spies who instructed her to stretch out the line and wait entered her home—the only part of the wall left standing—to rescue Rahab and her family.

PERSPECTIVES ON WAITING

When it comes to waiting, there are two perspectives: ours and God's.

Frequently we see waiting from the perspective of a microwave society, a generation raised on instant coffee, instant breakfast, and prayers like, "Lord, give me patience and give it to me *right now.*" We see waiting as a hindrance, as an erosion of our hope, a frustration to our faith.

God's perspective on waiting is totally different.

The record of Scripture provides the divine viewpoint—

that waiting can provide a rich source of strength, patience, and renewed motivation.

Waiting for Wings

In Isaiah 40, the prophet addressed a nation prepared to give up, a people at the point of despair. He accurately assessed the mood of his people with the words, "Why are you saying, O Jacob, and speaking, O Israel, my way is hidden from the Lord and the justice due me is passed away from my God?" (Isaiah 40:27). The nation felt so deserted that Isaiah used the desolate picture of burned out grass to describe his people.

The Israelites, facing imminent captivity, were convinced that God couldn't see how bad things were. They felt He had given them a raw deal. Drained of strength, overwhelmed with weariness, at the point of utter disaster, they needed a miracle—and they needed it now!

It was at this low point that Isaiah called on them to do one thing: *Wait on the Lord*. His call included an inspiring promise of renewed strength, of restored energy. They would bounce back. Those who had crashed and burned would mount up with wings to soar like eagles. Those whose strength had drained away because of the pressures of life would again run without growing weary. Those who couldn't even take a step without passing out would once more walk and not faint (Isaiah 40:29-31).

Have you been to the point where you desperately needed this kind of encouragement and insight? Have you spent hours and days, perhaps weeks or months, in the waiting room of a hospital, or sitting beside the sickbed of a loved one? Have you waited with what seemed to be not even a glimmer of hope for the provision of a need, for the fulfillment of a dream? Have you been continually frustrated in your attempt to solve a conflict or a legal problem? To overcome a persistent habit or addiction? To be reconciled with a wounded, bitter spouse, friend, or relative? There is hope— hope for those who "wait on the Lord."

So why does this promise often seem not to work for those

of us who wait? Part of the problem is our misconception of what it means to "wait on the Lord." Many people equate waiting on the Lord with "letting go and letting God," opening their mouths for God to fill, or some similar passive approach to the problems they face. I think such an approach misses the meaning of the word Isaiah uses. Let me explain.

Waiting to Make the Right Play

When I was growing up, baseball was the game of choice. Most of us Americans didn't even realize soccer existed—and football, even in such a football crazy state as Alabama, wasn't accessible to the common kids, at least not before high school. So we played baseball, or softball.

My favorite position was first base. At times I pitched—but I wasn't that good. Later I would play shortstop or third base on numerous church softball teams. But at that time I was the first baseman. If you like baseball as much as I do, you'll understand what I'm about to tell you. If not, just pretend you're caught up in the excitement of the seventh game of the World Series (the way I sometimes felt when playing in the Dixie Boys league in suburban Birmingham!).

Imagine—it's the bottom of the ninth inning. Your team is in the field, leading by one run. There's a runner on first base. Since you're the first baseman, you would normally be positioned at the bag. But the strongest left-handed hitter on the opposing team is batting, and your coach has instructed you to "play back in the hole" to try to guard against a base hit.

So here you are, shading toward the first base foul line, especially alert to prevent a potential extra-base hit down the line. Your eyes are on the batter as your pitcher winds and delivers. You hear the crack of the bat—and your mind instantaneously tells you it's a ground ball toward the second baseman. It's a potential double play. What do you do?

To put it most simply and biblically, you wait.

At this point, you're thinking, "Don, what do you mean, *Wait*? Don't you have to make a play?"

Absolutely. But—think with me carefully for a moment—

what does the first baseman do in this situation?

First, your responsibility is to cover first base, so you immediately take action. You do exactly what you can do. Without delay, you rush to cover first base. You plant the heels of both feet against the bag, just as you've been trained. Your eyes are riveted on the pivot man at second—in this case, the shortstop. You're prepared to stretch in whatever direction the throw comes—left or right, but always as far toward second as possible to cut down on the length of the throw. And you wait.

You didn't try to rush over to the second baseman to take the ball from him, run toward second base, and make the play unassisted. That was beyond your capability. You did what you could do—and waited on what you couldn't.

That, in essence, is what waiting on the Lord is all about. Let me put it in motto or axiom form:

Waiting on the Lord involves doing everything I can do— and leaving everything I can't do up to Him.

Such a simple lesson, yet so profound. So radically life changing for the perfectionists among us who occasionally like to pin on our Junior God badge and attempt to control others, or circumstances—even those things that are only within the realm of God himself to influence.

Yet what a rebuke to those of us who passively pull back into our shell, adopting the fatalistic pseudo-theology of "Que serà serà."

When I look at the people who waited on the Lord in Scripture—and when I consider contemporary people who have experienced hope during extended delays, I see this two-sided concept over and over again.

THE TWO SIDES OF WAITING

Waiting on the Lord means I do everything I am capable of doing. And it means I leave everything else up to God, and to others God holds responsible.

That's how a skilled first baseman functions during a

successful double play. That's also how a mother functions during labor and delivery.

The Labor of Waiting

Some time ago our daughter Karen presented my wife and me with a delightful, red-haired granddaughter. (We were especially delighted that Karissa was a girl, since Karen's sister Donna's two children were both boys. I was particularly thrilled that her hair was red, since my hair was red before it was infected by encroaching gray.)

I was scheduled to speak at a conference in a city not far from Karen's home the weekend she was due to deliver—and I told her clearly on several occasions how much I would appreciate it if she would just go ahead and have the baby while I was there. After all, it would be appropriate, efficient, and encouraging for me to be present for the birth of this new arrival.

Karen simply ignored me, and waited on the Lord.

In other words, she did everything she could do to expedite a safe and timely delivery of her baby. She rested, ate proper foods, exercised, and generally took good care of herself. She and her husband Thom attended all their childbirth classes. In fact, as the weekend progressed and I arrived at their home in Wisconsin that snowy Saturday afternoon, they laughingly told me that Karen had earlier taken a lengthy walk—in hopes of initiating labor.

But, since there was no compelling reason for their obstetrician to induce labor—other than a grandfather's selfish desire to see his new grandchild—they did the wise thing. Having done what they could and should do, they left the precise time of labor and delivery up to the Lord.

I became even more convinced that God has a sense of humor when, following my departure from their home on Monday morning, we received a phone call early Wednesday. It seems Karen had awakened in the night, when it was God's time for her to go into labor—and she did. By that afternoon my wife had flown from Texas to Wisconsin, and early the next morning she held our beautiful granddaughter in her arms. Unfortunately, as I write these words I am *still* waiting to see Karissa.

Karen and Thom had fulfilled the prescription for "waiting on the Lord." They had taken care of everything God wanted them to do, and left everything else in the hands of God and others, such as the physician who delivered the baby.

WAITING FOR THE CHILD OF PROMISE

This two-dimensional pattern can be seen clearly in the lives of people in the Bible. Case in point: Abraham and Sarah. For many years Abraham had learned and lived the importance of trusting God. At age seventy-five he was still childless, when God promised that he would in fact produce a son. Furthermore, although Sarah was sixty-five and past the normal child-bearing age, she was to be the woman to whom this son would be born. The two were thrilled!

Abraham's first response was right on target. Genesis 15:6 makes it clear that, in response to God's promise to remove his childlessness, he "believed in the Lord." Undoubtedly, Abraham and Sarah put their faith to work. Like married couples of all ages, they consummated their marital relationship, seeking to produce a child.

A year passed, and another. Over a period of time, the couple became frustrated, discouraged, tired of waiting.

Uninvited Help

Like many of us, they decided to take matters into their own hands. Sarah took the initiative. "Abe, here's my maid Hagar. The problem must be with me." So Abraham, in violation of God's ideal of one man for one woman, carried out the custom of his day. Hagar became pregnant.

The result was not simply the birth of Ishmael, but chaos, acrimony, and distress for Abram and Sarah's household, plus generations of conflict between the descendants of Isaac and the descendants of Ishmael. In fact, just about every time we read in a newspaper or see or hear news broadcasts about the persistent conflict in the Middle East, we're seeing part of the consequences of that unwise decision reached by Sarah and Abraham. What a vivid reminder of the vast superiority of God's timetable to ours. Can you imagine how much more tranquil our world might be had Sarah and Abraham *waited*?

But before we hasten to condemn them, let's put ourselves in their sandals. After all, a decade had passed since God's promise. Would we have been willing to continue to wait? My friend Dr. Joe McIlhaney, a Christian obstetrician-gynecologist, has done a great deal of work with childless couples. A frequent guest on my radio program, he is extremely sensitive to the ticking of the "biological clock" of women who are reaching the outer limits of their childbearing years. I'm sure that Joe would agree that Sarah had passed that typical limit decades before.

Finally, after *twenty-four years*, God again appeared to Abraham to remind him of the promise he had made.

"As for Sarah your wife . . . I will bless her and give you a son of her."

Abraham convulsed in laughter. Could a nonagenarian like Sarah bear a child? Could he, a centurion in years, still produce an offspring? "Dear God," Abraham responded, "What about Ishmael? Why not him?"

Tired of Waiting

After a quarter of a century, Abraham had grown tired of waiting. But now God graciously places a limit on the waiting period. "At this set time in the next year, Sarah will deliver. And, by the way Abraham, remember your response when I repeated the promise? You laughed. I want you to remember that, Abraham. So let's name your son Laughter."

Abraham had probably never heard the phrase "he who laughs last laughs loudest," but he certainly learned its meaning. Just envision yourself outside the family tent, wearing headphones attached to a machine with the capability of instantly translating Hebrew into English, or your language of choice. Sarah is inside preparing dinner. Perhaps Abraham is reading the sports section of his copy of the Palestinian Post which he hadn't had time to scan that morning.

"Abe," Sarah calls, "what's Laughter doing? Is he chasing the lambs again?"

Looking up from his paper, Abraham spots the young toddler in hot pursuit of the flocks' offspring. "Laughter, come here!" he cries. "Out of the mud! Let's get you cleaned up. Your mother has our meal ready." Throughout the day and into the evening, it's Laughter this, Laughter that.

They never forgot.

It was only a short time after Abraham had laughed when Sarah herself had laughed as a Visitor predicted she would bear a son. We probably would have laughed, too; for we do laugh, many times—even in the face of the Lord's promise, "Is anything too hard for the Lord?" (Genesis 18:14).

No question about it: waiting is hard. Ultimately, however, even though Abraham's hope wavered and flickered, it was never extinguished. Paul expressed it so clearly in Romans 4:18: "In hope against hope he believed . . . ."

HOW TO WAIT FOR GOD

Producing a child wasn't a difficult task for a ninety-year-old woman and a hundred-year-old man. It was simply impossible. There was just no way. Abraham was as good as dead. Yet in Romans 4, Paul points out three important steps that Abraham took as he neared the end of his wait.

Don't Waver in Faith

First, with respect to the promise of God, Abraham "did not waver at the promise of God through unbelief." Sure, he'd had his doubts. He'd struggled. He'd even suggested Ishmael. But now God had promised—and His promise had been confirmed. During that final year, it must have been exciting around Abraham's tent. I'm sure he treated Sarah delicately, talked to his servant Eliezar excitedly, and above all, approached God prayerfully. The old man was finally learning to take God at His word.

On a Sunday in March, 1982, after forty-five years of preaching God's word and fifty years of a happy marriage, Dr. Lehman Strauss saw his life jolted into a waiting mode. A phone call from his son Richard delivered the initial blow.

"Dad, the news is not good. Mother had a stroke."[1]

Canceling his speaking engagement at a Bible college in Illinois, Dr. Strauss immediately flew back to California. Over the next year, his routine changed drastically. He had traveled an average of 60,000 miles each year to some 400 speaking engagements. Now, suddenly, all scheduled speaking engagements were cancelled. As Dr. Strauss put it, "I have been in God's waiting room since my wife had her stroke. God in His faithfulness has enabled me to bear the trial. If Waiting 101 were an elective course in God's school, you may be certain, I would not choose it. But God didn't give me a choice."

Day after day Dr. Strauss turned to passages he had shared for years with others. Like David's prayer—"Thou art the God of my salvation, on Thee do I wait all the day" (Psalms 25:5). "Wait on the Lord, be of good courage, and He shall strengthen your heart. Wait I say on the Lord" (27:14). "The Lord is my shepherd I shall not want. He maketh me to lie down in green pastures. He leadeth beside the quiet waters" (23:1, 2).

Through eighteen days in the hospital—through month after month in a rehabilitation center, Dr. Strauss waited. Day after day, this man who had been so used of God to preach the Word to others, rested on the promises he had discovered. The waiting was incredibly difficult. But, like Abraham, he did not waver in unbelief. Both the patriarch Abraham and the preacher Dr. Strauss were fully assured that what God had promised He was able to perform.

Let Waiting Help You Grow

The second thing we can observe about Abraham in Paul's remembrance in Romans 4 is that as he waited he "grew strong in faith."

Catherine Marshall, the wife of dynamic preacher Peter Marshall, was told during a routine physical check-up on March 20, 1943, that she was infected with tuberculosis. It was a devastating word! The doctors ordered her to bed twenty-four hours a day. There she waited. And waited. In her book *Beyond Our Selves* Catherine notes, "Fifteen months later I had gained some fifteen pounds. Otherwise nothing was changed. The area of infection was as wide-spread as at the beginning."[2] Other specialists were consulted. They had no answers, and could only recommend more bed rest. When Catherine and her husband Peter asked how long, the doctors replied that they had no idea.

Writing in retrospect, Catherine described this time as three weary, endless years. Over and over she asked the question, "Why, oh why do I have to lie here month after month? Why can't the doctors do something?"

Yet it was during this time that Catherine, by her own confession, learned many important spiritual lessons. She became keenly aware that there were no shortcuts, that she had to deal directly with God who "was insisting through circumstances that He alone knew the shortest way to the sunlight of His presence."

She learned to deal ruthlessly and fully with sin in her life. She committed her life completely to Jesus Christ as Lord during that time. The seeds of her ministry of writing—a ministry that has touched thousands of people—were planted during this period of convalescence. She developed an increasingly strong faith in God's ability to heal. At first she was told there was no progress. Then x-rays began to show progress. And finally she was pronounced well. In addition, as her faith was strengthened, Catherine Marshall was able to reach out with word and pen and encourage others. Like Abraham, she "grew strong in faith."

Glorify God

Finally, Abraham gave glory to God. What was happening in the womb of his wife during this final year was what we today would probably refer to as a "Class A miracle." It was something that simply couldn't happen. But it did.

The other day I was walking across the campus of Dallas Theological Seminary toward the library to finish up a bit of research on another book project when I encountered Dr. Roy Zuck. After we had exchanged greetings, I asked him about his daughter Barb. He replied, "She's doing so well these days—has three children now!"

Barb's life is an incredible testimony to the glory of God. Dr. Zuck and I chatted about his experiences when Barb, his daughter, had remained in a coma following a serious accident. It seemed that she would never wake up—in fact, years later, Dr. Zuck wrote a book titled, appropriately, *Barb, Please Wake Up*. Finally, she did—and her subsequent recovery has given Dr. Zuck great occasion to give credit to God in the face of that extended delay.

As we stood outside the library watching the sun set over the Dallas skyline on that brisk February afternoon, Dr. Zuck reminded me of another of my professors, Dr. Robert Lightner, who told in another book about his recovery from what should have been for him a fatal plane crash.

I had studied under Dr. Lightner not too many years after that recovery. In fact, he was still feeling some of the physical effects. At first, he had been given little if any chance to survive—certainly no possibility of returning to ministry. The title of his book—*Triumph Through Tragedy*—reflects his oft-stated purpose of giving the rest of his life to glorifying God, who brought him through his ordeal. Like Abraham, Roy Zuck and Bob Lightner waited through lengthy periods of rehabilitation—and ultimately gave glory to God.

Solomon, in his wisdom, distilled the essence of waiting into two profound lines of Hebrew poetry:

Hope deferred makes the heart sick.
But when the desire comes, it is a tree of life.
(Proverbs 13:12)

Waiting for Mr. Right

Many of the single people I've known through the years can relate to the experience of my colleague Marty. When I was in the process of working on my first book project, her experience as an editor was invaluable. For years she had served with Campus Crusade for Christ, worked with Josh McDowell as an editorial assistant, and now was assisting me on several publication projects.

Like thousands of young Christian men and women, Marty was single, waiting for Mr. Right. On a couple of occasions, she and I discussed the reality that, statistically speaking, the chances of his appearing lessened significantly year by year.

Still she had continued to patiently wait. She didn't gripe. She didn't complain to God. She never engaged in hand wringing or soliloquies on "It's not fair." Nor did she rush out and grab the first eligible man. She waited.

But in waiting, Marty also took advantage of opportunities to meet eligible men. One day, at an organizational function, she introduced me to Jim, a Christian businessman. It turned out that he was to be Marty's "Mr. Right."

Today they are married, living in another state, where she is still involved in editing Christian publications. When they moved from Texas, they learned an additional lesson on the subject of waiting during the two years it took to sell their townhome in the depressed Dallas real estate market.

I'll never think about extended delay without remembering Marty. Hers is a powerful testimony of how hope need not be dissolved during delay, but rather can be strengthened.

LESSONS FROM HEBREWS

The book of Hebrews provides a wealth of practical help on persistence and hope while life is on hold. Like Paul, the author of Hebrews uses Abraham to point troubled first-century Christians to the anchor of our souls.

Stay with God's Perspective

The author's first admonition is: *don't stray from the foundation of God's perspective.* Abraham grew strong in faith because the promise, confirmed by God's oath, originated in a God who simply cannot lie (Hebrews 6:17, 18).

Someone has said you can trust some of the people all of the time, and all of the people some of the time, but you can't trust all of the people all of the time. And someone else added a corollary: you can trust God all of the time—since it's impossible for God to lie.

Life's circumstances must have seemed hopeless to the Christians addressed in Hebrews. The author describes these Jewish Christians as having endured great adversity following their conversion. This intense pressure apparently involved both what they suffered themselves, and their identification with others who suffered (10:32, 33). They needed steadfast endurance (10:36). To strengthen them, the author reminds, "Look back at Abraham. God, who promises the impossible, always delivers. He cannot lie."

Think God's Thoughts

Second, gain practical encouragement from thinking God's thoughts. The apostle Paul, quoting Isaiah, reminds his readers in Corinth that God's ways are not our ways, that the foolishness of God is far beyond the wisdom of man (1 Corinthians 1:27). This can be seen not only in God's perfect plan of salvation, but in his promise of protection and provision. The author of Hebrews, writing to Christians whose hope was stretched to the breaking point, promises them strong encouragement, a refuge, a safe harbor in which they can confidently anchor their souls.

Difficult days call for strong medicine. Extended delays demand strong encouragement—and God has delivered it.

When we are discouraged, God's strong encouragement is the perfect medicine, the ideal antidote. When we are at the point of despair, shaken by the winds of adversity, frustrated by the extended delay—this hope is the perfect refuge where we can escape despair.

Trust the Soul's Sure Anchor

The Hebrew writer also refers us to hope as an "anchor of the soul" (6:19). When our emotions are tossed up and down with the circumstances of life, and everything around us is breaking loose, we need nothing more than a sure anchor.

All the hymns and poems that have been written, all the references by preachers to this anchor of the soul, come right back to Hebrews 6:19. The small sailing ships on which Paul and others of the New Testament era traveled frequently approached narrow, dangerous harbors that were surrounded by rocks and reefs. Often, nearby sandbars would contain the wreckage of ships, mute testimony to the danger faced by those who dared attempt to sail into the harbor.

Approaching such a harbor, the wise captain would wait to be met by a pilot ship, a smaller boat with a function and purpose similar to today's tugboat. When the pilot boat was in position, the captain of the sailing ship would give the word and the crew would lower the ship's anchor into the smaller boat. As the crew of the ship continued letting out more line, the smaller boat would be rowed through the narrow entrance into the harbor. At this point, the crew would drop the anchor of the larger ship. Then the sailing ship, with sails lowered, would be pulled by the anchor line "past the obstacles, through the narrow opening and into the safety of the harbor."[3]

Remember How Christ Endured

Finally, notice that in Hebrews hope always directs us back to our Savior, Jesus, our personal High Priest and Guide. "For consider Him who endured such hostility . . . lest you become weary and discouraged in your souls" (12:3).

The author is saying, "Jesus has been there. He's endured the very worst—the cross—and He's promised to never leave us or forsake us" (13:5).

There will be delays—many extended far longer than we would prefer. There will be pain. Discouragement and frustration will come. But if we look to Jesus, the author and finisher of our faith, God will give us the grace to use such occasions to strengthen, rather than erode, our hope.

Try as we might, it would be hard to fail as 'royally'
as King David. Where would we start if we
decided to take a more royal road?

9

Hope Though We've Blown It Royally

$\mathcal{I}$t has been said that power corrupts, and that absolute power corrupts absolutely.

Charles Colson perhaps expressed it best: "Power is like salt water, the more you drink the thirstier you get."[1] America doesn't have royalty, but Chuck Colson and others who were a part of the inner circle of the Richard Nixon White House were perhaps the closest thing to it.

By his own admission, Colson had been reluctant to answer the call to public service. He actually would have to take a cut in pay. But the attraction of being a part of shaping history, and of influencing the President—finally it was enough to convince Chuck Colson to become a part of the White House staff.

From an inside office far down the hallway from the President's office in the old Executive Office Building, Colson maneuvered himself in a matter of months into the office adjacent to Nixon's. He became one of the most visible men in the administration—appearances on network television, a feature article profiling him in *Newsweek* magazine, frequent mention in Washington society columns. As he said:

I entered government believing that public office was a trust, a duty. Gradually and imperceptively, I began to view it as a holy crusade. The future of the republic, or so I rationalized, depended on the president's continuation in office. But whether I acknowledged it or not, equally important was the fact that my own power depended on it.[2]

They were almost like a royal circle, Colson and his associates—Kissinger, Haldeman, Erlichman, and John Dean. Yet their fall from glory to ignominy can be summarily described in one word . . .

Watergate

It's an impressive semicircular structure of several stories near the beginning of Rock Creek Parkway, one of the more imposing buildings fronting the Potomac River facing Virginia from the District of Columbia. But the Watergate complex is far less known for its architecture, and its famous and powerful residents, than for its role in the downfall of the Nixon hierarchy. Colson was a part in the conspiracy involving the so-called White House Plumber's Unit and the Watergate break-in and subsequent cover-up. For this, along with his efforts to smear anti-war activist Daniel Ellsberg for his role in obtaining the so-called Pentagon Papers, Colson moved from the seat of power to a seat in prison.

I first heard Chuck Colson speak in Washington. I'll never forget one of his initial comments—a response to a question in my mind and the minds of many others.

Colson was not a Christian when he blew it. He became a believer after he was imprisoned. It was while he was serving time in payment to society for his misdeeds that his faith had been nurtured and his Christian ministry shaped.

Here's the question Colson raised and answered:

"Frequently I'm asked whether I would have participated in Watergate if I had been a Christian when I worked in the White House. The implication of such a question is that Christians are immune to corruption. I'm always tempted to say of course not, but that's self-righteous nonsense. While Christians know that their faith requires high standards of righteousness, they are human, and often capitulate to the same temptations as anyone else."

A ROYAL FAILURE

While Chuck Colson wasn't royalty, David, the eighth son of Jesse of Bethlehem, was. Rising from the depths of obscurity—his own father forgot to invite him to the most important event in their family history, a dinner in honor of Samuel the prophet—David was anointed by the old prophet who forecast his rise to the throne.

But it was years later before David would actually become king. One of the most recognized figures in the Old Testament, the subject of countless Sunday School lessons and vast numbers of articles and books, David is a man who towers over the Old Testament—and even casts a shadow beyond our era to the Millennium where prophecy indicates he will serve as a vice regent of Jesus the Messiah-King.

David is a man of numerous significant, high-visibility life events. Like the skyline of New York City, his life was marked by an almost incalculable number of high points. Yet, like the twin towers of the World Trade Center, two events stand out more noticeably than the rest. Ironically, unlike those twin towers that guard the lower corner of Manhattan, the two major events in David's life stand in stark contrast. One was an monumental triumph, the other, an unbelievable disaster.

Each of the these two events can be called to mind with a single name—one that prompts our computer-like minds to access the story's details almost instantly.

Goliath.

Bathsheba.

Victory, Then Defeat

Our memory banks tick off the highlights of David's success story. His ability as a young man fresh from faithfully fighting off animal predators who threatened his small responsibility of safeguarding his father's sheep . . . his positive enthusiasm: "Who is this big bully who dares defy the armies of the Living God?" (Doesn't the Hebrew text quote David as saying somewhere, "The bigger they come, the harder they fall"?) . . . his refusal of Saul's armor and weaponry ("I'm not into heavy metal—just smooth rock) . . . his stunning victory over Goliath, the champion of the mightiest army of the known world of his day, a man who would dwarf most NBA stars of our day.

We recall David's eventual acceptance into Saul's household as a musician and court attendant ...the public acclaim as he conducted himself well and continued to win victories (the hit single, *Saul Has Slain His Thousands and David His Ten Thousands*, must have been at the top of the charts of all the radio stations in Palestine) ...his faithfulness to God during the years Saul sought to kill him—plus his continued loyalty to his friend Jonathan, and even Jonathan's lame son Mephibosheth ...his ultimate recognition as King, first in Judah, then of the United Kingdom ...decades of success as a ruler, a musician, the sweet singer and shepherd king of Israel.

What a man King David must have been!

Then he blew it—blew it R-O-Y-A-L-L-Y.

The record of the events beginning in 2 Samuel 11 almost sounds like a script for *Dynasty* or *The Young and the Restless*. David the King, the man at the pinnacle of success, the spiritual as well as political leader of his people—*this man* involved in a tawdry, illicit affair? Now the highlights tell a different kind of story:

Watching like a modern-day peeping tom from the high vantage point of his palace as a neighbor's wife bathed ... maneuvering to set up a secret liaison—one that would become disastrous both for him and for the woman's husband ...desperately maneuvering to carry out a cover-up—enlisting his friend and the ruthless lieutenant Joab in a Watergate-like conspiracy ... seeking to entrap Uriah into having sexual relations with his wife—so everyone would think the baby was Uriah's, although perhaps premature ...then, when that failed, actually putting out a hit contract, like some Hollywood-created Mafia don, to have Uriah terminated.

Hollywood has sought to glamorize the story of David and Bathsheba. But during the months between the murder of Uriah and his confrontation by Nathan the Prophet—and even following that confrontation—David's life was anything but glamorous, happy, or tranquil. He had been a man of leisure, choosing to delegate the risks and hassles of battle to Joab and his associates, relaxing in Jerusalem, enjoying the trappings of his power, the absence of conflict. But now . . . .

Disaster on the Inside

On the inside, David was experiencing full-scale disaster. Outwardly, no one could tell. It seemed like the cover-up had worked. In fact, the socialites in the capitol undoubtedly enjoyed the fete of another royal wedding when David married the widow of the heroic soldier. Then she bore him a son. Perhaps no one noticed that the baby seemed premature—or maybe those who wondered just assumed it was Uriah's after all. So, for David, life went on.

But two inner facts made that life painfully difficult: the feelings of David . . . and the feelings of God.

First, a word about God's feelings. The author of 2 Samuel ends the narrative about David, Bathsheba, Joab, and Uriah with the account of the wedding and the birth of a child. By implication, life continued as usual.

Except for one significant editorial comment: "The thing that David had done displeased the Lord" (2 Samuel 11:27).

LOVE AND HOLINESS

How difficult it is for us to balance two outstanding truths in tension: God is a God of infinite love . . . and He is also a God of infinite holiness. In gracious, long-suffering love He reaches out to sinful, fallen man. Yet because of His absolutely pure character, He hates sin—all sin—absolutely.

The Pressure Within

These twin forces of love and holiness combined to make David's mind a pressure-cooker. Listen to his own words recorded in vivid verbal technicolor in Psalms 32:

When I kept silence, my bones became old from my roaring all the day long. For day and night Your hand was heavy upon me. My moisture is turned into the drought of summer.

Who of us in the human family hasn't at some point kept silence regarding failure in our lives, refusing to confess to God, cultivating our denial, hiding our misdeeds from people? But the more David struggled to keep his sin hidden, the more intensely his conscience worked within. It's almost as though David used the phrase, "I aged twenty years."

A friend who is a psychiatrist once said to me after reading these verses, "This sounds like a man who is clinically depressed." David's strength was zapped, his resources dried up like the intense heat of summer.

Although Job used similar language to describe his emotional state (Job 33:14), David's was different. His feelings came as a consequence of his own misbehavior, and his persistent unwillingness to admit his guilt. The writer of so many of Israel's worship songs refused to face the music—so the internal music became louder and louder. It was as if David could not rest at night because of an intense, constant piercing sound, coupled with a draining inner thirst.

Though he probably would not have admitted it to those around him at this point, David must have felt hopeless despair. God's hand weighed heavily upon him. He knew the consequences of adultery, and of murder. He had blown it. Surely, eventually, he would pay the consequences.

Crossing Over the Line

David's feelings rivaled those of a friend who sat in my office one day—I'll call him Pastor Phil. His story is no different from that of thousands of other individuals from many walks of life. Energetic yet compassionate, Pastor Phil had been happily married, with two small children. I'd known him fairly well, and had rejoiced in the apparent success of his ministry and the blessing of God that seemed to rest upon him.

Then one day he called, tension in his voice, to request the meeting where he shared with his wife that he had been unfaithful to his marriage vows, and to God.

Like David, Phil had been attracted to someone who in a sense was one of his sheep, a member of his congregation.

She was married to a man who, like Uriah, was in the military. Unlike Bathsheba, she had initiated the contact with Pastor Phil—coming to see him for counseling.

As he sat on the couch in my office, tears leaking from around the fingers he held over his eyes, sobs shaking his shoulders, I was reminded of a truth that needs to burn vividly in the mind of everyone involved in God's service—Paul's warning in 1 Corinthians 10:12: "Wherefore, let him that thinketh he standeth, take heed lest he fall."

Composing himself, Phil acknowledged his failure. "I blew it," he said. "Even though my original motives were so pure, it wasn't long before I started feeling attracted to her. Things weren't going so well in my marriage either. And she needed comfort, encouragement.

"First it was an innocent hug. There was a line—and I chose to cross that line. I had drawn the line with other women, even talked about it with my wife and friends. But in this case, I knew where the line was, and I crossed it. Before I knew it, we were sexually involved."

Looking vs. Lusting

David also crossed that line. But first he *looked*—and every man understands the significance of that persistent look. It's the reason Jesus warned man against looking on a woman to lust after her.

It's important to remember that the initial look wasn't the sin. That came when David crossed the line—when he allowed the look to linger, and to come to the conclusion that Bathsheba was "very beautiful to look upon."

At this point, if he had been honest, David would have admitted his lust for Bathsheba and scoured it from his mind. Instead, he initiated a plan of seduction—an active pursuit. Tragically, Bathsheba didn't reject him. Both sinned, but his responsibility as a leader was greater. David lay with Bathsheba—and lost.

David lost royally, even though the subsequent four-stage cover-up must have felt like he was winning at the time. Uriah was a Hittite whose name meant, "Yahweh is my light." Apparently he had been converted to Yahweh, perhaps through David's own influence. He was one of David's thirty-seven elite military men—soldiers who actually risked their lives for the King. In destroying such a man, David lost. He failed. He had broken fellowship with the God he loved.

Time To Confess

Like David, Pastor Phil had lived for nearly a year with outward normalcy—but with the constant emotional weight of secret sin and its terrible inner consequences. David's callous external attitude had been reflected in sayings like, "Don't worry about it, Joab—the sword kills one as well as another." But such cynicism merely masked the inner turmoil of a man whose life had been marked by a heart for God—a heart that was now out of harmony with the Lord.

When a person reaches that stage of disharmony, it's time to confess.

Sometimes—as in the case of Chuck Colson—the legal consequences of our actions bring us to that point of hopelessness that tells us we've blown it royally. Humiliated, shamed, arrested, disgraced, the man who was once at the top now had to reach up to touch bottom. He reasoned that the consequences of his misdeeds would surely lead him to prison—and they did.

For Pastor Phil, the guilt of his personal inner dissonance finally broke through. When he came to talk with me, he had already shared his misdeed with his wife, and with a man who had been his mentor for many years in ministry. Seeking my encouragement and support as he prepared to share his personal failure with his church board, he had owned his sin, faced his guilt. Like David he could honestly say, "I acknowledge my sin to You, and my iniquity I have not hidden. I said I will confess my transgressions to the Lord, and You forgave the iniquity of my sin" (Psalms 32:5).

TIME TO CONFRONT

Sometimes the confession doesn't come without a confrontation. For David, it took a less than gentle nudge from God, delivered in the person of Nathan the prophet.

Picture the scene at David's palace in Jerusalem. There's a knock at the gate. A servant enters David's presence.

Servant: It's Nathan the Prophet.

David: Does he have an appointment?

Servant: No, but he says it's important that he see you. It's a matter of utmost urgency, he says.

David (glancing at his Rolex): Very well, bring him in—we'll meet here in the Oval Office—and serve coffee, please.

Nathan enters the room. The two men greet each other in the accustomed fashion. Refreshments are brought in and the conversation begins.

If David had worn a Rolex, he probably would have glanced at it frequently as Nathan began telling this story. Undoubtedly the thought ran through his mind, Get to the point Nathan. I don't have time for rambling stories.

But Nathan refused to be rushed. He described a rich man who owned many flocks and herds. Then he told of a poor man, who had but one female lamb. It was like a child—a daughter—part of the family.

As David grew increasingly impatient, Nathan verbally sketched the picture of an evening—a visitor to the rich man's home—a man unwilling to take from his own flock or herd, and who seized the poor man's lamb, killed it, and cooked it to feed his guest.

Without waiting for more detail, David exploded in rage. "As Yahweh lives, this man will die!"

We might assume that this kind of quick-tempered response was normal for David. After all, the Bible indicates that he was "ruddy" (1 Samuel 16:12)—perhaps he was red-headed! And there was his angry response to Nabal, Abigail's foolish first husband. When Nabal refused to provide food for David and his fugitive band, David was ready to kill him on sight (1 Samuel 25:10-13).

I'm inclined to think, however, that David's retort to Nathan here was the outburst of a guilty conscience—a man using the defense mechanism psychologists refer to as projection. Since guilt involves anger toward ourselves, it's easy, like a projector, to simply shine that emotion—in magnified, intensified form—onto someone else. In fact, this is the very thing Jesus described when He warned in the Sermon on the Mount against attempting to remove the speck from someone else's eye without first dealing with the timber lodged next to our own eyeball.

David's anger was inordinate. That cannot be questioned—after all, stealing and killing a lamb certainly wasn't a capital crime, even by the strictest interpretation of the Mosaic Law—which only demanded full restoration.

Visualize the stunned look on David's face when Nathan quietly interrupted his royal tirade with the simple words,

You Are the Man!

Without question, David was convinced he had just pronounced his own death sentence. Later Nathan would respond that "The Lord has put away your sin, you will not die" (2 Samuel 12:13), indicating that this was of primary concern to the fallen king.

But David certainly realized he had blown it. Absolutely. Royally. Totally. Overwhelmed with guilt, shame, and despair, he could but listen to the rebuke of the prophet.

Why have you thought so little of God's command? You killed Uriah. You took his wife to be yours. You wielded the sword of the Ammonites. And now, David, the sword will never depart from your house. You will experience unimaginable shame. Your wives will be taken by a man very close to you. Publicly, you will be shamed, humiliated throughout all Israel.

Moral failure. Abuse of power. White collar theft. The name doesn't matter; the effects are the same: overwhelming guilt, shame, feeling that somehow we've blown it to the point where we can never look anyone in the eye again. And for people genuinely concerned about their relationship with God, that's the worst part—the feeling that we'll bear that shame, even in our relationship with Him, for the rest of our lives. We'll never be able to be used of Him. Shame, without question, robs us of hope.

For Chuck Colson, for Pastor Phil, for King David, things looked hopeless—and each could blame only himself.

THE HIGH COST OF BLOWING IT

I could point to many other people for whom things have looked absolutely hopeless. So let me point to my friend Joel, who has, on a number of occasions, joined me on radio.

Seventeen, and Jailed

At the age of seventeen, Joel had had it. As he put it, "I found myself arrogantly standing in the doorway of my bedroom with hands stuffed deeply in my pockets telling my father that I hated him and everything he stood for."[3]

Shortly thereafter, Joel left his home in Alberta with just over twenty dollars in his pocket, planning to hitchhike to "freedom." He tried to tell himself he was finally free of the restraints and standards of his home—but by his own admission he was inwardly empty of everything but the burden of his guilt. Like David, Chuck, and Phil, he faced consequence after consequence—hitchhiking through snowstorms, sleeping beside the road, even spending almost three weeks in a juvenile prison in Portland, Oregon.

Like Chuck Colson, Joel didn't know Jesus Christ when he faced those consequences. Like David, Pastor Phil did. It does make a difference.

Unmarried, and Pregnant

Claudia knew Jesus Christ, too. An energetic, outgoing teenager, she was good at gymnastics, and had been selected as a cheerleader in her Christian school. Active in her youth group, she was personable, outgoing, seemingly the epitome of a Christian teenager.

But Claudia was in turmoil on the inside. Unsure of herself, she felt a desperate need to please others—and that led to her involvement with a young man named Al.

Al was two years older than Claudia, a man of the world,

into fast cars and a faster life-style than she had ever imagined. Soon he was the center of Claudia's life, although she concealed her relationship with him from her parents.

It doesn't take a lot of imagination to piece Claudia's story together. Before long, she and Al became sexually involved, and not long after that she learned she was pregnant.

Filled with humiliation, Claudia finally told her parents, "I feel so ashamed. I never intended for this to happen. I've ruined my life . . . and yours.

Her parents—active in the church and committed to Christ and to their family—were deeply saddened. They determined with Claudia to seek help—and to face the consequences of her sin. They would all go before the pastor and elders, and Claudia would make a clean breast of what had happened.

'I've Been Immoral'

I remember that meeting vividly. The tears in all our eyes. Claudia's halting voice. The love expressed as family and church leadership wept, hugged, and prayed together.

Afterward I asked one of my elders, "What stood out most to you about the meeting?"

Without hesitation, he voiced the same thing that had impressed me: "Did you hear what Claudia said? She didn't say, 'I got pregnant.' She said, 'I've been immoral.'"

Quickly I nodded agreement. "She didn't tell us the consequences, she simply confessed the sin. Would that we all could follow her example!"

David's anguish over his sin is reflected in Psalms 51. When you read the words of this Psalm, you don't hear David saying, "Lord, I got Bathsheba in trouble—I'm really sorry." What you hear is a confession of sin from the soul of a man who senses the enormity of what he has done—and who recognizes against Whom he has done it:

Blot out my transgressions.
Wash me thoroughly from mine iniquity, and cleanse me
from my sin.
For I acknowledge my transgressions: and my sin is ever

before me.
Against thee, thee only, have I sinned, and done this evil
  in thy sight.

(vss. 1b-4a)

It is in Psalms 51 that David comes to a crossroads—the critical crossroads faced by Chuck Colson, by Joel, by Pastor Phil, and by Claudia. On the one hand is an easy turn—the gentle slope in a downhill direction toward bitterness, self-pity, and, in all likelihood, repetition of the sin, not to mention an open door for sins of other kinds to slip in.

In the other direction—a sharp turn uphill, toward repentance, confession, forgiveness, restoration to fellowship—and even the hope of restoration to service, to ministry.

David took the uphill turn. So did the others of whom I've written in this chapter. Tragically, many people haven't. I could fill page after page with the stories of those who haven't. Perhaps you could too. But that's not my point.

The point is to show that hope for restoration is possible —even when we've blown it royally, as King David did. And the crux of the matter is expressed from two viewpoints in Psalms 51. I think it's important enough to devote the next chapter to what's involved.

What did King David learn that might help
us to resist the temptation to give up
when we fail in colossal ways?

10

Hope for a
Royal Recovery

*W*e met some people in the previous chapter who, like King David, had blown it royally. But in each case —in the life of Chuck Colson, and of Joel and Pastor Phil and Claudia—something was at work that enabled them not to give up. Something put them on the royal road to recovery. What did they discover that can help others of us who may be tempted to lose hope because of the depths of our failure?

THE INGREDIENTS OF RECOVERY

I think the crux of the matter is in verse 6 of that Psalm we noted—Psalm 51, where David poured out his confession of sin. Specifically, the key to recovery is found in two perspectives in Psalm 51:6:

Behold You desire truth in the inward parts. And in the hidden part You will make me to know wisdom.

The Ruthless Truth

First, from God's point of view.

God desires absolute, inward truth.

We must break through our denial, and become ruthlessly honest about what we have done. We must face the magnitude of it, recognize the true nature of it, and admit against whom it has been carried out.

We are creatures so prone to denial. We frequently laugh denial off as something addicts are guilty of—yet in a sense, by virtue of our fallen human nature, each of us is addicted to sin, and even to denial itself. It is that fundamental flaw of which Jeremiah wrote when he said, "The heart is deceitful above all things, and desperately sick. Who could know it?" (Jeremiah 17:9).

David understood the problem. It must have been his own propensity for denial which motivated him to write such words as, "Let the words of my mouth, and the meditation of my heart, be acceptable in your sight, O Lord my rock and my Redeemer" (Psalms 19:14).

And, "Search me, O God, and know my heart, try me and know my thoughts and see if there be any wicked way in me. And lead me in the way everlasting" (Psalms 139:23-24).

Paul hints at this same problem in his letter to the church of Rome:

For we know that the law is spiritual, but I am carnal, sold under sin. For that which I do, I understand not. For what I would, that do I not. But what I hate, that do I (Romans 7:14).

As Paul acknowledges in his despair, it is only through the power of God's Spirit that this denial can be broken and joy restored. David affirms his agreement in Psalms 51:11-12:

Do not cast me away from Your presence,
And do not take Your Holy Spirit from me.
Restore to me the joy of Your salvation,
And uphold me with Your generous Spirit.

And how does this impact us when we've blown it—royally or otherwise? In the fact that we must be absolutely honest—honest with God and honest with others—in a setting of accountability.

This means I stop minimizing the problem. I stop professing to have matters under control. I stop pretending things are okay. Certainly I don't overstate the extent of my wrong—but

I am aware of the far greater danger of understating and devaluing it.

God's Wisdom

The other side of Psalms 51:6 gives the added perspective we desperately need when we've blown it royally—God's wisdom:

In the hidden part, You shall make me to know wisdom.

How desperately we need wisdom—God's wisdom—when we've failed. We need wisdom to know whom to tell, wisdom to break free from the clutches of our sin, wisdom to deal with the consequences we face.

David needed such wisdom. And when God granted it, He saw David's broken spirit, his contrite heart, his desire to please Him. And God gave David direction for restoring the joy of his salvation.

After praying for God's Spirit, David promises, "Then I will teach transgressors Your ways, and sinners shall be converted to You" (Psalms 51:13). In time, David is given the opportunity to do just that—through his leadership in Israel and his influence outside her borders.

These two components—truth or honesty on our part, and wisdom provided by God—are the two essential ingredients for rebounding, for recovering when we've bottomed out through personal failure.

POWERLESSNESS FOR PURPOSE

That's what happened in the life of Chuck Colson. Confronted with the claims of Christ, the man who would be kingmaker finally bowed the knee to the King of Kings . . .

And was promptly sent to prison to face the consequences of his crime.

Yet it was in prison that Chuck Colson learned what came to be the most important lesson of his life:

When the frustration of my helplessness seemed greatest, I discovered God's grace was more than sufficient. After my imprisonment, I could look back and see how God used my powerlessness for His purposes. What He had chosen for my most significant witness was not my triumphs or victories, but my defeat.[1]

Some years ago at a broadcasters' meeting, I first heard about the establishment of Chuck Colson's ministry, Prison Fellowship—a ministry which became the focus of his life. I learned that in 1984 Colson met with high government officials in Lima, the capitol of Peru. But this meeting was far different from those Colson had arranged and participated in as a member of the Nixon inner circle.

For Chuck Colson had gone to Peru not to meet with government officials but to visit Lurigancho, the largest prison in the world.

By his own admission, Chuck Colson could not and did not have the power or influence to demand a meeting with Peru's highest government officials. Yet because of his ministry through Prison Fellowship to prisoners both in the U. S. and abroad, and because of the impact his ministry had on the terrorists and other criminals incarcerated at Lurigancho, they eagerly met with him. They were eager to hear what a man who now held no government power had to say about the power to change the lives and attitudes of men in prison.

So what's the point? It was when Chuck Colson went to prison that God began preparing him for what would be the most important phase of his life—and the one with the greatest eternal significance. If Chuck had given up hope just because he blew it royally, he would have missed out on this priceless opportunity.

ONE MINISTRY FOR ANOTHER

So it was with Pastor Phil. Acknowledging the wrong he had done to his family, his ministry, and most of all his God, he courageously stood before his people, carefully explained how he had failed, and offered his resignation. Their marriage strained by both the betrayal of trust and the future uncertainties, economic and otherwise, Phil and his wife moved from their comfortable pastorate back to the city where his mentor lived.

Placing himself under the accountability of several godly men he respected, and seeking both personal and family counseling from a Christian professional, Phil began working to rebuild his life. And work he did, taking on a variety of jobs, including moving furniture, before finally obtaining a position as manager of a grocery store.

It was during this time that Phil came in contact with several other men whose lives had been shattered as a result of similar failures—men who shared his feelings that any hope of future ministry or spiritual success had evaporated.

Out of these contacts, Phil began laying a foundation for a new ministry, one of reaching out with encouragement to others whose experience paralleled his. Phil's wife, with whom he has rebuilt the close relationship they once had, now shares his ministry goal. She is well-qualified for this, since she so clearly understands the pain, loneliness, and suspicion suffered by wives of men who experienced this kind of ministry failure.

Presently Phil is involved in a counseling ministry, using his training and personal experience to communicate God's wisdom, just as Nathan did for David. Someday Phil and his wife hope to establish a more widespread ministry to provide healing, growth, and restoration for moral casualties.

ABOUT JOEL AND CLAUDIA

And Claudia? Spurning without hesitation the option of abortion, she decided to have her baby. Shortly after the birth of her son, she and Al were married. Although life hasn't always been easy for her—the marriage broke up shortly after the birth of their second child—Claudia is currently involved in a Bible Study support group and is receiving Christian counseling. In addition, she is working part-time in a ministry of encouragement to hurting people in which she is able to use her cheerful voice, compassion, and keen awareness of God's ability to give people a second chance—even when they've failed.

Joel, too, has come to know clearly the God of the Second Chance. It happened dramatically on September 10, 1972, when he placed his trust in the Savior whom he had resisted for so long. The very next day Joel entered Bible School. Today his ministry involves communicating encouragement and the wisdom of God, both as pastor of a large church and through his writing ministry.

PAINFUL CONSEQUENCES

So David lived happily ever after? Well, not exactly. There were consequences, scars, painful circumstances.

The Law of Sowing and Reaping

Just as Nathan had promised, there was chaos, misery, and conflict in David's household from that day forward—not because God is some kind of cosmic killjoy, but simply because He has established certain universal principles—one of which is the law of sowing and reaping. It's the principle expressed so clearly in Romans 6:28: "The wages of sin is death." And it's further amplified in Galatians 6:7-8: "Do not be deceived, God is not mocked. For whatever a man sows, that shall he also reap."

The ultimate "wage" of sin is spiritual death, separation from God—the plight of every human being who refuses to reverse the process by trusting Christ for forgiveness and life. Physical death, the end result of all disease, accident and disaster, is another consequence of sin.

Sometimes sin's consequences occur immediately, sometimes much later. They *will* occur.

Almost before the door had closed behind Nathan, the young son born to David and Bathsheba became violently ill. For seven of the worst days of David's life the child hung between life and death. David prayed, fasted, spent sleepless nights, refused to eat.

Finally, the child died—and David's servants feared he might take his own life.

But when he learned of the child's death, David responded appropriately to the consequence. He cleaned himself up, went to the Lord's house and worshipped, then returned home to eat. His servants were shocked. "What is this! You fasted and wept while the child was alive. But it died—and now you can eat?"

David's response was both theologically and practically sound: "I prayed and I fasted, because I hoped God would allow the child to live. But that wasn't God's choice. The child has died; now it's time to get on with life."

David refused to be bitter or to dwell on what might have been. Instead, in an expression of understanding that I've personally used to encourage the parents of infants who have died, David told his servants, "I can't bring him back again can I? I shall go to him, but he will not return to me" (2 Samuel 2:23).

GETTING ON WITH LIFE

Several elements of David's response have practical implication for us. First, he felt free to pray to ask God to spare him from the consequences—but he accepted the consequences God permitted without bitterness.

Second, he applied God's truth—in this case, the truth concerning his own rightness with God and the prospect of his reunion with the child who had died—to his sad circumstances.

Third, David comforted his wife Bathsheba. He resumed normal marital relations, and this led to the birth of another son. The prophet Nathan, who became David's close friend, named the boy Jedidiah—but we know him better by his other name—Solomon.

David not only moved on with the activities of life, accepting the consequences of his deeds; he maintained a close relationship with Nathan the prophet. In fact, it is remarkable that even to the point of David's death—and beyond, as Solomon is crowned king—a close relationship continues between Nathan, David, Bathsheba and Solomon.

Caring Enough to Confront

What a practical lesson to us of the value of appropriate confrontation. Paul was right when he encouraged the Thessalonians to confront those who are out of line, in the same breath with which he urged them to cheer up those who are about to give up, and support those with chronic weakness (1 Thessalonians 5:14).

I thank God for people who've cared enough when I needed it to confront me—and for people who've responded positively and continued to be my friend after I've confronted them. That is how it should be.

David experienced a mixture of restoration and continued consequences, mercy and pain, similar to what those of us who fail today experience. We don't want things to be that way. We'd like for all the consequences to be lifted the moment we voice repentance. Like certain famous televangelists, our plea is, If God has forgiven me, I should be restored immediately—and completely.

That extreme is no more appropriate than the other extreme—washed up, ruined, hopeless, no ministry whatsoever, an out-and-out reprobate who's at least as big a failure, or perhaps bigger, than _____ or_____ (most of us can mentally fill in the blanks without too much trouble).

God graciously allowed David to continue to be married to Bathsheba—and He blessed their union with the birth of Solomon. God continued to use David as king, and allowed his friendship with Nathan to flourish.

Yet the consequences Nathan had originally predicted continued to plague David throughout his remaining years. His son Amnon raped his own sister Tamar. In turn, Amnon was murdered by his brother Absalom—the first of a trail of devastating acts that eventually forced David to flee his palace in humiliation. They finally led to the murder of Absalom by Joab, the very man David had entrusted with the job of having Uriah put to death. *What comes around, goes around.*

Living with Twin Truths

How important it is for us to remember these two balancing truths. God's forgiveness is absolute, complete, and unconditional. Yet the consequences of sin may continue to haunt us. Despite all that, we are never to give up.

Was David forgiven? Absolutely. Thoroughly. Totally. His transgression was forgiven—his sin covered—his guilt not charged—the deceitfulness of his heart removed. Those four statements of the early verses of Psalm 32 echo the reality of his forgiveness:

You are my hiding place. You shall preserve me from trouble. You will surround me with songs of deliverance (Psalms 32:7).

And the result of his confession? Forgiveness and restoration to fellowship, protection from trouble—access to God through prayer. As he continued to walk with God, he could voice a promise still true for us today.

David not only acknowledged God's protection from trouble; he further accessed God's direction to keep him from future sin. In Psalms 32:8 God speaks to David:

I will instruct you and teach you in the way which you shall go. I will guide you with my eye upon you. Don't be like the horse or mule without understanding, whose mouth must be held in check with bit and bridle.

Like a modern motorist at a railroad gate crossing, David was to stop at every point, look to God for guidance, listen to his instruction. To do so would lead to the full experience of God's loyal love, which results in gladness and joy.

AFFECTED BY THE FAILURE OF OTHERS

Perhaps we, like David, have blown it royally. Or perhaps we are caught in hopeless circumstances as the result of the failure of others.

That's what happened to Joshua, captain of the Lord's hosts. This leader of the nation that had struck terror in the hearts of every tribe in Palestine had just completed the successful conquest of Jericho. On the advice of his crack espionage team, he sent only two or three thousand soldiers to take on Ai, a much smaller, more vulnerable city.

Unknown to Joshua, however, sin had infiltrated the camp. An obscure Israelite named Achan had violated the ban against taking booty, bringing back a coat, plus a sum of silver and gold.

The consequences for the mighty Israeli army were devastating. Their military troop was put to flight—and thirty-six men were killed! What a contrast to the fantastic victory at Jericho, where there had been no casualties at all. The people's hearts melted with fear. Joshua, at the point of despair, tore his clothes, as was the custom of his day, and fell on his face before the Ark of the Lord.

Unlike David, Joshua hadn't personally failed. Yet, like members of David's family, he suffered the consequences of the failure of someone close to him. Joshua's over-confidence—and that of his people—had been shattered. He was at the point of despair.

THE LANGUAGE OF DEFEAT

Perhaps you can identify with Joshua's feelings as we consider five statements of a man ready to give up. Perhaps you've even said them yourself at some point.

First, Joshua questioned God's purpose in bringing them to this point in the first place. Keep in mind that this is the man who had followed in Moses' giant footsteps for forty years, who had confidently led Israel across the Jordan at flood stage, who had been commissioned by the captain of the Lord's hosts, who had given the command, "Shout! For the Lord has given you the city of Jericho."

He now uses the same tongue, lips and tonsils to question God's purpose in the first place.

Alas, O Lord God, why have you brought us over the Jordan just to deliver us to the Ammorites? (Joshua 7:7).

Even though God has clearly directed, Joshua's mind is filled with questions. How helpful the old warning—*don't doubt in the dark what God has shown you in the light*.

Second, Joshua questioned his own pursuit of God's leading. We can hear him ask himself, "Why didn't we just stay on the other side of the Jordan?" It's so easy to let the emotions of the moment cause us to forget the clear instructions of God in our lives in the past—and take the edge off our commitment to fulfill them.

Third, Joshua felt he had to have an answer for the situation—even while acknowledging his own helplessness. "O Lord, what will I say when Israel turns their backs before their enemies?" (vs. 8).

How like ourselves to make the perfectionist assumption that it's our job to get things moving in the right direction when there's been a setback—yet how contrary to the purposes of God! Yes, like Joshua we can be a tool, an encouragement, a source of leadership and motivation. But ultimately the job is not ours—it's God's.

'What About Our Name?'

Fourth, Joshua was more worried about his own reputation and that of his people than about God's purpose. It does not seem by accident that he verbalizes concern that the Canaanites and other tribes would cut off "our name"— before he even raises the question of "Your Great Name" (vs. 9). Such a perspective constitutes one of the most subtle dangers we face whenever we have failed—the danger of being more preoccupied with our reputation than with God's testimony.

Some time ago Terry, a man I know well, lost his job due to a combination of a failure on his part and false accusations by others. For a while he struggled with questions. What will others think? What will happen to my reputation? Finally, through the encouragement of close friends and meditation on God's Word, Terry became convinced that God would take care of his reputation—if he made God's testimony a priority.

Within twenty-four hours, a respected Christian leader, the head of a ministry with which Terry had worked over a period of years—phoned to invite him to lunch. Assuring Terry of his continued love and support, the leader explained the purpose of his meeting. It appeared that untrue rumors had circulated among some in the leader's staff. The leader had carefully investigated, tracking them to the source. Knowing them to be false, he had confronted all those involved—and he wanted to assure Terry that he had taken this action to stamp out those rumors. Imagine Terry's encouragement—he had made God's testimony a priority, and God had taken care of his good name!

Finally, Joshua struggled with the concern that somehow God wasn't big enough to take care of His name in light of the Israelites' failure. Now Joshua knew better than this. He was aware of how God had worked in Moses' life—in spite of Moses' previous failures. He had seen how God could use Israel, despite the unbelief of an entire generation. Despite forty years of funerals in the wilderness, he had seen God's power at the battle of Jericho. Surely he should have known that God's great name would remain great despite the failures of His followers.

Minding Our Own Business

In spite of many vivid lessons from his own lifetime, from his personal observation, and from Moses his mentor, Joshua was trying to assume God's responsibility while neglecting his own. How like our reaction today!

That's why, in a sense, God says, "Joshua, what are you doing lying in the dirt? Get up, you'll catch cold—and you won't get anything done. Israel has sinned. The sin has been covered up. That's why you have to take action to deal with the matter" (see Joshua 7:11-13).

And Joshua did so. At daybreak the next morning, he followed God's instructions by putting the offending family to death in a place that would be named the Valley of Achor—a Hebrew word meaning trouble.

In a sense, Joshua had blown it, too—even though he hadn't been guilty of the original sin. But he took action when confronted by a loving God in a place called the Valley of Achor.

Ironically, other than the sad record of Joshua 7, there are only two other references to the Valley of Achor. In one, the prophet Isaiah predicts a day of millennial bliss in which the Valley of Achor will be a place of rest for the herds of people who have sought the Lord (Isaiah 65:10).

The other reference regards the ministry of the prophet Hosea, whose wife failed him morally. Using his own life as an illustration of God's compassionate and unfailing love for the adulterous nation of Israel, Hosea holds out God's gracious promise to bring her tenderly into the wilderness, give her vineyards, and the Valley of Achor for a "door of hope" (Hosea 2:15).

A door of hope! Think of it!

How encouraging to know that when we—like Israel and David, like Joshua and Chuck Colson, like Pastor Phil and Claudia and Terry—have blown it, God still offers, even in the Valley of Trouble, a door of hope.

Although we're in more danger from giving up than from false hope, there are actually some situations when to hope is to defy God.

11

When Hope Doesn't Apply

$\mathscr{A}$t this point in the book you may be thinking, "I'm always supposed to be hopeful, positive, persistent. I'm never to quit. I'm always to forge ahead. Persistence, if not the quintessential quality, is certainly in the highest demand.

"So should I *always* persist?" you ask. "Is it imperative that I *never* quit?"

Yes . . . and No.

"Whatever does that mean?" you ask.

Ever hear of beating your head against a stone wall? It's a surefire way to get a headache—and it's not a very effective way to make a dent in a wall—much less tear it down.

As discussed elsewhere in this book, the Berlin Wall—that seemingly impenetrable barrier between East and West—has come down. But it didn't happen because some persistent capitalist—or communist—kept beating against the wall with his or her head.

There is a time to persist—a time to hope. It's important that this be our overriding perspective.

This chapter, however, is about balance, about recognizing that there are times when hope doesn't apply. It's about deciding when persistence isn't called for—when to hope or to persist is simply to beat your head against a wall.

That, in effect, is what Baby Doe did.

A few months ago my wife and I had the opportunity to visit with friends in Denver. We drove around the metropolitan area, and up into the mountains to the northwest of the city. We learned much about the lure of this special part of the world.

Baby Doe, whose name now graces a chain of restaurants in numerous metropolitan areas—located where possible on a mountain or hill overlooking the city—is an example of someone who persisted too long, who kept hoping when the basis for hope had expired.

John Tabor was one of the fanciest, and best known of the Colorado miners. He made millions as a result of the success of his "Matchless Mine," as he named it. Located near Cripple Creek, Colorado, it was one of the most famous—and most successful—silver mines in the entire mining industry.

At the height of his career, Tabor decided to divorce his wife. He had become attracted to a beautiful divorcee named Baby Doe.

The marriage of Tabor and Baby Doe was called by many "the social event of the early west." Robin Leach would have been right at home with the rich and famous who attended—including the President of the United States. Had the event taken place today, reporters from the newspaper tabloids and their video counterparts would have been pushing and shoving to obtain every possible scrap of gossip and information.

It seemed that John Tabor and Baby Doe had it all.

It wasn't long, however, before misfortune struck—Mr. Tabor lost his money. But he never lost the hope that, somehow, his mine would eventually come through and bail him out.

MISPLACED CONFIDENCE

Just before he died, Tabor admonished Baby Doe, "Have faith in the Matchless Mine. Never give it up. It will give you back all that I have lost."

For the next thirty-six years, Baby Doe lived near the

Matchless Mine. She guarded it. She expended all her meager resources and energies to fight off repeated attempts to oust her. She experienced one crushing blow after another.

Finally, in 1935, Baby Doe died—not with her wealth restored, but in abject poverty, in a dilapidated shack near the Matchless Mine.

Her hopes were never realized.

Does Baby Doe have anything to say to those of us living in the final years of the Twentieth Century? Without question she does. If she could somehow return from the grave, stand before us, and explain in twenty-five words or less the heart of what she learned during those thirty-six years following the death of her wealthy miner husband, I believe she'd say something like this:

"There is a time to give up. There is a point beyond which persistence is pointless."

Baby Doe's message has relevance for us, I believe, for two reasons. First, it's biblical. Second, it makes sense.

In preparation for writing this chapter, I examined a number of scriptures in which the concept of persistence or hope is combined with the negative, the word No. Although less common than positive exhortations to hope or persist, I believe that formula should not be ignored.

And it's not inconsistent with Jesus' words in Luke 18:1 to the effect that we should always pray and never give up.

BRAD, MOSES, AND A HARD HEART

Case in point. Julie and Brad had been married for seven years when they came to me for counsel to try to save their marriage. Both were Christians, but, as Julie put it, "Brad had the seven-year itch." He had become involved with a secretary at the firm where he worked, and his affair left Julie devastated. Brad seemed repentant, although he was reluctant to quit his job—something Julie really wanted him to do.

She, in turn, decided the affair was the straw that broke the back of the marital camel that had been overloaded for seven unhappy years. Their visit to my office was to be the final stop on the express line to the divorce attorney. After a few futile sessions meeting with them, I learned from Brad, as a result of a phone call late one evening, that Julie had filed for divorce.

Never Give Up?

I encouraged Brad not to give up—to continue praying, to work on areas of his own life—such as patience, trustworthiness, compassion, understanding, and the ability to communicate. I also urged him not to follow his inclination to keep calling her every day—sometimes several times a day—begging her to just give it another chance. I suggested, as other counselors have in similar circumstances, that such an approach is frequently counterproductive.

Then one day Brad showed up in my office unexpectedly. He simply had to see me that day. He was more upset than I'd ever seen him. Tears streaked his face as he poured out the awful news he had received only that morning.

Julie was involved with someone else. She had fallen in love with an account executive at the office where she worked —and they planned to be married within three months.

Now Brad was really desperate. Being personally involved as pastor and counselor, I sensed the measure of his desperation. It was an extremely trying ninety days for him—and a learning experience for me.

During that time we didn't give up. Brad prayed, communicated, read, kept seeing a professional Christian counselor, talked with his wife whenever he had the opportunity, wrote happy notes, sent presents.

Finally, in June of that year, Julie married the account executive.

The following day Brad walked into my office, collapsed on the sofa, looked at me, exhaustion written on his face, and said, "So do I give up now?"

I'm the guy who'd been telling him all this time, "Never, never, never give up." But by then I really had no option. I had to tell Brad, "Give it up."

In the process of interpreting the Mosaic Law that God delivered on Mount Sinai (Deuteronomy 24:1-4), Jesus explained that God permitted divorce—even remarriage—not because it was His perfect will but because of the hardness of human hearts.

However, it was carefully stipulated that if divorce and remarriage occurred, the wife was not to return to her former husband from whom she had been divorced. To do so was simply forbidden.

On the basis of that biblical principle, I had to tell Brad that it was time to give up hope of being reunited with Julie. He would see her when he visited the kids. They would have a relationship, because of the children. But she would never again be his wife, nor he her husband.

Not Giving Up Can Mean an Addiction

I thought about Brad and Julie the other evening when a man living in a midwestern state phoned my radio talk show to share a perplexing family problem. "It's like my wife is addicted to her ex-husband," he lamented. "She's always thinking about him, always talking about him. Sometimes I wonder who she's really married to. She says she loves me. We've been married for several years now, but she just can't get him out of her mind. It's really affecting our marriage."

I can't imagine a marriage not being affected in such a situation—in the most adverse manner. Clearly, this man's wife was addicted to her former husband. Also, she had failed to reckon with the fact that the former union had been broken. She continued hoping, but her hope ticket had already been used up. Here's what I mean:

Recently a Dallas newspaper carried the story of the arrest of a man who had played a key role in cleaning up the savings and loan scandal in Texas. Now, however, the man—who was the C.E.O. of a company with offices in Dallas and Chicago—had allegedly bilked American Airlines out of hundreds of thousands of dollars.

His scheme was simple. He would purchase a valid ticket on American, thus guaranteeing he had a reserved seat. But when he boarded the aircraft, he somehow found a way to use a ticket that had already been used on a previous flight. I'm not sure how he did it—the airlines have safeguards to prevent this—but somehow he found a way. The point is, he was using a ticket that had already been used up. It was no longer valid.

We are probably tempted to give up more often than to persevere beyond good judgement. Our "hope ticket" is usually still valid. But there are other times when hope simply doesn't fit, such as a wife clinging to her ex-husband after both have remarried.

WHEN DOES HOPE NOT APPLY?

So how do we know when hope doesn't apply? The best way to find out is to examine Scripture itself. Clearly, hope doesn't apply when to hope would violate Scripture. The case of Brad and Julie illustrates this principle.

Second, hope should be suspended when we find ourselves pursuing an expectation that would violate the character of God. There's an interesting observation in the Sermon on the Mount that illustrates this. In preparing His listeners for the Kingdom of Heaven, Jesus shows them that their personal righteousness—the kind advocated and exemplified by the Scribes and Pharisees—isn't good enough.

As one example, Jesus, recognizing that the Pharisees loved their neighbors and hated their enemies, encouraged his followers to love their enemies and "do good to those who hate you." His recommendation for implementing this principle is quite specific—that we share our financial resources "hoping for nothing again, and your reward shall be great, and you shall be the sons of the highest; for He is kind to the unthankful and to the evil" (Luke 6:35).

In this case, *not* to hope or hold an expectation for a return on our investment in the needy is to exemplify the same gracious spirit as the Father who freely gave His Son that we, his enemies, might have life.

This is another one of those truths that must be held in balance. Jesus' words do not necessarily mean it is my responsibility to give away every resource at my disposal to every person standing on the street corner holding a sign that says "Will work for food." Caring for the needs of my own family, and supporting God's work, are of higher priority.

However, if I close my feelings of compassion toward those in need, I should not profess to be exhibiting God's love. If the only funds I disperse are those from which I expect a return on investment, I should not claim to be a person of compassion.

This teaching from Jesus flies in the face of those who promulgate a so-called "prosperity gospel." You've heard how it's supposed to work. A person invests so-called "seed money" in the Lord's work—almost invariably in the ministry of the one who is doing the teaching. Then supposedly at some point in the near future, the contributor miraculously becomes prosperous. Such an approach stands in stark contrast to Jesus' warning to "hope for nothing in return."

Hoping Against God's Will

Third, hope expires when we crash headlong into God's sovereignty. There are times when God says certain things are simply not humanly possible. For example, God confronts Job with the hopelessness of attempting to defeat Leviathan, that awesome creature described in Job 41:9.

There is clearly no hope of life or heaven for those who have refused to trust Christ. Paul makes this clear when writing to the Ephesians (2:12), and in his words of encouragement to the Thessalonians regarding their "blessed hope," the rapture (1 Thessalonians 4:13).

Sir Francis Newport, the English infidel, recognized this truth. The story is told that, as he lay dying, he said to his fellow infidels, "You need not tell me there is no God, for I know there is one, and that I am in His angry presence. You need not tell me there is no hell, for I already feel my soul slipping into its fires. Wretches, cease your idle talk about there being hope for me! I know I am lost forever."

Why would Sir Francis Newport voice such a sentiment? He had persistently refused to admit his need of the Savior, and to trust Christ. Thus he knew clearly that, for him, there was no hope.

The most common intersecting point for human hope and divine sovereignty—and the most recognizable—is a point we are confronted with in some fashion every day of our lives. It is the point of death.

DEATH AND HOPE

Few people learn this lesson quite like King Hezekiah of Israel. A godly ruler who lived near the end of the period leading up to the Babylonian captivity, he had just witnessed God's miraculous overthrow of Sennacherib of Assyria. In response to Hezekiah's prayer, what seemed hopeless had actually come about.

Lord Byron, in his classic poem "The Destruction of Sennacherib," gave rhyme to the story of the mysterious death of 185,000 Assyrian soldiers—and the subsequent assassination of Sennacherib by two of his own sons when he returned to his homeland.

Shortly after this astounding victory, King Hezekiah became sick—in fact, he was at the point of death. A visit from the prophet Isaiah confirmed the news: "Set your house in order, Hezekiah, you will die and not live" (2 Kings 20:1).

As he had before, King Hezekiah prayed. Centuries before Jesus told His disciples to pray always and never give up, Hezekiah gave flesh-and-blood implementation to this strategic principle.

And as He had with the prayer regarding the army of Sennacherib, God again responded positively. Isaiah was sent bearing a second message—God would allow Hezekiah to live fifteen additional years. The prophet's message was miraculously confirmed when the angle of the sun was reversed ten degrees—King Hezekiah observed the miracle on the sundial built by his father Ahaz (vss. 9-11).

To celebrate his delivery, Hezekiah wrote a song in which he praises God for His gracious gift of life. The poem climaxes with the exultant statement, "For You have cast all my sins behind your back" (Isaiah 38:17). In the following excerpt, Hezekiah draws a true observation from the obvious:

> For Sheol cannot praise you. Death cannot celebrate you. Those who go down into the pit cannot hope for your truth. The living, he shall praise you. The parent to the children shall communicate your truth (Isaiah 38:18).

Hezekiah may have been the first poet to record such a song, but he probably wasn't the last. When a person has died, it's over, it's done. There is no more hope—no hope of praising God, of communicating with your children or leaving a lasting legacy, no hope of changing what has been done in this life. In short, death brings hope to an end.

David expresses this same premise in Psalm 39. He, too, had been delivered from an early grave in response to his prayer to God (39:13), and he, too, responded with a song of praise and hope (vs. 7). Earlier he had observed that there is no benefit or productivity possible in the grave, no possibility of proclaiming God's truth (Psalm 6:5).

The death of David's infant son, born of his sinful union with Bathsheba, had given David a graphic reminder of this lesson. Before the child died, David recognized that the power of life and death rested in God and God alone; so he cried out to God, appealing for his son's life. But when that point of hope was passed, David didn't hesitate to recognize it, and to change his behavior.

A Choice Against Heroics

Not long ago, a young couple we'll call Jim and Valerie faced a similar dilemma. Six-year-old Bethany, the second of their three children, had been diagnosed with a genetic degenerative disorder called neuronal ceroid lipofucinoses. They wept in their grief after being told by the best of medical authorities that Bethany had zero chance of recovering—that she would almost certainly die within three to five years, and probably much sooner.

Bethany grew weaker and weaker. She was unable to walk, and required constant care when she was at home. Her mother had little relief except for a few hours a week when Bethany attended a special school for the disadvantaged.

One day Valerie received an urgent phone call from the school. Bethany had simply quit breathing. A member of the school faculty had given her CPR while a staff member dialed 911 to summon an ambulance. During the initial hours of her treatment, Bethany's breathing stopped four more times. Finally, at Cook Children's Medical Center in Fort Worth, Jim and Valerie listened intently as the doctor explained the problem—and presented them with some tough options.

The couple agonized over the issues, then finally reached a painful, difficult decision. Because of her situation, they would allow Bethany to be given oxygen and kept comfortable. But the doctor was to note on Bethany's charts that she was not to be placed on a breathing machine. Nothing would be done to take her life prematurely—but neither would her life be prolonged by heroic measures.

In making this difficult decision—one with which my wife and I concurred as we talked with Jim and Valerie—these anguished young parents were simply recognizing that the power of life and death rests in the hands of a sovereign God. We are to do all we can—then leave the outcome up to Him.

Flora, a widow of some years, never seemed to learn this lesson. Her husband suffered a stroke shortly after retiring at the age of sixty-five. For several months he lived in a coma. The doctors told Flora there was little if any hope of his recovering. She faithfully attended to him, spending most of her waking hours at his bedside—even though, except for one or two occasions, he never responded to her words, gestures, or presence.

Finally, after months of agony on her part, Flora's husband died. Those who were close to her hoped she would be able to process her grief and get on with her life. But it wasn't to be.

Following the funeral, Flora developed a habit of going to the cemetery every day, and spending hours at her husband's grave site. When this pattern of behavior persisted for months, Flora's grown children became concerned. They talked with her, her pastor counseled with her, all to no avail. Flora's standard response went something like this: "He's still with me as far as I'm concerned. I can feel his presence when I'm in the cemetery. I talk to him—and it's as though he answers me back."

Unwilling to work through her loss and move on, Flora lived in the past, failing to recognize the reality—and the finality—of death. She needed to face the fact that there was no hope for relating to her husband. Death, at its heart, is separation; but Flora has refused to acknowledge this truth.

THE RESURRECTION FACTOR

"But wait!" you may be saying at this point. "What about the resurrection? Doesn't God give victory over death?"

Absolutely. There is no question about it. But again, truth must be held in balance.

Perhaps the man who can best help us balance this truth is the man who had two funerals.

Now, I'm not talking about Tom Sawyer. Many of us fondly remember the story of how Mark Twain's fictitious character staged his own death, then crept in to watch and listen to determine who would really mourn his passing.

The person I'm talking about actually did die twice. As we have already recalled, His name was Lazarus. He was the brother of Martha and Mary, and a close friend of Jesus. He had fallen so seriously ill that Jesus had been summoned with a view to healing him. But when the Savior's arrival was delayed, Lazarus died.

Perhaps "stuffing" her grief, Martha somewhat angrily insisted that if Jesus had simply arrived in a timely fashion, her brother's life could have been spared. And when Jesus insisted, "Your brother will rise again," Martha essentially said what any Bible believing Christian would say today. "I know he will rise again in the resurrection at the last day."

Hindsight is always 20/20 vision, and it's easy for us to say, "Martha, you should have known before it happened that the Lord could raise your brother." But who among us would have suspected? Who would have believed? Who would have even thought it possible? Sure, Jesus could have healed

Lazarus—probably kept him alive, and even restored him to health. But raise Lazarus from the dead?

That's one of the things that makes Lazarus' raising all the more remarkable. This was the exception that proved the rule about life and death. It was an intervention by the Creator, suspending the laws governing creation that He and His Father had established.

What John's Gospel doesn't record is the account of Lazarus' subsequent death. But die he did—again. And they undoubtedly held another funeral for him. Hebrews 9:27 makes it clear: it is appointed unto men once to die. Lazarus was simply given an extra appointment.

Hope doesn't fit when death has occurred—other than the hope of resurrection and an after-life.

A WOMAN'S REALISM

Hope is simply inappropriate when wisdom dictates it's time to quit hoping. Case in point, Ruth's mother-in-law, Naomi. She changed her name from "Pleasant" to "Bitter" after encountering a multiple dose of life's painful adversities.

Had Naomi taken a modern-day stress test such as the one devised by Holmes and Rahe, her score would probably have been off the chart. First there was the famine, which meant economic reversal, the loss of income. Then came the relocation from Israel to Moab, followed by the adjustment to a foreign culture, a place where everything from religion to diet was totally different. More stress occurred when, counter to family custom and biblical mandate, Naomi's sons married Moabite women.

Naomi's stress came to a climax with the death of her husband, followed shortly by the loss of her two sons. Bitterly she told her friends and relatives in Bethlehem, "Don't call me Pleasant. Call me Bitter. I went out full, and the Lord brought me home empty" (see Ruth 1:20).

But before her return to the land of her youth, there's a scene in which Naomi attempts to say good-bye to her daughters-in-law, Orpah and Ruth. With Orpah, Naomi is successful in her farewell. Ruth, on the other hand, persists.

In the course of the conversation, Naomi employs sanctified common sense:

> Go back my daughters, why would you go with me? Do you think I will bear additional sons you may marry to be your husbands? I'm too old to have a husband. If I should say I have hope, if I married tonight and immediately bore sons, could you wait until they were grown? Not a chance, my daughters (Ruth 1:11-13).

Naomi's perspective regarding the hope of marrying and having additional children was not only wise for her day—it's insightful for ours. Granted, she speaks from the throes of bitterness toward God, feeling the pain of her adversity. But she's absolutely right. There's little question that her biological clock had long since stopped ticking—and she has the common sense to recognize this fact of life.

At this point I suspect at least some of you are saying, "Wait a minute. What about Sarah? She was ninety years old—and *she* had a baby." I couldn't agree more that, just as God is sovereign regarding death, He's certainly in charge of births. As Hannah acknowledged freely, it is God who opens and closes the womb. Sarah, laughing behind the tent door when she hears the word that she's about to become pregnant at the age of eighty-nine, is another strong witness to the sovereignty of God in the area of birth.

You don't even have a biological clock left at the age of eighty-nine, much less one that ticks! Furthermore, Sarah's husband Abraham was "as good as dead" as he approached age 100. Yet God chose to give them a child.

But Sarah, like Lazarus, is the exception who proves the rule. I mentioned earlier that my friend Dr. Joe McIlhaney, one of the country's premier obstetrician/gynecologists, has done extensive research into fertility. A frequent guest on my radio call-in program, he is recognized as an authority on everything from *in vitro* fertilization to laparoscopic surgical procedures to repair tubal and ovarian damage. His work is proof that modern medicine can work wonders.

Yet Joe would be the first to tell you that *God* is in control of the business of who gets pregnant and when. This skilled specialist believes that God has just now begun to allow us to understand some of the processes He uses. Ultimately, however, he says he's reminded daily that God is in charge.

HOPE AND CHILDHOOD DISCIPLINE

Another area in which wisdom recognizes that there is a point beyond reasonable hope is in the matter of rearing children. There's a time beyond which parents no longer have the opportunity to shape the lives of those children, to mold them into men and women of character. That's the point Solomon makes in Proverbs 19:8—"Discipline your child while there is hope. Don't hesitate just because he cries out."

This is a verse my dad took seriously. A sergeant in the Marines during World War II, he allowed those experiences to reinforce the discipline he had learned from his father—my grandfather. As I mentioned earlier, my dad's discipline was no laughing matter. It hurt.

Quite a contrast to a man I know well—I'll call him Lew. Marrying somewhat late in life, he and his wife were blessed with two children. Although he was extremely successful in his corporate career, Lew was never quite able to pull it off as a dad. His parents had been super strict on him, and he determined he would be the kindest, most sensitive, and loving father a son ever had—and he was.

Unfortunately, Lew never gave his son the discipline he so desperately needed. The balance just wasn't there. Finally, when his son became a teenager, Lew began to realize his mistake. Getting into the Word and reading Christian books, he saw that his son, even in his persistent misbehavior, had been crying out for the strict discipline of a loving dad.

But when Lew tried to reverse his field, he found it just didn't work. As Solomon warned, it was simply too late. By then there was no hope of turning his son around—unless God chose to miraculously intervene.

MIRACLES AND CONSEQUENCES

In this area, as in so many others, we may hope for a miracle. We'd like to see God move the sun backward as he did with Hezekiah, or break open the grave, as he did with Lazarus, or open a long-closed womb as he did with Sarah. But God usually chooses to allow the natural laws and consequences He has established in the universe to operate.

Christian recording artist Phil Driscoll is a good illustration of the point. Anyone who has ever heard Phil sing knows how much he enjoys music. One of the most talented men ever to pick up a trumpet, Phil, by his own admission, doesn't have nearly the vocal ability he once possessed.

Recently, in Washington, D.C., I heard him pull off an unusual musical achievement—sing the bass solo from the "The Trumpet Shall Sound" section of "The Messiah" and play the trumpet part for the same solo! But why doesn't Phil have the voice he once had?

The problem, in a word, was cocaine. For many years, while he was with the rock group Chicago, Phil ingested large quantities of cocaine. Unfortunately, his voice was permanently impaired. Perhaps there are times when Phil might hope for a miracle, wishing that God would miraculously reverse the damage done years ago. Instead, Phil simply uses the talent he has left—working within his limitations rather than wasting futile energy trying to change permanent damage already done.

The lesson for us is obvious, but one we frequently forget. We are to fulfill our responsibilities—doing what we can, leaving the rest to God. For Phil that involves playing the trumpet and singing Christian songs. Like Phil Driscoll, many of us have been impaired in some way or another by the scars of the past—perhaps as a consequence of our own sinful behavior, or maybe as the result of factors beyond our control. Whatever the case, we must simply press on, doing what God has given us to do—and leaving the rest to Him.

A TIME TO PULL THE PLUG

Jim Hedlund and his wife Norma invested almost a quarter of a century in missionary work among the Shuar people, a community of former headhunters in Ecuador's eastern jungle region. The radio station they established, Radio Rio

Amazonas, served as the main communication link between these isolated jungle people and the outside world.

Some time ago, Jim and his staff faced a difficult decision. They had sought to continue their radio ministry in the face of increasing political and social unrest, declining listenership (partly from higher costs for batteries and radios), plus actual personal danger to radio station staff members from political activists. Jim put it this way:

> Things heated up to such a degree that our lives and property were in constant danger. The life of the Shuar program director and the lives of his family were threatened repeatedly. Although the threats did not materialize, the net effect was that his desire to continue in radio was killed. He had served a total of twenty-three years in various positions in the radio work. He liked his work. He was good at it. But he was the first to say that the time had come to discontinue at least the Shuar language programming segments.[1]

Reaching a decision to discontinue a ministry is an almost unheard of thing for many Christian organizations. But in this case, it was a decision marked by wisdom and courage—and it was eventually validated as a wise choice. The former station manager is now serving in a literature ministry that affects all of Ecuador. Ministry efforts to teach the Shuar people face-to-face through the local church are being stepped up. In addition, outside agitators who have sought to use radio to foster their own anti-Christian beliefs, as well as drive a wedge between Christians, have been thwarted.

Some might view all this as giving up. But those who know Jim and Norma Hedlund, and those who were aware of the situation, recognize this decision as a product of wisdom.

Either Way, God Is Sovereign

The prophet Ezekiel records two situations in Israel that illustrate the balance between human wisdom and divine sovereignty, especially as it relates to the matter of persistence.

In the first case, the prophet uses poetic language to lament the loss of Israel's princes—the kings who resided in Jerusalem at the time of the captivity. The lioness Israel nourished a cub who became a powerful young lion, noted among the nations. This lion, King Jehoahaz, was led captive in chains to Egypt. When this happened, Ezekiel notes, "Now when she saw that she had waited and her hope was lost, then she took another of her whelps and made him a young lion" (Ezekiel 19:5). Ezekiel's point is obvious. Jehoahaz had been taken captive, with no hope for recovery—it was time for Israel to choose a new leader.

Contrast this picture with the prophet's prediction regarding the dry bones (Ezekiel 37). "Our hope is lost," the nation concludes (vs. 4). Ezekiel doesn't condemn this thinking—he simply counters it with a remarkable revelation of God's plan to bring a dead nation to life. Using vivid language to describe the restoration of sinew and flesh to bones, restoring breath and vitality and renewing spiritual awareness, the prophet points out that, though humanly speaking all hope is lost, Israel as a nation will be restored.

Even though in both cases human wisdom was forced to acknowledge that hope had expired, a sovereign God could reverse either situation. Ezekiel records that in one instance He would. In the other, He didn't. Can we rightly honor Him in one situation but not the other?

PEOPLE WITHOUT HOPE

Not only does hope not fit when death has occurred, or when wisdom dictates that it has expired, there are also certain individuals for whom hope doesn't fit.

The Wicked Fool

The first of these we might describe as the wicked fool—the unbelieving, self-sufficient person often identified as a fool in the book of Proverbs. Three times King Solomon documents the futility of the expectation of those he classifies as wicked—those whose life and belief show them to be separated from God. Their expectation comes to naught (10:28), to death (11:7), and ultimately to wrath (11:23).

A definite regression can be seen in the life of the person who has no use for God today. He may achieve great exploits, perhaps amassing a fortune in the world of business and industry. She may accomplish some remarkable medical or scientific development, or even become a significant political leader. Yet, God says that, in this life, whatever such persons do adds up to zero.

Furthermore, the wicked fool will eventually die. And after his death he faces only an eternity of divine wrath. What a hopelessly bleak picture painted by the wisest human being who ever lived—and all because those he describes chose to live as though there were no God.

A Fool and His Money

Bob grew up in abject poverty, the son of an extremely poor family. Perhaps that's why he was frequently fond of saying, "All that really matters is money." Another of Bob's proverbs was, "Remember the Golden Rule—the one who holds the gold makes the rule!"

That's how it was with Bob. He started with one company, eventually took over a second, then a third. Assembling a management team of people equally dedicated to the bottom line, he became known as a shrewd, even ruthless businessman. But he didn't mind. When people referred to him as a local version of Donald Trump, he'd chuckle and say, "I may not be as well-known as The Donald, but then I've never lost an airline either."

Bob's often-stated hope was to make enough money with his multiple businesses to retire by age forty, then spend the rest of his life either playing golf or sailing—the two passions that occupied the few nonworking hours he permitted himself. His hopes appeared to be a possibility, until tragedy struck. Shortly after his thirty-ninth birthday, Bob suffered a massive heart attack. Doctors had warned him he needed to give up smoking, cut down on cholesterol, exercise more, and, above all, change his attitudes and life-style in terms of work. His wife and friends had begged and pleaded, but to no avail.

Just as the doctors warned, a second heart attack occurred six months later. And shortly before his fortieth birthday, Bob was retired—feet first, to the cemetery.

In many ways, Bob's career bore a strong resemblance to

that of a man of whom Jesus spoke. This man tore down his barns to build larger storage facilities for the grain he'd planned to harvest and enjoy. "Fool," the Lord said, "this night your life will be required of you."

Bob's story is also similar to Israel's response to God, whom Jeremiah portrays as a potter, asking the nation, the work of His hands, to submit to His sovereign shaping and change their ways. Their response was, "There's no hope of that" (Jeremiah 18:12). Likewise, in response to a warning from the prophet Isaiah, the nation simply refused to recognize their truly hopeless plight (Isaiah 57:10).

The two prophets' statements sound almost opposite, but their content is remarkably similar. Both represent—and challenge—the expression of fools who refuse to submit to a sovereign God, and who are therefore without hope.

Less Hope than a Fool

Ironically, Solomon identifies two classes of people who have even less hope than a fool. One, described in Proverbs 26:12, we might call "The Arrogant Deny-er"—the one who insistently asks, "Me? Need God?" This person, in chronic spiritual denial, simply refuses to see his desperate plight. The man is like Herod in Acts 12, smiling expansively when his followers cried, "It must be the voice of a God and not a man." Herod didn't realize he was only an hour away from death, because he refused to give God the glory.

Then there is the hopeless person we might label "The Hasty Blurter," described in Proverbs 29:20. During his early career, David encountered such a man. His name was Nabal, and he was a man quick of tongue and sharp of word. David's young men had been sent by their captain to seek provisions (1 Samuel 25:9-11). Nabal's vitriolic response was, "Who is David? There are plenty of outlaws today. Why should I support David?" Not long after, Nabal, having escaped David's sword, suffered an apparent heart attack and died following a night of partying.

For the hasty blurter, the arrogant deny-er, the wicked fool, God says simply, "There is no hope."

Bob had some of all three of these characters in him. As one of his former associates said at the cemetery following his funeral, "He lived hard, climbed high, and died young."

What an epitaph.

A Forbidden Relationship

Let's consider one final example of a person whose hope was best unrealized. Sally and her husband Fred had only been married for a short time—and already Sally wasn't happy. Since he had been a victim of abuse, and because he was under a great deal of stress at his work, Fred was unable to focus on the marriage relationship, or on Sally. Communication suffered, as did their intimate life.

Sally, who was a big fan of daytime soap operas, began fantasizing that perhaps she was in love with someone else. Sure enough, two men attracted her attention because of their ministry visibility, commitment to Christ, and compassion for people. One was her pastor, and the other the teacher of the adult Sunday School class Sally and Fred attended.

As she later confided, Sally went back and forth thinking about these two men, speculating about what it would be like to be married to one or the other. Eventually in her own mind she became convinced that, somehow, God was in these thoughts. Her husband was going to die, or something would happen, and she would be able to marry one of these two.

Finally Sally mustered up the courage to set up a counseling appointment with her pastor. Gingerly she broached the subject, discussing her feelings and her hopes regarding the Sunday School teacher. Her pastor, however, noted carefully some of the comments she made, and recognized a potentially dangerous counseling phenomenon called transference. Immediately he referred Sally to a professional Christian counselor with whom he often worked.

Sharing his concerns, first with Sally, then with the counselor, the pastor made it clear that Sally's hopes were totally misplaced. God never intended for her to consider or even think about being intimately related to someone other than her husband. Rather, it was God's will that she concentrate her thoughts and energies on her present marriage relationship. Her hope needed to be refocused away from the possibility of finding someone else, and onto the prospect of a better relationship with her husband.

It took time, but Sally was finally able to process her feelings, grieve the loss of her fantasies, and concentrate on her marriage. Not surprisingly, it was at this point that her husband actually began paying more attention to the relationship—with a significant improvement in every area of their married life.

HOPE, WISDOM, AND THE WORD

Some final observations regarding when hope doesn't apply. First, the witness of Scripture is clear. For those who are rightly related to God, there is hope. For the ungodly, the person in whom there is no faith—there quite simply is no hope. In short, ultimate hope rests in God himself.

Second, hope in any situation will be governed by God's sovereignty. When Jeremiah wrote to the Israelites who had been taken captive, he shared a heavy burden. Seventy long years would pass—but then the nation would be restored. Captivity was a necessary part of God's discipline. Yet, according to Jeremiah 29:11, it was evident that God's purposes for Israel were peaceful, not evil. He would provide His people with a future and a hope!

Third, in any given situation, we humans desperately need God's wisdom to fine-tune our expectations. Proverbs 24:14 notes, "So shall the knowledge of wisdom be unto your soul. When you have found it, then there shall be a reward and your expectation shall not be cut off."

It is God's wisdom that can give us the proper perspective on any of life's myriad of circumstances, showing us just what and what not to expect, so that our expectations and hopes will be precisely what God intends for them to be.

Finally, the key to obtaining the wisdom needed to align our expectations with the will of God is His written revelation. Psalm 119 is the longest single chapter in Scripture. All but a very few of its verses have something significant to say about God's written revelation, His Word. Seven times during this lengthy portion, the psalmist connects hope to the Word:

> I have hoped in Your ordinances ...I have hoped in Your word ...I hope in Your word ...I have hoped for Your salvation and done Your commandments ...I hoped in Your word ...Uphold me according to your word, that I may live, and let me not be ashamed of my hope.

The implication of the psalmist's prayer for us is evident. To the degree that we make God's Word our foundation for decision making and daily living, we need never be ashamed of our expectations or hopes. For they will be consistent with God's purposes, attuned to His wisdom, submitted to His sovereignty. As a result, we'll know when hope does or doesn't apply.

Attacks from both Satanic and human enemies
claim many victories for hopelessness.
How strong is our defense?

12
Hope in the Face
Of Attack

*T*his is a test. For the next sixty seconds this station will conduct a test of the Emergency Broadcast System. This is only a test."

When I first became involved in radio during my years at Dallas Seminary, I obtained a radio license known as a "third ticket," officially called a third-class radiotelephone operator's license. This piece of paper, which I obtained following the successful completion of a test which is no longer required, enabled me to sign onto the station log, take transmitter readings, and fulfill all the responsibilities of operating a radio broadcast station.

At that time, no part of the responsibility for a broadcast operation was taken more seriously than the Emergency Broadcast System, referred to as EBS. Tested regularly, this system was designed to notify Americans in the event of an emergency—articularly a nuclear attack. In the post-U.S.S.R. era, such concerns seem to have gone the way of bomb shelters—but we took them very seriously in those days.

The U. S. government had developed stringent safeguards to see to it that a genuine attack would never be confused with a false alarm or a test. On a regular basis, sealed envelopes containing updated authenticator codes were sent to every broadcast facility in the United States.

Despite all the safeguards, however, the unthinkable happened one day. The signal for a real attack was mistakenly given. The wire services picked up the bulletin and distributed those chilling words, *"This is not a test."*

The response to this bulletin was both enlightening and frightening. The majority of the U. S. radio stations that received the bulletin either chose to ignore it, or figured, correctly, that it was a mistake.

Incredible events have occurred to change the face of the world in which we live since the Cold War days of the Sixties and Seventies. In 1989, the Berlin Wall came down—and within months, Germany was reunified. Then in 1991 the Soviet Union fell apart from within. Yet the collapse of what seemed to be our biggest adversary did not remove the danger of attack from other adversaries, such as Saddam Hussein, Moammar Khadaffi, and their like.

Few things can be as discouraging as sudden, unexpected attack—which often leaves the victim feeling helpless and hopeless. Numerous events, from the carefully planned terrorist effort during the Munich Olympics of 1972 to the commandeering of TWA Flight 847 and the hijacking of the cruise ship Achille Lauro in more recent years, are living evidence of the nerve-shattering fear and dread such attacks can generate.

ENEMIES, HUMAN AND OTHERWISE

Attacks can produce hopelesness and despair in the lives of Christians as well. Sometimes they come from vicious human enemies who, for greed, guilt, or whatever other motivation, may launch an assault.

Frequently such attacks are motivated by Satan, the supernatural enemy of our souls. Being armed and ready for these attacks, and responding in the appropriate way, can keep us from becoming defeated, disillusioned, and despairing—in short, from losing hope.

When I was growing up, people thought Halloween was some kind of a joke. We laughed at witches, goblins, and "spooks." Invariably, at school or trick-or-treating, some kids would dress as the devil—horns on the head, a dangling tail, cloven hooves, and a pitchfork.

This tradition of what the devil looks like apparently has a dual origin. During the Middle Ages, so-called "miracle plays" provided a popular form of entertainment. Audiences apparently derived a great deal of excitement from watching "Old Nick," or "his Satanic majesty"—horns and tail and all —sneaking up on the hero or heroine.

The other root of this picture of Satan is in Revelation 12:3, which somewhat corresponds with this imagery. A great red dragon with seven heads and ten horns appears during a time of intense tribulation on earth. His vicious activities—particularly directed against the nation of Israel— make it clear that this dragon is none other than Satan himself.

Now my purpose at this point is not to fully expound the doctrine of Satan and demons. Numerous evangelical works have done so in excellent fashion. However, it is impossible to consider hope and persistence without recognizing one of hope's fiercest foes—the powerful, evil spirit whose strategies and minions have sapped the persistence from many a saint.

SATAN AND MARTIN LUTHER

Several years ago, my wife and I were privileged, along with several members of the church I pastored and other Christian friends, to take a tour behind the Iron Curtain in East Germany. The occasion was the 500th anniversary of the birth of Martin Luther. We traveled to numerous sites in both East and West Germany, including Worms, where Luther is said to have verbalized his stand on the authority of Scripture with the words, "Here I stand, I cannot do otherwise . . . My conscience is captive to the word of God, I cannot and I will not recant anything . . . God help me."[1]

One memorable afternoon as we drove south, then west, from Leipzig in East Germany, we spotted our destination for that day—a castle, rising high above the East German landscape. At the crown of the steep hill, above the town of Eisenach, was the Wartberg Castle, where Luther was hidden after he was declared to be an outlaw because of his stand against church authorities at Worms.

As we were shown through the vast, musty old castle, one room in particular intrigued us. Located near the top of one of the towers, its window commanded a view of the surrounding countryside and the town below. Yet it was a dark room, and quite musty. In the corner of the room there was a desk, and on the desk, an inkwell. It was here, we were told, that during his work on translating the Bible from the original Greek and Hebrew languages into German, Luther struggled with depression and felt himself under intense Satanic attack.

We were told that Luther felt the presence of Satan so strongly that, on one occasion, he actually threw an inkwell at the devil, whom he perceived to be physically present in the room with him.

SATAN'S OVERALL PURPOSE

Luther's persistent battles with satanic oppression and discouragement are certainly not unique. Attacks on both well-known and obscure Christians are consistent with Satan's life purpose, as explained by Jesus in John 10:10: "The thief comes not but for to steal, to kill and to destroy."

Explaining to his sometimes dense disciples His own unique role as the genuine shepherd of the sheep, Jesus contrasted His ministry with that of those who came before him. They were thieves and robbers, He said—apparently speaking of the Pharisees or of the false Messiahs who had tried to win the hearts of the people.

Since He had already accused His adversaries the Pharisees of being "of your father the devil," the disciples wouldn't have to strain their brains too greatly to put the picture together. Jesus, the good shepherd, had come to give His life for the sheep, so they might have life, and have it more abundantly. Satan, on the other hand, came as a thief— to steal, to kill, and to destroy.

Originally created as the Anointed Cherub, the most powerful being in God's creation, Satan, or Lucifer as he had been named, rebelled against God, and fell from heaven.

Now his energies are bent on defying God and destroying those who follow Him.

Paul was undoubtedly familiar with Jesus' warning to the disciples recorded in John 10:10. With his analytic mind, he must have carefully thought through what Jesus meant. Perhaps he was able to identify Satan's strategies in his own life, based on the information passed on to him about Satan from the teaching of Jesus. Furthermore, Paul had ample opportunity to experience Satan's assaults firsthand—at least that's the perspective we are given in 2 Corinthians.

Satan's Strategies

How does Satan "steal, kill, and destroy" today?

One of several of Satan's major strategies identified by Paul is to blind the mind of unbelievers to keep the light of the gospel from breaking through to produce life (2 Corinthians 4:3, 4). If you've ever witnessed to an individual time after time, and wondered why they couldn't seem to grasp the clear, simple truths of the gospel, this was probably the reason. It's as though Satan has put blinders across the spiritual eyes of people who *will* not believe.

This was but one of Satan's numerous devices or strategies Paul identifies in this letter he wrote in the face of attack—attacks from certain people who were his enemies, and attack from Satan himself. Throughout 2 Corinthians Paul pinpoints a number of diabolical activities and strategies employed by the evil one.

From our contemporary perspective, it is possible to see Satan "stealing" sheep through energizing the activities of cults which deny the truth of salvation by faith, substituting a gospel of works, and offering New Age philosophies that make false doctrine sound like God's truth.

Satan today may kill people, by bringing disaster into their lives—perhaps through terrorist activities such as the bomb that blasted PanAm Flight 102 from the skies over Lockerbie, Scotland, and took over 250 lives.

Our enemy can also be seen motivating some people to take their own lives. The rise of suicide, which today is the tenth leading cause of death in the world and probably the second leading cause of death among teenagers, seems to be ample evidence of Satan's strategy to bring people to the point of self-destruction.

Frequently Satan brings about moral destruction by presenting temptations that appeal to the lust of the flesh or eyes or the pride of life (1 John 2:16).

AN ATTACK ON A CHURCH

Throughout 2 Corinthians Paul portrays Satan not as a Halloween character in a red flannel suit and wielding a pitchfork, but as a powerful adversary seeking to sidetrack us from whatever God intends that we do to serve Him.

Paul's first reference to Satan, presented against the background of church discipline, warns against the enemy getting "an advantage of us, for we are not ignorant of his devices" (2 Corinthians 2:11).

A Pharisaical Spirit

Some time earlier, a moral failure of great magnitude had occurred in the church in Corinth. Apparently a member of the church was openly living with his stepmoter. The attitude of his fellow-believers reflected shameless pride in their tolerance toward the man. Paul had written to call for the believers to break fellowship with this man for as long as his sinful life-style continued (1 Corinthians 5:11, 12).

Apparently the man soon repented; but, going to the other extreme, the believers in Corinth refused to restore him to fellowship. So Paul identifies the strategy of Satan as trying to produce a lack of love, or a pharisaical spirit that divides the brethren.

Paul warns, "Let him who thinks he stands take heed lest he fall" (1 Corinthians 10:12)—in the context of assuring them of God's provision for victory over temptation (vs. 13). This seems quite appropriate also for Christians today who may be tempted to voice the pharisaic prayer, "God, I thank Thee that I'm not as other men . . . certainly not as this moral failure."

Blinding the Mind

A second of Satan's strategies directed against the church at Corinth was the very one mentioned earlier—blinding the minds of unbelievers to keep them from responding to the gospel (2 Corinthians 4:3, 4).

It is significant that Paul's reference to this Satanic strategy is bracketed by two of his reminders to "never give up" (vss. 1 and 16). In light of this Satanic technique Paul calls for personal integrity in word and deed (4:2) as well as steadfast persistence.

Many missionaries have had the privilege of working in cultures in which they have seen large numbers of people turn from darkness to the light of the gospel. Such was not the experience of my friends Gordon and Daphne McCrosie, who seemed put on the spot at a missions conference I attended several years ago.

I was moderating a panel discussion in which a number of the other missionaries were sharing exciting stories and dramatic statistics about how God had blessed their ministry. On the other hand, Gordon and Daphne, after decades of ministry among Islamic peoples in North Africa, could count the genuine converts under their ministry on the fingers of one hand.

After the panel discussion, several people asked me, "Why didn't he just give up? How could he continue with no more converts than that?"

Perhaps that's the point Paul is making as he acknowledges this strategy of the "god of this age." Gordon and others who work in Islamic and similar cultures have certainly encountered firsthand the barrier of spiritual blindness. Not only does the adversary blind those to whom the gospel is presented; he then seeks to play mind games with the individual missionary who hasn't experienced large-scale positive results. "You must be an inferior missionary. You're certainly of no use to God! There must be something wrong with you. You might as well quit! You're of no value!"

A number of missionaries I've talked to have had such

thoughts hurled at them frequently by the enemy. Yet, confident of their personal calling, certain of the power of the gospel, and secure in their promised victory, most have utilized the spiritual armor provided for us to stand firm, and have not given up.

Aligning with Unbelievers

A third strategy of Satan identified in 2 Corinthians is to link Christians in a "yoke" with unbelievers (6:14). For the Corinthians, this must have been a critical issue. In a church that fancied the external and supernatural, tolerated the immoral and unbiblical, and often fought against the genuinely apostolic, it is not surprising that many had begun living, perhaps in marriage or in business, in a "yoke" with unbelievers.

The basis for Paul's warning is rooted in the Old Testament law in which cattle were not to be bred with diverse kinds (Leviticus 19:19), oxen were not to be plowing in the same yoke with donkeys (Deuteronomy 22:10), and Israelites were not to marry pagans (Deuteronomy 7:3). For Christians to take on such a yoke is as unthinkable to Paul as a joint venture involving both Christ and Satan (vs. 15).

Stella was a godly young lady, faithful to her Lord during high school. While studying at a Christian college in preparation for a life of Christian service, she met Jack. He was handsome, outgoing, well-to-do, fun-loving—in short, everything Stella was looking for in a husband—that is everything except one. Jack was not a Christian.

"I think I can win him over," Stella rationalized. Unfortunately, evangelistic dating is not a strategy recommended anywhere in Scripture. Stella and Jack married, and it wasn't long before spiritual things became of little importance to one whose life had been set aside to serve her Redeemer. A tragic divorce, following a great deal of emotional pain, finally brought Stella back to her faith—but at incredible cost.

Assault on the Mind

Paul refers to a fourth Satanic strategy in Corinth in terms of an assault on the mind. He speaks of an attack "against the knowledge of God," which he counters by waging spiritual warfare designed to bring "every thought into captivity" to Christ (2 Corinthians 10:4, 5).

The apostle identifies himself as meek and gentle in personal presence. Nonetheless he recognizes that believers are in a state of spiritual warfare. He further reminds us that we possess weapons not to be used physically, but powerfully through God to defeat Satan's attacks (10:4).

Since these attacks are against "the knowledge of God" (vs. 5), Paul may have in mind systems of thought such as atheism. Today we may think of secular humanism, or New Age philosophies. But Paul's focus is not just on *systems* of thought. His concern is that we bring every individual thought captive to the obedience of Christ.

Defensive Armor

During high school, my limited experience with football taught me a number of valuable lessons—in addition to reminding me of the limitations of my own physical skills. One of those was the value of the headgear. Frequently during practices and games I witnessed collisions—and was sometimes involved in them—that could have led to serious injury or even death, if not for the carefully-designed protective helmets we wore.

The Roman soldiers with whom Paul was so familiar also wore carefully designed helmets to protect themselves against their enemies. Twice Paul calls upon believers to utilize a helmet—"the helmet of salvation" (Ephesians 6:17), and the "hope of salvation" helmet (1 Thessalonians 5:8)—the only two references to helmets in the entire New Testament.

Mark Bubeck, a gentle-voiced pastor and author, has written a number of excellent books on spiritual warfare. During seminary days, Mark worked on a construction project. He was careful to follow the helmet rule—no matter whether you were at the most dangerous part of construction or on the fringes, helmets had to be worn at all times. If you took your helmet off on the construction site, you were subject to immediate dismissal.

It was during the same period of Mark's life, however, that he learned the value of the helmet of which the apostle Paul spoke. Let's allow him to tell his own story:

A dark time in my life still lurks in my consciousness as one of life's fiercest moments. It happened in the early years of my marriage. I was in my second year of seminary, taking a full academic load, working part-time, and struggling financially to make ends meet. There were some unresolved conflicts in my spiritual life, and they were putting greater emotional and psychological pressure on me than I realized. Suddenly, one day as a result of a minor crisis, something snapped in my emotional well-being, and total panic swept in ... Only those who have gone through such a valley will understand the hellish nature of the experience.[2]

Relating his emotional trauma to a similar experience in the life of noted preacher Charles Haddon Spurgeon, Mark Bubeck acknowledged that "fear of a nervous breakdown" helped fuel his downward spiral.

It was only after the encouragement of a seminary prof, who had been through a similar experience, that Mark began to recover. Surprisingly, Mark identified one of the most encouraging turning points as a time when his prof shocked him into an awareness of truth with a surprising observation:

"Mark, if God wants you to go through a nervous breakdown, you will have to want to have a nervous breakdown more than anything else in the world."

Like Job, Mark found himself face-to-face with one of Satan's major tools—fear gnawing like a fierce animal at his mind. Thankfully, he had a friend willing to share encouragement—and since encouragement involves the infusion of courage to help "cast out fear," the encouragement took root and helped.

Acknowledging a nervous breakdown as "the thing he feared most," Mark began drawing on the Lord for peace. In addition, through this emotional crisis, Mark developed a sensitivity for others in pain and spiritual danger that perhaps would never have otherwise occurred—and he learned many lessons he was able to apply later in such books on spiritual warfare as *The Satanic Revival.*

How does Satan wage war against our minds today? Sometimes by throwing confused thinking at us, thoughts of despair, thoughts of agitation. Perhaps even thoughts of intellectual pride and arrogance.

Whatever the case, God's goal is for us to utilize our spiritual resources—the weapons of our warfare—to bring every thought captive to the obedience of Christ.

Error that Sounds Like Truth

A fifth Stanic strategy identified by Paul to his readers in Corinth is to make false doctrine sound like God's truth (11:3). Motivated by his jealousy for their exclusive commitment to Christ, much as the father of a bride would be jealous over any involvement on her part with someone other than her bridegroom, Paul expresses a significant fear. The same serpent who deceived Eve through his craftiness might corrupt the minds of the Corinthians! Later in the same chapter, Paul warns of pseudo-apostles—deceitful workers who masquerade as followers of Christ. He points out that this isn't surprising since Satan *himself* (the emphatic word in 2 Corinthians 11:14)—the prince of darkness—is transformed into an angel of light.

Some time ago, after I had been involved for several years in the Christian counseling field, I was approached by a man who wanted me to assist him in establishing a Christian treatment program in another part of the country. He was a man of great intellect, keen business skill, and an intense interest in spiritual things. In fact, many of the things he told me sounded like just what I believed.

However, I discovered his perspective on spiritual things to be much more eclectic than mine. During one conversation, he told me all religions have an element of the truth. He and I did not come to an agreement on working together. His beliefs were close—but not consistent with Christ's statement, "I am the way, the truth and the life. No man comes to the Father but by Me" (John 14:6).

Step into the religion or psychology section of any large bookstore in a suburban shopping mall or major metropolitan area today. You will see shelves filled with books by authors with wide-ranging ideas about life, death, and spirituality. Tune the dial through your cable channels—or if you have a satellite system, scan the skies. You will hear a bewildering variety of voices and perspectives on issues related to life and godliness.

The key to discerning the truth amid this variety is to follow the first-century example of the Bereans. They listened to Paul and other teachers, then paid them the supreme compliment of checking their teaching out to see if it fit with the Scriptures (Acts 17:11). After all, one of Satan's greatest strategies is to make error sound like truth.

The Weapon of Pain

The final strategy of Satan pointed out by Paul affected the apostle himself. That strategy is simply to produce pain. With characteristic humility, Paul uses the third person to describe the wondrous revelations God had given to him—even heavenly scenes (12:1-6). Then, reverting to the first person, he identifies something "given to me, a thorn in the flesh, a messenger of Satan," bringing turbulence into his life (12:7).

We don't know what this "thorn" was—speculation has ranged from eye problems to migraine headaches to chronic depression. Whatever it was, we know this: it was extremely painful to Paul, physically or emotionally, or both. And it hindered his effectiveness for ministry.

Cindy, one of the most gifted counselors I have ever met, has learned, like Paul, to live with a thorn in the flesh. Born an illegitimate child, she suffered intense physical, emotional, and sexual abuse at the hands of five different men during her growing-up years. This abuse led to intense personal emotional pain, and even physical difficulties. Yet Cindy has experienced enough grace from God not only to deal with the emotional pain of her life, but to turn that pain into a point of sensitivity in the lives of others. Like Mark Bubeck, she has learned the lesson the apostle Paul acknowledges in 2 Corinthians 1.

Facing intense trouble during a missionary trip to Asia Minor, encountering pressure beyond what he had strength to face, Paul wasn't even sure he would survive! Yet he considered his experience an occasion to trust in "God who raises the dead" (vs. 9). Furthermore, God's comfort in all his adversity was designed to enable him to encourage others in their time of trouble, based on the encouragement he had received from God.

STRESS ATTACK

Had Paul taken one of our modern-day stress tests, he probably would have doubled the usual high-stress score! In 2 Corinthians, he acknowledges stress upon stress, problem upon problem—frequently as a result of enemies. Time after time he was confronted by critics who questioned his apostolic authority, disparaged his ministry, and challenged his motives.

Perhaps nowhere does he describe this attack so graphically as in 2 Corinthians 4. After pausing to reflect on the glory of the gospel message with which he has been entrusted, he acknowledges that "We have this treasure in jars of clay, so the power and glory may be of God and not of us" (4:7). Then he describes in general the waves of attack he will more specifically catalog later.

The four graphic contrasts Paul lists in these verses are pictures from the battle of a gladiator surrounded by enemies, or a soldier locked in mortal hand-to-hand combat. Paul was hemmed in, but not so cornered as to have no room to maneuver. He was perplexed, but not at the point of despair. He felt relentlessly pursued, but not abandoned by the One who was always on his side. He had been tripped up, but not totally destroyed or put out of commission. (vss. 8, 9).

Paul admitted that because of this opposition he faced trouble on every side, conflict from the outside, and fears on the inside (7:5). Later, he quotes his detractors more specifically: "His letters, they say, are weighty and powerful. But his presence is weak, his speech contemptible" (10:10).

We may surmise from Paul's comments in defense of his

ministry that a variety of other charges had been leveled against him, ranging from ripping off the Corinthians to displaying ignorance in his public speaking.

Just reading what Paul went through in the face of this opposition is enough to tempt most of us to give up. Hard work, frequent travel, exhaustion, physical pain, hunger, thirst, cold, nakedness, frequent fasting, physical confinement, mental stress and anxiety, danger to the point of death, physical beatings—few of us have been attacked as Paul was!

A Parable of Spiritual Warfare

In a modern parable about spiritual warfare, Frank Peretti writes of a mythical pastor named Hank who, along with his wife Mary, faced incredible hardships.[3] Satanically motivated and humanly carried out, these covered a wide range: church members told vicious half-truths about his ministry, undermining his credibility. Resisting his spiritual purposes, a young lady—Satanically motivated—attempted to seduce him, then physically attacked him when he refused her advances. Finally she had him arrested for attempted rape.

Though fiction, Peretti's scenario is rooted in the reality of events which have occurred with surprising frequency in the lives of many people, not only in Paul's day but ours as well, who have sought to remain true to God's standards. Like those individuals, Pastor Hank and his young wife Mary could have given up.

Instead, they appealed to a higher Power—precisely the course of action followed by the apostle Paul. His life at risk, the apostle identifies the God of the resurrection as the source of his past, present, and future deliverance (1:9, 10).

Sometimes we forget we are already on the winning team. The battle has been decided. Satan is powerful, and impossible to defeat in our human strength. Yet he stands defeated! The Cross is his death sentence, and the clock is inexorably ticking toward the time when his sentence will be carried out.

Overcoming Stress

In the meantime, a simple editorial comment from the apostle John in Revelation 12:11 gives us a threefold clue as to how to appropriate God's resources so we will not give up in the face of Satan's attacks.

First, the tribulation saints against whom Satan vented his wrath overcame him by the blood of the lamb. In essence, they understood the power of the shed blood of Jesus Christ—how the Cross was the decisive point at which the serpent Satan's head was crushed, the point where the mortal blow had been delivered.

The author of Hebrews makes it plain that, apart from the shedding of blood, there is no forgiveness. Equally true from John's perspective, apart from Christ's shed blood and finished work, there is no victory. However, both forgiveness and victory are ours. We stand both accepted and protected by the One who shed His blood for us and rose again. As Paul triumphantly noted in 1 Corinthians 15, since death, the final enemy, has been destroyed, we can continue to thank God who has given us the victory through Jesus Christ—and we can utilize that victory to remain firm in faith, unshaken in our hope, and abounding in God's service.

Second, the saints overcame Satan by the Word to which they gave witness. The Word of God is what Paul identifies as "the sword of the spirit" in Ephesians 6—*the* offensive weapon in his extended description of the weapons of our warfare. Putting on the whole armor of God, utilizing prayer as our vital communications link with the God who has given us victory, we are in a position to do as Jesus did when confronting Satan's temptations—one of which involved giving up His mission. We can respond with the "thus says the Lord" of Scripture whenever we are tempted.

Finally, John describes God's saints as victorious because "they did not love their lives to the death" (Revelation 12:11). In short, they were sold out—100 percent committed to Jesus Christ.

That's another lesson I learned from my somewhat uneventful career in high school football. Those who go about it half-heartedly are most at risk of suffering injury. On the other hand, those who work hard, follow the coach's instructions, and give 100 percent, are far less likely to become casualties of the conflict. So it is in the spiritual warfare which is an integral part of our lives.

Paul could count on victory from the God who raised the dead. So he could also assure the church at Rome that not even Satan and the very demons of hell itself can separate us from His love; for "If God be for us, who can be against us?" (Romans 8:35).

And here in 2 Corinthians Paul voices his praise to God, the Father of our Lord Jesus Christ, for the salvation He had provided, to the Father of Mercies for the loyal love Paul enjoyed, and to the God of all Comfort for the total encouragement He made available (1:3).

For Paul, sufferings abounded—but his encouragement from God was equally abundant. Yes, he had to fight wild beasts in Ephesus. Earlier, he was nearly torn apart by a rioting mob in that city. Five times he suffered the thirty-nine strokes with the "cat o'nine tails"—a horrible whip composed of multiple thongs embedded with bits of metal and glass designed to flay the skin from the back, which often took the life of the one scourged. But in spite of this opposition—despite the humans and demons who instigated it—Paul was encouraged through his God.

But that's not the whole story.

THE PEOPLE DIMENSION

Paul not only was encouraged by God—he frequently received his encouragement from God through people. After explaining how he entrusted himself to God when at the point of death, he acknowledges, "You also helping together by prayer for us . . ." (2 Corinthians 1:11).

Certainly the encouragement was mutual—"We are your rejoicing, even as you are ours . . ." (1:14). Paul, Silas, and Timothy, through their ministry in Corinth, had become "helpers of your joy" (1:24).

Paul is quick to acknowledge the human dimension of the encouragement he received, and to point out just how crucial it was. Describing himself in 7:4 as "filled with encouragement, exceedingly joyful in our trouble," he notes that:

God, who comforts those who are cast down, encouraged us by the coming of Titus. And not by his coming only, but by the encouragement with which he was encouraged in you when he told us your earnest desire, your mourning, your fervent mind toward me so that I rejoice the more (7:6-7).

There's a chain of encouragement helping to support Paul during these stormy events. God is the first and crucial link. He characteristically encourages those who are cast down.

The second link overall, and the first human link in the chain, is Titus, who arrived to give Paul a positive report. Titus was a good friend, a valued colleague in ministry. And Paul was encouraged by his presence.

The third link was Titus' positive message, a message made possible because the Corinthians had encouraged Titus. They then became the final link in the chain. Their earnest desire for Paul, their sorrow over their past wrong, their warmth toward the apostle who had fathered them in the faith, all were encouraging to the apostle. "Therefore," Paul could say, "we were comforted in your comfort, and exceedingly the more we rejoiced because of the joy of Titus, because his spirit was refreshed by you all" (7:13).

The subject of encouragement is so vast it actually deserves a book of its own. But it is important to understand that, in the face of human and Satanic attack, during times of adversity, human encouragement can be God's primary means of keeping us from giving up. If the apostle Paul needed human encouragement to maintain faithfulness and personal integrity, how could we possibly not need it ourselves? Perhaps this is why Paul seeks to encourage the Corinthians not to give in nor to give up in the face of the pressures they encountered. This is why I view 2 Corinthians as a crown jewel of encouragement. It is the essence of what encouragement is all about.

PORTRAITS OF ENCOURAGERS

If we were to look for the perfect example of encouragement in Scripture we would probably find the virtue best exemplified in the Holy Spirit—whose title "the Encourager" (Grk. *parakletos*) is so prominently displayed throughout Jesus' final words to His disciples in the Upper Room (see John 13–16). Several of the Spirit's traits—not speaking of Himself, focusing on Christ, providing insight into things to come—while not reproducible in the same fashion in our lives, can nonetheless serve as role models for human encouragement.

Furthermore, Scripture is replete with examples of human beings who provided significant encouragement to others in the face of serious adversity. David, for example, when threatened by King Saul, found major encouragement from Saul's son—and his loyal friend—Jonathan.

Needed: More Barnabases

Barnabas, in the New Testament, was recognized as a "son of encouragement." He provided encouragement for Paul when he faced rejection by the early church shortly after his conversion. He encouraged the early church to contribute generously to meet the needs of poor saints in Jerusalem.

This doesn't mean that Barnabas was just Paul's "Yes man." He was so loyal an encourager that he wanted what was best for Paul more than he wanted simply to please him. For example, Barnabas took issue with the apostle when Paul objected to allowing John Mark to participate in their second missionary journey (Acts 15:36–41). Perhaps Barnabas' loyalty both to Paul and to Mark played a role in Paul's eventual acknowledgment of Mark's usefulness, as the apostle approached the end of his life (2 Timothy 4:11).

Every year in her Christmas column, one of America's premier syndicated advice columnists describes her role with language that seems to give the most accurate definition of encouragement—"to comfort the afflicted and afflict the comfortable." Surely Barnabas had something of the sensitivity as an objective encourager that this requires. We need more encouragers like Barnabas.

Remember Onesiphorus?

It was near the end of Paul's life. As he wrote his final letter to Timothy from prison, he gave Timothy, who had been in a ministry of mutual encouragement along with Paul, two important words regarding encouragement. The first was a picture, the second a plea.

The picture, found in 2 Timothy 1:16-18, reminds me of one of those old portraits of someone long dead that might be found in the attic of an old house. It's a picture of an obscure man named Onesiphorus. I've come to consider him one of my personal heroes of encouragement.

Paul points out several ways Onesiphorus provided the apostle encouragement. First, he often refreshed Paul's spirit. The word Paul used for refreshed, found only here in the New Testament, is a compound word which means to lift up the soul. In short, Paul says, "This man lifted my spirits!"

Have you ever known anyone who often lifted your spirits? Many people would give large sums of money for such a friend. More to the point, are we this kind of influence on those near us who are in need of encour-agement?

Second, Paul describes Onesiphorus as unashamed of his chain. This man was not embarrassed to be identified with Paul, even though Paul carried the label "criminal."

Third, Paul noted that Onesiphorus carefully sought him out when he was in Rome—and found him. That may not sound like much to us today. But remember, there were no telephone directories, published Mapscos, service stations where one could stop for directions, or directory assistance operators. Rome was an immense city, the biggest of the world of that day. Yet Onesiphorus sifted through the haystack until he found the needle—his friend Paul.

Finally, Paul observed that, in a variety of things, Onesiphorus had ministered to the apostle at an earlier time in Ephesus, a ministry already familiar to Timothy.

Since I believe God has given me the spiritual gift of encouragement, I've spent more than a little time considering the life and ministry of Onesiphorus. On the basis of what evidence we have, he may have been one of the key people who encouraged Paul not to give up in the face of his innumerable adversities. As obscure as he is, I've often thought, regarding Onesiphorus, "May his tribe increase."

And I hope to be considered a member of his tribe.

Come Before Winter

After the picture, a plea—and a final word about Paul and encouragement. For those of us raised on the American self-reliant, independent model—and for those who might have known the arrogant, independent, fire-breathing apostle of an earlier era—it's a remarkable plea.

After challenging Timothy to faithfully preach the word, to be diligent in season and out of season, and to demonstrate fully his ministry, Paul pulls back the curtain for a personal word: "Timothy, make haste to come to me quickly" (2 Timothy 4:9).

The apostle is honest. He is near the end of his ministry, and he feels abandoned. Demas has bailed out, as have Titus and Crescens. Only Luke is present. Further, Paul needs Mark. The apostle who once strongly resisted Barnabas' efforts to give Mark another chance now admits, "He is profitable to me for the ministry."

In addition, Paul asks Timothy to meet certain physical needs—to bring him a coat. As always, He is aware of mental and spiritual needs, and asks Timothy to bring his collection of books—especially his copies of the Scriptures.

Paul further requests encouragement as he ventilates his feelings about the harm done him by one of his chief opponents—Alexander the coppersmith. The apostle doesn't engage in bitterness or gossip—he simply shares his honest feelings with a friend, turns vengeance over to God, and warns his colleague Timothy of the danger posed by this enemy.

Acknowledging God's strength and deliverance, trusting God for future protection from every foe—human, animal, or demonic—Paul nonetheless repeats his request to Timothy, "Be diligent—come before winter" (4:21).

Somehow this verse has to rank right up there with John's brief statement that "Jesus wept"—in showing us that it's all right to be human, it's okay to receive encouragement, it's appropriate to express vulnerability and need. Because, in the face of attack—and attack will come—we can count on the God of all encouragement. And we can count on God's encouragers.

THUS WILL WE PRAISE HIM!

David, the psalmist and king, has been humiliated and attacked, forced to flee for his life in the face of his own son, to a place far away from his capital city, the place where he was accustomed to worshipping his God. The king cries out in his heart for God (Psalms 42:1-2), and reviews honestly his feelings of despair (vss. 2-3). He can still affirm previous times of joy and encouragement when he wasn't isolated from God's people.

As important as it was to David—and to us—to receive encouragement from other people, the king finally confesses that his hope ultimately is in God. Three times in Psalms 42 and 43, David concludes his verbal cycle with the words, "I shall yet praise Him" (42:5, 42:11, 43:5).

Perhaps you, like David, are facing multiple attacks. Be encouraged—hope and encouragement in ample supply are still available.

Brent, like the apostle Paul, had suffered a serious personal attack. A successful, innovative businessman, the CEO of his company, Brent had sought to expand his business into a nearby city—but had been stymied by a competitor who had also attempted to smear him in the city where his corporate headquarters was located.

When confronted by this obstacle, Brent felt intensely angry. But instead of seeking revenge, he admitted his anger to a close friend and business associate. Together, the two men prayed. They turned vengeance over to God, on the basis of Romans 12:19.

Just a little over a week later, Brent's phone rang at home. It was his business associate—the man with whom he had prayed—asking, "Have you seen this morning's paper?"

Brent hadn't, but he listened incredulously to the news his

friend shared with him. In a copyrighted story, his adversary—the man who had sought to discredit Brent's own business integrity—was himself facing charges that would in all likelihood discredit him and his business.

As Brent said to his friend, "I'm sure glad we didn't try to get revenge. God took care of the situation much better than we could ever have imagined."

When we are attacked, let us remember that our best defense lies in Paul's self-answering question: *"If God is for us, who can be against us?"*

13

Hope: Antidote for Despair

$\mathcal{S}$ince it was a Saturday evening service, I decided to begin my message a little less formally. Those who were attending the conference were primarily singles and "singles again." During the twenty-four hours the conference had been underway, I had already learned two important things about them. Most of them were extremely knowledgeable about the Bible. And many of them, caught in difficult circumstances, were at the point of giving up, feeling despair.

"How may of you can identify the greatest chapter in the Bible on love?" I asked.

Hands went up all over the building. Without waiting to be called on, several spoke out, "1 Corinthians 13."

"What about the greatest chapter in Scripture on faith?"

Fewer hands were lifted, but still the number was substantial. Again, two or three called out, "Hebrews 11—the faith chapter!"

"Now let's get serious," I continued. "What's the greatest chapter in the Bible on hope?"

Only a couple of hands went up. Several people looked at each other, as if to say, "I'm not sure." At least, I thought, these two bold souls decided to take a stab at it.

A slender brunette with long hair and a quiet voice spoke up: "1 Peter 1?"

"Excellent New Testament choice," I countered, "but probably a bit limited in terms of the extent to which it deals with hope."

A husky young man wearing casual clothes and looking as though he had invested a significant amount of time in a weight room, suggested, "1 Corinthians 15."

"Excellent choice," I replied, "if you're looking at the New Testament. In fact, I would consider 1 Corinthians 15 to be the major New Testament chapter on hope. But, in my opinion, there's one other chapter in Scripture that I have to rank right up there with Hebrews 11 on faith and 1 Corinthians 13 on love."

I noticed several people thumbing furiously through their copies of Scripture. Others simply sat, waiting.

"Have you ever heard of the book of Lamentations?" I continued. "It's right after Jeremiah, and its third chapter, the longest in the book, is considered by many students of Scripture to be the ultimate chapter on hope."

DESPAIR TODAY

The reason I introduced Lamentations 3 to the group at this Singles and Singles Again conference is because, over the last decade, I've sensed an increasing degree of hopelessness and despair. We've noted that depression has been called "the common cold" of emotional problems in America, and that, statistically, you have one chance in four of experiencing clinical depression at some point in your life. Before showing how the book of Lamentations relates to this issue, let's look more closely at the need.

Karen's Story

Clinical depression affects strong, healthy men, bright, personable women—and active, energetic, vivacious teenagers like Karen.

As her sister was fond of saying, "Everybody likes Karen. She's everybody's friend!" The daughter of a pastor, Karen had been exposed to Christian teaching literally from the cradle, and had trusted Christ at a very early age. She had become active in her youth group, and consistently brought unsaved kids to attend the youth sessions. At times her father and mother would observe that Karen seemed to have redeveloped the concept of friendship evangelism for teenagers.

Diligent in her studies, Karen still found a great deal of time to spend with people. Those who knew her and her family thought Karen's life was in control. Even though she enjoyed spending time by herself, curled up with a good book, no one—not even her family—suspected that Karen was depressed.

As Karen neared her sixteenth birthday, however, her mother sensed that something wasn't right. Entering Karen's room to call her to supper one evening, Karen's mom found an open bottle of syrup of ipecac—a syrup that induces vomiting. Warning lights begin flashing in her mom's mind. What was going on?

The next day, as Karen's dad drove her across town to the Christian school she attended, the radio was tuned to the "Focus on the Family" program. Psychologist Dr. James Dobson, the program's well-known host, was interviewing a young lady who was recovering from bulimia, an eating disorder which leads to frequent binge eating and purging, using forced vomiting or laxatives. As Dr. Dobson and the young lady explored the dynamics of bulimia, Karen's dad noticed that she was paying closer attention than usual to the broadcast, particularly when Dr. Dobson's guest described her life as "hopeless and helpless, out of control."

'Helpless and Hopeless'

Later, as she reflected on that point of dawning awareness, Karen was able to share with her family how she had also come to feel that her life was hopelessly out of control. On the surface things seemed fine, yet Karen often felt lonely and unloved. Several traumatic events had happened to her, some of which were so painful she had blotted them out of her conscious memory. Yet, like many depressed people, Karen had come to feel that she was helpless and life was hopeless.

After Karen admitted her bulimia to her parents, the

family made arrangements to have her enter a Christian treatment facility. Karen's therapist pointed out to her, and to her parents, that bulimia was primarily a symptom of Karen's underlying depression and her crisis of personal identity.

As she gained insight, Karen began the recovery process. After six weeks of lengthy, often difficult treatment, she finally seemed ready to reenter normal teenage life. She was discharged from the hospital unit on her sixteenth birthday, and took an extended vacation with her family and two teenage friends.

Returning home, Karen was able to resume her active role in school and her youth group, and her involvement with her acquaintances. She even began trying to encourage a couple of her teenage friends who seemed depressed to seek counseling.

Cardiac Arrest

It was five o'clock one August afternoon when Karen's dad received an urgent call at the church study. It was Karen's mother. "Hurry home! Karen just collapsed!"

Rushing into the living room a few minutes later, Karen's dad spotted his daughter lying on the floor unconscious, her mother kneeling beside her. Realization dawned on both parents almost at once. Her medicine—Karen likely had taken an overdose of her anti-depressant medicine!

Making a split-second decision, Karen's father chose to drive her to the hospital himself, rather than waiting for an ambulance. Hurrying through rush-hour traffic, they reached the emergency room in ten minutes. Karen was wheeled into the trauma unit, where the "twelve longest hours of our lives" began to unfold. Nearly an hour passed before one of the emergency room doctors could take time to come out and talk with Karen's anxious parents.

"Why did you decide to drive Karen to the hospital yourself instead of calling an ambulance?" the doctor asked Karen's dad.

He replied, "I'm really not sure. I just prayed about it and felt it was the thing to do."

"It's a good thing you did," the doctor said. "Less than four minutes after you brought her in, Karen went into cardiac arrest. If she hadn't been here, we would have lost her for sure!

"However, I don't want to kid you. Her chances right now are still extremely slim. And if she makes it, we don't know what kind of permanent damage may have occurred to her brain or other vital organs."

Three times during the next twelve hours, Karen's heart stopped beating. All three times the cardiac arrest was reversed. A crowd of concerned friends from the church gathered in the waiting room. Some cried. Others simply sat with Karen's family. All prayed.

Finally, hours into the next morning, Karen was wheeled from the emergency room to an intensive care unit. For the first time, her parents were able to go in and stand beside her bed. Tears stained the eyes of both parents when they came out to report to friends, "It looks like that breathing machine is all that seems to be keeping her alive."

Again the doctor consulted with her parents. "I have to be honest," he said, "it really looks hopeless."

JEREMIAH'S HOPELESSNESS

As in the case of Karen and her parents, life looked hopeless for the prophet Jeremiah. Despair came crashing into his life because of events which seemed to rob Israel of hope. For hundreds of years, Israel had defied God's laws, worshipped false gods, and become more complacent and comfortable with their pagan practices. Even the Sabbath rests God had prescribed for the people and their fields had been neglected.

Over and over, God had sent prophets to warn Israel that one day the nation would suffer the consequences of her disobedience. But for the most part they were ignored. Finally, in 722 B.C., the ten northern tribes were swept away under the might of the Assyrian armies.

Judah and Benjamin, taking the name of the larger tribe, Judah, maintained the southern kingdom for a little more than

150 years. Then in 588 B.C., the armies of Babylon placed Jerusalem, the capital, under siege.

An alliance with Egypt failed to block the invaders. One by one, the cities of Judah were crushed, until only Jerusalem remained (Jeremiah 34:6-7). One of my seminary professors said it must have been as if the River Jordan had overflowed the entire land at flood stage, with only one person, Jeremiah, standing on tiptoe, atop a slippery rock, with his nose just above the flood waters—and he could go under at any time!

As the siege continued, the fabric of society began to unravel. Idolatry, already entrenched, flourished as people cried out to any and every god for help. Yet the people were so filled with paranoia they were willing to kill God's prophet Jeremiah as a traitor and a spy—in response to his telling them the truth about the reason for their calamity.

Things became so bad that starving mothers ate their own children (Lamentations 2:20, 4:10). Finally, the thirty-month siege came to an abrupt end as the walls were breached on July 18, 586 B.C. (2 Kings 25:2-4). King Zedekiah and his army were captured as they fled the city (2 Kings 25:4-7).

By August 14 the destruction of Jerusalem was in full swing. The armies of Babylon burned the Temple and the king's palace. Every other major building in the city was destroyed. The walls were torn down. By the time the devastation was finished, the city had been reduced to an abandoned heap of smoldering rubble.

For Jeremiah, who had been raised in a priestly family just north of Jerusalem in Anathoth, witnessing this destruction firsthand must have felt like a knife in the heart. After all, this self-described "weeping prophet" had warned the people he loved, but they had rejected the message and sought to have him put to death.

HOPE AMID TEARS

As he wrote this obscure, seldom-preached book called Lamentations, Jeremiah graphically expressed his personal despair and that of his people. Yet even in this darkest hour of Israel, he observed a dramatic ray of hope—one that can even help reverse the feelings of depression and despair we may experience today.

Jeremiah's nick-name might be changed from weeping prophet to weeping poet—for he composed four alphabetic poems designed to turn the heart of his people back to God and to hope. Elsewhere in Scripture, only Psalm 119 contains more elaborate poetic structure than Lamentations.

The impact of the book, however, is not in its structure but its intense emotion, as Jeremiah expresses both his agony and his hope:

> Let us search out and examine our ways, and turn back to the Lord;
> Let us lift our hearts and hands to God in heaven.
> (Lamentations 3:40,41).

> Turn us back to you, O Lord, and we will be restored; renew our days as of old.
> (5:21).

As he writes these poems, Jeremiah ventilates his personal feelings of anger and grief, leading Chuck Swindoll, in a radio message, to describe Lamentations as "the other side of eat, drink, and be merry."

In chapter 1, Jeremiah focuses on the desolation of the city of Jerusalem. Five times he asserts, "There is none to comfort her." In the first portion of the chapter Jeremiah writes in the third person, standing, as it were, on the outside looking in at the suffering city. The last portion of chapter 1, written in the first person, expresses the pain of standing on the inside looking out.

Chapter 2 gives the reason for the desolation—God has poured out His wrath in judgement. Again, the first portion is written in the third person (vss. 1-10), and the following verses in the first person.

The Hope Chapter

Lamentations 3, the chapter I've characterized as "the hope chapter of the Bible," is the longest in the book. Walter

C. Kaiser, Jr., in *A Biblical Approach to Personal Suffering,* describes Lamentations 3: "Like a pool of light in the midst of the thickest darkness, this chapter rises above all others in the hope and consolation it offers."[1]

While some Bible scholars see this first person account as a literary description of a typical sufferer, it seems more logical to take these words at face value as coming from Jeremiah himself. The essence of his perspective in verses 1-18 is simply, "Life looks hopeless." The first three verses describe the suffering as coming from the hand of God— "Surely he has turned his hand against me, time and time again throughout the day."

The intense sorrow of this time is described in verses 4-7: "He has besieged me and surrounded me with bitterness and woe." For Jeremiah, even prayer seems no longer an option (vss. 8, 9), and there is no way to escape (10-13).

Incidentally, if you compare verses 1-9 with the Twenty-third Psalm, you will discover that Jeremiah's words constitute a reversal of that great song of David. The prophet totally lacks the feeling of being shepherded and cared for. Instead, he describes his personal humiliation and bitterness (vss. 14, 15), and laments the despair brought about by his disgrace (16-18).

While it is certainly remarkable that Jeremiah felt such intense despair, it is equally remarkable that God saw fit to record the desperation he expressed in Scripture. What an example to assure us of God's love and understanding when we experience feelings of despair. What an encouragement for us to be honest about such feelings. I would encourage you to find a quiet place and read through these verses two or three times, ending with verse 18. Ask yourself, "Are there times I've felt this way? Do I feel this way now?"

Hope Depleted

As I spoke to that Singles and Singles Again conference in New Jersey, I observed how Jeremiah employed the wide range of vocabulary of Old Testament words for hope. Describing hope depleted, he cries out, "My strength and my hope (*toheleth*, or expectation) have perished from the Lord" (vs. 18). If an accountant were to develop a balance sheet from these sources, he would point to the loss of peace, prosperity and strength. The other side of the ledger would point to gains of affliction, misery, bitterness, and pain. Surely hope has been depleted in Jeremiah's heart and mind.

I am convinced that this is exactly how Karen must have felt that bright Monday afternoon when she took all her antidepressant pills at once.

That's also how Jack must have felt one evening as he sat in his car in front of a convenience store near his house following an intense argument with his estranged wife. Taking a .38 caliber pistol from under the front seat, Jack placed the barrel of the revolver under his chin and pulled the trigger.

When I was called to the emergency room an hour later, Jack had somehow managed to survive. The bullet had penetrated his mouth cavity and the roof his mouth, tearing up his sinuses, destroying his vision in one eye, and lodging just to the side of that eye. Miraculously, it had missed his brain. As pastor of the church he sometimes attended, it fell my lot to call Jack's parents and tell them of the despair he felt and the self-destructive action he had taken.

This low level of hope must have been the experience of Jolynn. She, too, attended a church I pastored. Like Jack, her marriage had collapsed. When custody of the children was awarded to her husband, it seemed the final straw. Filled with bitterness and despair, drained of peace and strength, Jolynn dressed, went out to the garage, started her car, then sat in it with the motor running. She was found about noon when one of her daughters returned to pick up the rest of her personal effects. I received the phone call a short time later, after Jolynn had been rushed to the hospital.

For Jolynn, it was too late. Jack somehow survived. As for Karen, the hours stretched for her family and friends in the waiting room. The question hung in the air like a fog: "Is there hope? Will she make it?"

In the case of the prophet Jeremiah, his depleted hope left his mind focused on affliction, misery, bitterness, and pain.

As he summarized his feelings, "My soul still remembers, and sinks within me" (3:20).

Hope Rekindled

Then suddenly, in the middle of what must have been the blackest of nights, it seems that Jeremiah reaches up to switch on the brightest of lights—a ray of hope in the face of despair and grief, a beam that originates in the faithfulness and loyal love of God.

Even though Jeremiah's situation seems hopeless, there are two hopeful points that, although they are not stated in the text, are evident from careful examination of the passage. First, Jeremiah is still alive. Second, he is still thinking. On many occasions as I've talked with suffering people caught up in feelings of despair, I seek to lovingly remind them of these two cardinal truths. I may ask them, "Are you still alive? Are you still able to think?"

The fact is that it is Jeremiah's thinking that provides the spark from which his hope is rekindled. In a sense, Jeremiah illustrates the principle of Romans 12:2: "Be transformed by the renewal of your mind." His perspective is literally transformed as his mind or thinking is renewed.

How many times have we allowed ourselves to linger in the overwhelming rush of emotional pain, rather than exercise our minds and *think*? For many years *The Unshackled* broadcast, produced by the Pacific Garden Mission of Chicago, has told the stories of people whose lives have been shattered and drained of hope, but who have been transformed through the power of Christ. In almost every one of these dramatizations, Jack O'dell, producer of the program, states its purpose in these words:

"The program that makes you face yourself and think."

For Jeremiah, it's time not only to face himself and think, but to turn toward God. Of course if such thinking provides the spark to rekindle Jeremiah's hope, the fuel for this flare of hope comes from God's loyal love. Let's consider the prophet's words, noting that there isn't even a paragraph break between his thoughts of despair and this flash of hope.

This I recall to my mind, therefore I have hope.

Through the Lord's mercies we are not consumed, because His compassions fail not.

They are new every morning; great is Your faithfulness.
(Lamentations 3:21-23)

As we examine these verses, we discover four major logs upon which the fire of hope is rekindled. The first is God's loyal love.

The word here for this kind of love is *hesed*, translated mercies in verse 22. It is one of the most significant terms from the Old Testament, appearing about 250 times. Using the plural to describe the greatness of this concept (he does the same thing with "compassions"), Jeremiah employs a word common to his day to describe the covenant loyalty and love that bound a god to his people.[2] According to Nelson Glueck, the word described an ethically-binding relationship of relatives, hosts, allies, friends, and rulers. "*Hesed* is fidelity to covenantal obligations, real or implied. [In addition . . .] the *hesed* is freely given. Freedom of decision is essential. The help is vital, someone is in a position to help. The helper does so in his own freedom, and this is the central feature . . . ."[3]

OUR NEED + GOD'S LOVE = HOPE

This is what Jeremiah seems to have in mind as he recalls God's loyal love. He and his people desperately needed help. Even though Israel had violated her covenant with God, that covenant was still in place. Israel had been given the freedom to choose, and had chosen to disregard the terms of the covenant. Yet because of His great love, God exercised His freedom, maintaining His covenant love and fidelity.

In communicating the Ten Commandments to Moses, God had used the term *hesed* to describe His response toward those who were in a loving relationship with Him (Exodus 20:6). God used the same words to describe His attitude toward Israel even after the worship of the golden calf (Exodus 34:6-7).

Frequently this term is associated with the concept of

mercy (the word *rehem* or mercy is used in connection with *hesed* fifteen times in Scripture). A classic example is David's description in Psalm 103 of the God who "crowns you with loving kindness and tender mercies" as he calls upon God's people to "forget not all His benefits." In essence Jeremiah, in writing Lamentations 3, is following the instruction of David in Psalm 103:2-4.

I'm not an expert at building fires, but I've watched experts build them. A dry spot is necessary, as is a source for the flame, and the appropriate kindling—but at some point, a big solid, long-burning log is important. Usually such a log should be placed in the fireplace first, then the other ingredients such as the kindling arranged around it. That's the approach Jeremiah takes here. He provides a foundation for hope with the Lord's loyal love.

Out of a Womb of Compassion

Then the prophet adds a second ingredient—the Lord's tender compassions. He notes that they are not exhausted, but "fail not." This term for compassions, *rehem*, also used in the plural to show its intensity, actually comes from the Hebrew root for "the womb." In essence, what Jeremiah is expressing in these two terms is the decisive nature of God's loyal love, plus the intense emotional nature of His feelings toward Israel. The prophet points out that God feels toward His disobedient people the same way an expectant mother feels toward the baby she is carrying in her womb.

Here is another large and solid log upon which to rekindle the flames of hope. No matter how far God's people have pushed Him, He will never abandon them forever. His feelings toward His people, and His ultimate choice to love them, will never cease.

What marvelous encouragement to those of us faced with hopeless circumstances! Frequently our despair has grown from roots of personal feelings of guilt or shame. We may have failed, or we may perceive ourselves to have failed. Worse yet, we may see ourselves as failures. It is at this point that we often buy into the false belief that "those who fail (including myself) are unworthy of love and deserve to be punished."[4] And we punish ourselves by turning anger inward—which leads to depression. Jeremiah's antidote for such feelings is to rekindle our hope with a careful look at God's loyal love and tender compassions.

A third log to be added to this fire involves what we might describe as the Lord's daily provision. "They are new every morning" (23a). The prophet reminds himself—and us—that there will never be a day when God's loyal love and tender compassions have been exhausted.

Perhaps in the back of Jeremiah's mind is the example of God's provision of manna for his people in the wilderness. Every day, six days a week, for forty years, God provided fresh food for an entire nation (Exodus 16:35). On the day before the Sabbath, He provided enough to cover both days. In short, although there were no supermarkets, no nearby farms, and certainly no convenience stores, the 2 million-plus Israelites wandering through the wilderness never missed a meal! Each day God provided exactly what they needed.

As we think back over our lives, undoubtedly there have been days when we may have wished for more, times when we may have felt that provisions were lacking. So often, from our perspective, the timing is off, needs go unmet, catastrophes happen. Yet the truth is, not a single case can be documented in which God has failed to exercise his loyal love or his tender compassions for even one of us his children. The difference is one of perspective.

Out of Divine Provision

There is perhaps no better example of this kind of divine provision than can be found in the life of George Muller. Converted to Christ at the age of twenty after a youth of excess and drunkenness, Muller entered missionary training in London.[5] An illness brought about a change in plans, and Muller wound up as a pastor in Bristol, England, a city swept by a plague of cholera.

In 1836, Muller's Scriptural Knowledge Institute opened a home for orphaned girls—the beginning of a ministry that, by 1870, provided housing and care for 2,000 resident children.

Although Muller never made an appeal for money, his children never went hungry or without clothing. By the 1880s, more than £1 million had been contributed to the Scriptural Knowledge Institute—an incredible sum!

By the end of his life, Muller had raised almost £1.5 million for God's work, without ever making public appeals for funds. Muller died with only £160 to his name—but with a legacy of testimony to God's faithfulness and covenant care.

This brings us to the fourth of the great logs from which the fires of hope are rekindled. "Great is Your faithfulness," Jeremiah exults (vs. 23b). Few hymns have been as loved as the lyrics by Thomas O. Chisholm based on this passage and set to music by William Runyan:

Great is Thy faithfulness,
Great is Thy faithfulness,
Morning by morning new mercies I see.
All I have needed Thy hand hath provideth.
Great is Thy faithfulness
Lord unto me.

It is virtually impossible to sing this hymn with the mind and heart and remain in the depths of despair, no matter what the circumstances. I've personally been encouraged countless times by hearing or singing this grand hymn, which reflects the light of the rekindling of hope expressed by the prophet Jeremiah.

Hope Refocused

We might expect the prophet to end his discourse at this point—but he doesn't. Having rekindled his personal hope, Jeremiah now refocuses this hope with the words:

The Lord is my portion says my soul, therefore I hope in Him.

The Lord is good to those who wait for him, to the soul who seeks Him.

(3:24, 25)

What a remarkable contrast from the prophet's focus in the previous paragraphs. At this point, his focus is on the Lord, rather than on the adverse circumstances surrounding him. The expression he uses here seems to flow out of his personal knowledge of Numbers 18:20. There, in the context of preparing for the division of the land among the tribes, God explains to Aaron the priest, "I am your portion and your inheritance." Rather than focus on personal possessions or real estate, the priestly tribe was to find its essence and sustenance in the Lord himself. As a descendant of Aaron, Jeremiah is reminding himself that since everything he has is wrapped up in the Lord, God will provide for him.

Since we are a royal priesthood (1 Peter 2:9), this truth applies to us today. Our hope and inheritance are wrapped in the person of God and our position in Him. Personal significance comes not from achievements, possessions, status in life, or the acclaim of others, but from our relationship to God. As Peter expressed it, in Him we have "all things that pertain to life and godliness, through the knowledge of Him who called us, by glory and virtue" (2 Peter 1:3). The psalmist expresses this concept almost word for word in Psalms 119:57, and another great hymn utilizes it in the title "My Hope Is in the Lord."

IS GOD GOOD?

In focusing our attention on God, Jeremiah immediately deals with the major struggle faced by most of us in times of despair. He asserts, "The Lord is good" (25a). In fact, all three verses of this poetic triad (25-27) begin with the Hebrew word *tov*, or good.

Cindy's family struggled with the question of God's goodness after learning that, early one Saturday morning, she had been brutally gunned down by a would-be bandit in the convenience store in which she worked. At the age of nineteen, with a heart for God, in the process of preparing to serve him, Cindy's life had been brutally ended. Her youth minister expressed the question that must have been on each of their hearts: "Where is the goodness of God in all this?"

Louise also struggled with the goodness of God. Growing up in a dysfunctional home, Louise at times felt abused verbally and emotionally by a mother who herself had been abused physically and sexually by an alcoholic father. Later Louise herself suffered sexual abuse at the hand of a youth pastor, then by an older student at the Christian college she attended. Bitter and depressed, she frequently voiced the question, "Where is the goodness of God?"

These and other circumstances serve to remind us that, in an evil and perverse world, the goodness of God is a central and foundational truth. Furthermore, Jeremiah reminds us, God's goodness will ultimately be seen by those who wait and hope for Him.

Here Jeremiah uses two other words for hope: *yakow* (vs. 24), to wait with hope; and *qavah* (25), a term also used to describe waiting, expectation, or longing. He couples this with the word seek (*darash*), a term referring to the process of inquiry. His point is evident. In circumstances where we tend to question God's goodness, we must wait for Him to act, and seek His will, humbly asking direction from Him.

So it was in the life of David. The city of Ziklag, where his family and friends lived, had been sacked and burned by the Amalekites. His own men were questioning his leadership. David himself was at the point of despair. Yet Scripture reminds us, "David encouraged himself in the Lord his God" (1 Samuel 30:6). At a point when he could have asked, "Where is the goodness of God in the face of this atrocity carried out against my people?" David remembered a fundamental truth of Scripture—despite the existence of a wicked world, God is good.

Sometimes it's hard for us to remember this truth today. When hundreds of teenagers like Karen are seeking to take their lives, and many are succeeding . . . when studies indicate that one woman in four and one man in twenty has suffered sexual abuse at some point during childhood . . . when marriages continue to break up at the rate of almost 50 percent, leaving devastating scars on the lives of innocent children, we may be tempted to ask ourselves, "Where is the goodness of God?"

Jeremiah's message to us is clear. Focus on His person and goodness. Wait for Him to act.

Waiting on the Lord

That was the course of action taken by Bart when his personal life and professional career were almost ruined by the untrue assertions of a former colleague, out to get even for a perceived insult. Bart faced the real possibility of a successful professional practice coming to an end. But his reponse was to share his hurt and anger with several good friends who joined him in praying that God would act. Bart expressed his willingness to "wait on the Lord."

He didn't have long to wait.

Only a few weeks later, events confirmed that indeed God had acted. The prominent individual who had sought to discredit Bart's life and practice was himself totally discredited. Bart was completely exonerated, and able to resume his professional practice. By waiting on the Lord instead of following the human desire to take action and to seek revenge, Bart—and his friends—were able to acknowledge the goodness of God.

Similar concerns ran through the minds of Karen's parents as they spent hours waiting outside the intensive care unit. For three days, Karen was connected to a respirator. Doctors warned of the possibility of liver and kidney damage, even of permanent brain damage resulting from the extended time on the breathing machine. Loving friends encouraged Karen's family by word, and frequently just by their presence, to focus on the goodness of God. All waited.

PERSPECTIVES ON HOPE

In Romans 15:4 the apostle Paul expresses the desire that we "through patience and comfort of the scriptures might have hope." The power of the Word drives us back again and again to such writings as the book of Jeremiah, just as he drew hope from the recorded acts of God. Only in God's Word can we gain His unique perspective on hope.

Hope Extended

It's one thing to come to a momentary awareness of hope. It's yet another to extend that hope in the face of hopeless circumstances. Yet this is precisely what the prophet does in verse 26: "It is good that one should hope, and quietly wait for the salvation of the Lord" (vs. 26).

Here the prophet uses yet another word for hope—*chul*. This word, also found in Job 35:4, is an appropriate parallel for the word translated "quietly wait" *(dumam)* in the second part of the verse. It is so hard to remain still when one is forced to wait. Minutes stretch into hours, sometimes into days, weeks, months, or even years. Yet waiting, as we saw in chapter 1, is of the essence of hope.

Verse 27 is intriguing: "It is good for a man to bear the yoke in his youth." Nagelsbach describes youth here as the period of "still fresh unbroken strength, in opposition to the period of broken and diminished vitality."[6]

It may be easier to endure adversities of life when we are young and strong, or even when we are in the prime of life. Yet God knows what we are able to endure, and when. As the apostle Paul asserted, "He will never suffer us to be tested above what we are able to bear" (1 Corinthians 10:13), providing either a way of escape or the grace to endure. Ultimately, as Jeremiah has noted, it is God's deliverance from hopeless circumstances for which we are waiting.

We must recognize that while there are times when God delivers us in this life—as He frequently delivered David from the murderous hand of King Saul, and as He delivered Peter from prison—at other times He chooses not to do so. David's beloved friend Jonathan died an untimely death, as did Peter's brother James. Yet Scripture indicates that both for David's close friend and for Peter's godly brother, the ultimate deliverance of the Lord was into His presence and beyond the circumstances of this life. Thus, hope in God's deliverance may be realized in this life—or it may even take place through the doorway of death.

Hoping Even 'in the Dust'

The next triad of Jeremiah's poem contains a reflection of the nasty reality of life.

> Let him sit alone and keep silent, because God hath laid it on him.

Let him put his mouth in the dust—there may yet be hope.

Let him give his cheek to the one who strikes him, and be full of reproach.

(vss. 28-30)

There are times when we wait without a word, almost without a prayer, it seems. There are times when our face seems to be in the dust, when we must endure patiently the blows of those who attack us and bring us reproach.

Karen's family experienced a measure of this—sitting for hours in a quiet waiting room . . . going for brief visits to the intensive care unit . . . hearing the sound of the apparatus that continued to help Karen breathe . . . waiting for a word, for the squeeze of a hand. At times, their mouths were as dry as a person's whose face is in the dust, as they wondered with the prophet if "there may yet be hope."

At times, they even felt like the words of well-meaning but ill-advised fellow Christians fell on them like blows: "If they had only_____ , this wouldn't have happened."

Haven't we all been there at times? Sitting quietly, feeling that God has placed more on us than we can take? Lying prostrate, faces in the dust, wondering, "Where is the hope?" Feeling the blows of those whose words add insult to injury?

Despite these honest feelings, Jeremiah doesn't lose the perspective he regained when he refocused his thinking on God's loyal love.

For the Lord will not cast off forever,

Though He causes grief, yet He will show compassion according to the multitude of His mercies.

For He does not afflict willingly, nor grieve the children of men.

(vss. 31-33)

Here is Jeremiah's overall perspective. First, all grief will come to an end. The Lord never permanently abandons those who are His. Second, the Lord's loyal love and tender compassion far outweigh any sorrow He permits to invade our lives. Third, He does not willingly send affliction or grief.

Although He may permit it, as in the case of Job, life's pain originates in those who are evil, in Satan and his demons, in the wickedness of people, and in the consequences brought about by our own sin or even the sin of others.

As James, the Lord's half-brother reminds us, God is not the originator of that which is evil (James 1:13). Instead, He is characterized in His person and His actions by absolute perfection (vs. 17). As James so wisely cautions, we must not be fooled into thinking that God is ultimately to blame for the temptations of life (vs. 16).

Rather, we must be swift to hear, slow to speak, and slow to wrath (James 1:19), hearing and obeying God's life-changing Word (vss. 21, 22). There can be no question about it. Our response must follow that called for by James, and by Jeremiah:

> Why should a living man complain, a man, for the punishment of his sins?
>
> Let us search out and examine our ways, and turn back to the Lord.
>
> Let us lift our hearts and hands to God in heaven.
>
> (vss. 39-41)

BACK IN THE LIGHT

Perhaps you are wondering What happened to Karen? Where is she today? Remarkably, she recovered from the physical effects of the overdose of the medication she took. She didn't recover hope immediately—that took time.

But during her initial stay in that emergency room, as consciousness returned, Karen began reflecting on God, and on her hope in Him. Later, during another stay in a Christian therapy unit, Karen further refocused her hope and began working through her emotional pain. The support of loving family and friends helped.

Ultimately Karen spent a successful stint as a summer missionary in Canada, started a home-cleaning business while in college, and met and married a student at Dallas Theological Seminary who, by her own admission, reminded her of her father. (As she put it, with a big smile on her face, "They are both involved in ministry, and both have red hair.")

Today Karen and her husband are involved in a ministry to teenagers. Recently she gave birth to their first child, a cheerful, red-haired daughter. Frequently, she has the opportunity to talk to young girls who are suffering from depression, bulimia, or anorexia. Like Jeremiah in his darkest days, Karen has learned that biblical hope is the ultimate antidote for despair.

Does she have difficult times? Yes. Does she anticipate feeling despair? No. Her hope now provides an anchor which she is committed never to give up.

Hope—strong enough to bring down the defenses of Saul of Tarsus and the Iron Curtain—also creates character and builds a solid future.

14

Living in the Light of Hope

*H*e was the last person you would ever expect to become a Christian—much less a champion of the spread of the Christian faith across the known world. Born in Tarsus, the capital of the Roman province of Cilicia, he was raised in that major cosmopolitan trading center located on the banks of the Cydnus River in the shadow of the Taurus Mountains.

At an early age he learned the trade practiced by many of his fellow citizens—making tents from the cloth woven from the hair of goats kept on the nearby mountains. Religiously, his upbringing hardly seemed destined to prepare him for what he would become. Perhaps growing up in a city in which men of every race, class, and background rubbed shoulders helped prepare Saul of Tarsus become the apostle Paul, and fulfill his mission to the world of his day.

We noted in chapter 4 how Paul *taught* hope. In this chapter we shall follow his life and work to see how the apostle *lived* what he taught.

I can remember making the observation that there was more likelihood that the Berlin Wall would be torn down or that the Soviet Union would disappear than that Paul would become a chief proponent of the faith of Jesus Christ.

Funny how hindsight teaches us, isn't it?

Although Paul's father had undoubtedly moved from Jerusalem to Tarsus to make his living in the commerce of that city, he didn't stray far from the strict religion of the Pharisees, in which he raised Paul. Since the apostle referred to himself as a Hebrew of the Hebrews, his family was apparently not long removed from Palestine, and they still followed scrupulously the tenets of the Jewish faith. At an early age, Paul's parents sent him back to Jerusalem to study under the most noted teacher in Israel, the man referred to as the Great Rabbi in the Beauty of the Law—Gamaliel.

THE SCOURGE OF CHRISTIANS

It was apparently shortly after the completion of his rabbinical training that Paul was first exposed to the Christian faith. It was at the expense of a man named Stephen, who had been dragged before the Jewish Sanhedrin by angry men who were unable to resist the wisdom of his words.

The message Stephen communicated in response to his charges left no question in the minds of his hearers. Stephen accused them of defying the God they claimed to serve, and pointed to the slaying of Jesus Christ the Just One as evidence that these self-appointed guardians of the Law had actually become its biggest violators (Acts 7:53).

The response of Saul's colleagues to Stephen was sudden and violent. Dragging him from the hearing room of the Sanhedrin, they ripped off their coats, picked up rocks, and stoned Stephen to death. Ironically, the young man at whose feet they laid their coats was none other than Saul of Tarsus. Stephen's final words—"Lord Jesus receive my spirit . . . Lay not this sin to their charge"—must have left an indelible impression on Saul's young mind.

Yet his immediate actions seemed to give no hope for a positive response to Stephen's message about the death and resurrection of Christ. For not only did the young man Saul consent to Stephen's death, he ravaged the church, entering house after house to drag followers of Christ from the safety of their homes and have them thrown into prison.

This stage in Paul's life reminds me of my first visit to the

Berlin Wall. It was during the tour of Europe to commemorate the 500th anniversary of the birth of Martin Luther, which I mentioned earlier.

Although we covered portions of France, Belgium, Switzerland, and what was then West Germany, by far the most eagerly awaited portion of our journey lay behind what was then referred to as the Iron Curtain. The anticipation of our group rose palpably and the tension increased noticeably as we drove into the border staging area where East German officials were to scrutinize our passports.

Our tour guide grimly reminded us, "When you leave the United States to travel abroad, you give up a measure of your rights as American citizens. When you leave the free world to travel behind the Iron Curtain, you give up a much greater degree of your freedom."

One of the members of our traveling group was not even allowed to enter East Germany—apparently because she held a sensitive defense-related job. Thoughts raced through our minds as stern-faced soldiers wearing the uniform of the DDR—the German Democratic Republic—detained us for what seemed like an eternity (actually several hours). What were we getting ourselves into? Would some incident occur that might delay—or even prevent—our return to the free world? Finally we were allowed to travel on toward East Germany, after being warned of the dire consequences of turning off the direct road into the East German capital.

Behind the Wall

Arriving in a dark, seemingly deserted city after midnight, we finally located our hotel. Several of us were stranded on an elevator for almost half an hour as we made our way to our rooms.

The next day, a group of us walked toward the famous Brandenburg Gate, where the Wall literally sliced the main artery of this magnificent old city in half. We had been warned not to approach too close to the Wall—and we took the warning seriously. Numerous foot patrols could be seen near the Wall itself. We were also duly impressed by the sight of several soldiers with automatic rifles who stood careful watch atop the many guard towers.

We began to pick up a sense of what we had been told—how the Wall itself symbolized the hopeless plight of the East Germans, denying them access to freedoms and the standard of living enjoyed by the West. The looks of grim despair on the faces of the citizens we passed on the street, the feigned cheerfulness of our East German tour guide who tried—unsuccessfully—to cast a positive light on the society in which she lived—all worked together to confirm the utter hopelessness felt by those living "behind the Wall."

In a sense, Saul of Tarsus was also living behind his own kind of wall. Breathing threats and murder against the disciples of Jesus, he requested authorization to travel the approximately 160 miles from Jerusalem to Damascus, to arrest any followers of the Way.

It was during this journey of almost a week that an event occurred which was to radically change the course of Saul's life. From this point on he was referred to by the name Paul, which ironically means "little one." Near the end of his journey, he was suddenly confronted with a light brighter than the sun at noon. Falling to the ground he heard a voice —one he had no trouble recognizing—asking, "Saul. Saul. Why are you persecuting Me?"

It was at this point that the steel will, determination, and drive of this unique, gifted man came under the influence of Jesus Christ. "Lord," he responded, "what will you have me do?" In a sense that question provided the direction for the rest of Paul's incredible career as the apostle who lived in the light of hope.

Within a few days he was preaching Christ in the synagogue of Damascus. His startled listeners could only ask, "Isn't this the man who destroyed those who called on this name in Jerusalem? Didn't he come here to arrest followers of Christ?"

Before long, they were plotting to have him killed. Paul even found himself in a spiritual "no man's land" when he returned to Jerusalem—the disciples were afraid of him, not trusting the authenticity of his conversion. But Barnabas, the gifted encourager, took Paul under his wing, introduced him to the apostles in Jerusalem, and vouched for the reality of his faith.

Later Paul would rank his encounter on the road to Damascus right along with the other appearances of the risen Christ—"And last of all, He appeared to me also . . ." (1 Corinthians 15:8). Like Thomas the doubter, Paul had seen and believed. As a result, his persistent pursuit of spreading "the hope of the gospel" throughout the world in which he lived became the driving force of his life.

The Wall Is Breached!

November 9, 1989. To many people it was a day just like any other. To the citizens who had lived for so many decades behind the tyranny of what Churchill had termed the "Iron Curtain," in the shadow of the Berlin Wall, it was a day that marked the beginning of a breathtakingly new direction. For it was on this date that the gates of access were opened, the stern-faced soldiers withdrawn, and the citizens of East and West Berlin given the opportunity to go back and forth.

I remember the stark contrast the following summer when, for the second time, my wife and son and I visited the city of Berlin. This time we drove in a rental car, arriving one late sunny August afternoon. Gone were the long lines waiting at the checkpoints. When we drove through the very area where we had been detained for so many hours several years before, there was only one officer present—and he was just sitting there, completely ignoring the passing traffic.

By this time in Europe it was possible to cross from one country to another with no more difficulty than driving from Texas to Louisiana or Oklahoma in the States. So we drove almost without slowing down into what at the time was still East Germany—although already the process was underway that would ultimately lead to the reunification of the two Germanys.

After locating our hotel and spending a restful evening, we arose and headed the few blocks east toward the Wall. The shock, the surprise at what awaited us, surpassed even our expectations. In numerous places, the massive concrete had been moved. The once impassable barrier had been breached! People were walking back and forth, unhindered, at the Brandenburg Gate where armed guards once stood with orders to "shoot to kill." Not only was it possible to buy pieces of the Berlin Wall at numerous souvenir stands; entrepreneurs from East Germany were actually renting hammers and chisels to the tourists so they could literally chip off their own "piece of the Wall"—which is exactly what my son Brent and I decided to do.

After chipping pieces from the wall for about half-an-hour, we walked down the tree-lined Unter Der Linten, the broad boulevard leading from the Brandenburg Gate into the heart of East Berlin. We couldn't help noticing the total difference in atmosphere. I even stopped to chat with an East German soldier. It was a pleasant exchange, although his dozen-word English vocabulary was just a bit larger than my German.

We visited Wittenburg, where Luther had nailed the ninety-five theses to the church door in a declaration that sparked the Protestant Reformation. A couple of days later we stopped for lunch near St. Thomas Church in Leipzig, far behind the old Iron Curtain. In an open-air restaurant we encountered an East German couple about our age. Our conversation confirmed that things were radically different.

They told us in their limited English how thrilled they were that the Wall had come down. Now they were looking forward to something they had never dared hope to do—visiting West Germany, where relatives lived they had not seen for decades. They even hoped someday to come to the United States. Without question these people had been infused with fresh hope.

The events in Eastern Europe underscore the value of hope—the difference it makes in the lives of those who have lived in hopelessness. From the words of Vaclav Havel of Czechoslovakia:

> I'm not an optimist because I'm not sure that everything ends well. Nor am I a pessimist because I'm not sure that

everything ends badly. I just carry hope in my heart. Hope is a feeling that life and work have a meaning. You either have it or you don't, regardless of the state of the world that surrounds you.

Life without hope is an empty, boring and useless life. I cannot imagine that I could strive for something if I did not carry hope in me. I am thankful to God for this gift. It is as big a gift as life itself.[1]

THE NEW MAN IN CHRIST

What difference did living in the light of hope make in Paul's life? We have seen that Paul and the other writers of the New Testament do not use the word *elpis* or hope to refer to a mixture of anticipated good *or* bad, as the pagans did. Centering his hope on Christ and His victory over the grave enabled Paul to use the word in two very positive ways. He spoke of it in the sense of a "happy anticipation of good."[2] And he viewed hope as an important quality of character to be developed by believers in the face of adversity.

The Impossible Certainty

Now Paul knew hope as a paradox—the experience of the impossible actually having occurred. Two common threads tie these seemingly opposite concepts together. First, hope frequently reflects something which, humanly, would not be possible. Paul spoke of Abraham "hoping against hope" that he and his wife would have a son, even though they were far beyond child-bearing years (Romans 4:18). In this spirit, Abraham lived to see the promise come to pass.

The second thread is the certainty reflected in this New Testament concept. Today we use the word hope much more like Plato than like Paul. "I hope maybe it will happen," we say, "but maybe it won't." It's almost as if we use "hope so" in contrast to the phrase "sure of." But Paul viewed hope as that which "does not disappoint" (Romans 5:5). The heart of the New Testament hope was a "favorable and confident expectation" regarding the unseen and the future.[3]

On the Monday following our dramatic weekend visit to the Berlin Wall, we stopped off in the small village of

Wiedenhausen, located just off the Autobahn about sixty kilometers north of Frankfurt, to visit our friends Cleon and Gail Rogers. Five years before, there would have been no hope of our visiting Cleon in the summer of 1990.

The reason for this was quite simple. Cleon, who had served for many years in Germany as a missionary, a theologian and a seminary president, had developed cancer of the colon. He had undergone surgery—as he liked to put it, the surgery left him with a "semicolon." He had also had chemotherapy and radiation treatments. But not only did the cancer persist, it spread to his liver.

The doctors in Germany gave him no hope. They told him to expect a fairly normal first year. By the second year, his health would be in serious decline, they said, and by the third year he would be dead. His daughter was a nurse and his son was studying to become an M.D. They sadly concurred with the medical opinions. Everyone agreed: for Cleon there was no hope.

Cleon's case reminded me of a gentleman named Harvey who was a member of a church I had pastored. He had learned in the spring that he had cancer of the liver. I talked with him on several occasions after the diagnosis. He really seemed too tired to fight it. By late fall of that same year, I conducted his funeral.

The Impossible Happens

In contrast, Cleon did not grow weary or give up in the face of the adversity he was suffering. He refused to give in to the notion that things were hopeless, despite medical opinions to the contrary. In addition, he availed himself of every bit of medical help possible. Most important, Cleon and Gail and their family never stopped praying, and never stopped encouraging their friends and others to pray. I remember receiving many letters from them during the time of his illness, giving us details and encouraging us to "keep praying."

And sure enough, things began to stabilize. I was reminded of this recently while having lunch with another friend, Dr. Alden Gannett, who had been invited to conduct a visiting lectureship at the seminary where Cleon was serving as president. Following the lecture, the night before they were to leave, the Gannetts and Rogers spent more than an hour praying and reading the Word together. Then, at the very moment the Gannetts were scheduled to catch their flight home from Frankfurt, Cleon was concluding a visit to his doctor. He returned home just in time to answer their last-minute phone call from the airport with the news: "Incredibly, the news is no cancer. Praise the Lord!"

When we visited the Rogers, five remarkable years had passed. As we sat in the living room of their cheerful home on a picturesque hill in that little village in Germany, drinking tea and catching up on ministry and family news, we heard firsthand the account of how, just the year before, the doctors had declared Cleon cancer free. The medical professionals had absolutely no explanation. However, the Rogers understood. They had simply persisted in prayer, while carefully following the medical treatment prescribed. They left the results in God's hand—and God saw fit to make him cancer free.

"If Cleon had given up," said Gail, "I'm sure he wouldn't be sitting here now. In fact, I'd be a widow. It was tiring for me, and more tiring for him, but he never gave up. It was his mental and spiritual attitude that made the difference."

Visiting with Cleon reminded me of another missionary—a young man named Kit Marple. He and his parents were serving as missionaries to Mexico, living in the Rio Grande valley of Texas, when Kit was diagnosed as having inoperable cancer. His doctors decided to operate. The surgery lasted almost an entire day; but the prognosis was poor: Kit could not survive more than a few months.

Our church family and others around the country were notified of Kit's plight, and Christians in many locations prayed. Meanwhile, Kit continued to pursue the best medical care possible.

Two years later, at our church missions conference, I had the privilege of introducing Kit as he stood before the church family on Sunday morning to share the exciting news. Just weeks earlier, the doctors had pronounced him cancer free! Despite the prognosis that there seemed to be no hope, there he stood, cured.

Perhaps as you read the stories of Cleon Rogers and Kit Marple, you're thinking to yourself, *But I know of situations where that didn't happen.* It may have involved a friend or a close relative of yours. You prayed. You pursued the best possible medical care—and now you struggle with the fact that your loved one or your close friend didn't make it.

Perhaps that struggle even includes a measure of bitterness toward God—of persistent anger relating to your grief and loss. Perhaps a perspective from Paul's life can help.

As I mentioned, Paul's perspective on hope seemed to be twofold. Whenever he spoke of hope without the definite article, he seemed to be identifying a positive, persistent quality of character. It describes the person who lives with the expectation that God will ultimately "work all things together for good" in his or her life.

When Paul used hope *with* the definite article—"the hope"—he seemed to be speaking of a specific future event, either for Israel, or for the believer.

Both look forward toward a future goal—not simply with optimism, but with an expectation based on faith. For Paul, "hope" is a positive, persistent character quality involving genuine trust in a sovereign God. "The Hope" focuses on the absolutely certain future awaiting those whose trust is in the living God.

HOPE AND SALVATION

For Paul, the development of the concept of hope was an integral part of his understanding of salvation. Both aspects of hope as he presents it flow directly from our salvation. Nowhere does he make this more clear than in Romans 5.

Having explained our desperate need for justification, acknowledged God's gracious provision of that need, and illustrated through Abraham how it is received by faith, Paul concludes: "Therefore, being justified by faith we have peace with God through our Lord Jesus Christ" (Romans 5:1).

Building on this foundation, Paul points to other resources—first, we have access by faith to the grace in which we stand. Furthermore, we rejoice in the hope of the glory of God. Clearly this reference is to the future of the believer—because of our faith in Christ, we have the privilege of joyfully anticipating the coming time when, instead of falling short of His glory (3:23), we will actually share His glory.

Paul gives a more extended discussion of this concept in Romans 8. Four times in five verses (20-24) he uses the term hope in explaining "The glory which shall be revealed in us." This glory is beyond comparison with our present adversity. Paul points to the fallen creation to illustrate and underscore the future aspect of hope. Hope seen isn't really hope. Hope not seen is to be waited for with patient endurance.

Hope for Creation

This future hope for creation has implications for a variety of ecological issues today. One day the headlines warn of the depletion of the ozone layer. The next day television newscasts show pictures of animals killed in oil spills, or medical wastes washing ashore on beaches near densely populated East Coast cities. Demonstrators crowd before television news cameras, protesting the dumping of nuclear and other toxic wastes.

At times, it does seem we have harmed this planet irreparably. Cancer, AIDS, and similar dread diseases, the catastrophic effects of pollution—in many instances the effects of the harm we have done to each other and the environment may cause things to seem hopeless. Yet the hope of the believer, according to Paul, has implications for the hope of the planet as a whole. Ultimately the God of hope is still in control of His creation. How encouraging to know that the inward groaning of the Spirit we experience as believers—not to be confused with the outward moaning and groaning we frequently engage in—is a sure sign of the anticipation of the redemption of our physical bodies (Romans 8:23). It is in this hope we are saved—even though we may not see it now.

What reassuring words of encouragement for every person facing the hopelessness of HIV infection, and ultimately

AIDS—especially for those who are accidentally infected by medical utensils or HIV-contaminated blood. Likewise for the person suffering chronic pain for which there is no relief. There is hope!

But there is another side to this business of "rejoicing in hope." Paul has encouraged his readers at Rome to rejoice in hope of the glory of God. Then he gives them a principle that is much more difficult to swallow:

> And not only so, but we rejoice in tribulations also, knowing that tribulation produces steadfastness, and steadfastness proven character, and proven character hope, and hope does not disappoint (Romans 5:3-5).

Rejoicing in Adversity

It's one thing to rejoice in a bright future, to look ahead with joy at the sweet by and by. It's another to rejoice during the nasty here and now. But that's precisely what Paul says we are able to do, in light of our relationship to the God of hope. We actually can rejoice in adversity! And we do so because adversity is part of the process through which God is working in our lives to strengthen and develop our character today. We don't like it, necessarily. We certainly don't enjoy it very often. But Paul says we rejoice in it—because it's proof that God is indeed shining His love into our hearts through His Holy Spirit.

Paul learned this lesson firsthand, through his own illness. Among the many adversities catalogued by the apostle in 2 Corinthians was a particular "thorn in the flesh"—as we saw earlier. It was something painful, something in which Satan had a hand, something raised as a roadblock in Paul's way. We don't know if it was cancer, an eye disease, or some other problem.

Paul took the same approach Cleon Rogers and the Marple family took. He prayed. Three times he asked God, "Remove this thing." Now there can be no doubt that Paul was a man of great faith, a man of persistent hope, a man of sterling character, and persistence—a man who didn't give up. So what happened to the apostle of hope?

He continued to suffer from his thorn in the flesh.

And the only reply he received from God was, quite simply, "My grace is sufficient for you."

What happened? The sovereign God determined that, at this point, it wasn't in His plan to heal Paul.

But it *was* in His plan to teach Paul through his experience those character development stages Paul shared with his friends at Rome. How are we able to rejoice? Because we have come to know or perceive that something good can come out of adversity.

HOPE AND GROWTH IN CHRIST

In January of 1991, when we moved our *Life Perspectives* radio call-in program to a late-night release time, it took some adjustment—but we were thrilled with the response of the audience. At the close of the final program of the initial week of late-evening broadcasts, my wife Kathy and our producer, Pat, both left. Kathy ran to the store to pick up a few items for the weekend, and Pat returned to her home.

About ten minutes later I heard sirens in the distance, just as the phone rang. Putting aside the question that immediately came to my mind, I answered—then learned that the answer to the unphrased question was Yes—there *had* been an accident involving Kathy.

It was a chain reaction collision involving four vehicles. Kathy had come to a stop in order to turn into the grocery store parking area, careful to give her left-turn signal as she waited for oncoming traffic to clear. Pat had stopped behind her, and a couple riding in a large pickup truck were directly behind Pat.

The fourth driver didn't even slow down. He slammed into the truck behind Pat, setting up a chain reaction. Kathy was the only person uninjured; and our car was the least damaged. Pat's vehicle was totalled—and a year later she still suffers pain in her back and neck as a result of the accident. The two people in the pickup truck—which graciously shielded both Pat and Kathy from more serious injury—were seriously hurt.

Yet the chain-reaction nature of the mishap actually lessened the magnitude of the consequences for both Pat and Kathy. The accident in itself wasn't good—but things certainly could have been worse.

In a sense, Paul is describing a chain reaction in Romans 5. The first blow happens when we collide with some kind of trouble, affliction, or pressure. Pressure hurts us—but it also produces one of the most important qualities we need in our lives—steadfastness or perseverance. This is the quality of which James speaks when he writes, "The trying of your faith produces steadfastness" (James 1:3).

The Value of Pressure

My experiences with athletics—a bit of football in high school, a touch of "small college"-style basketball in college —helped teach me the value of pressure in developing strength and capacity.

When I went out for basketball in college, I discovered our coach had a plan for building our endurance that seemed to come right out of the imagination of Marquis de Sade.

Now, I don't want to give the wrong impression about our coach—he was a dedicated Christian man and a fine athlete in his own right. The problem came from the things he had us do to build endurance!

Small-college basketball didn't get much smaller than ours—at that time, the college didn't even have a gym (they built a beautiful facility shortly after I left, and they play in an even nicer one today). The college was located near the top of Red Mountain, on the south side of Birmingham. We held our practices and played our games in the Five Points YMCA Gym, located several miles away, and several hundred feet down the mountain.

Our coach was possessed with the notion that if we dressed in our dormitories, then ran to practice and back, it would help us build the stamina necessary to compete on the basketball court.

Running down Red Mountain, around Highland Avenue, then down the final several blocks toward Five Points wasn't so bad. For one thing, we were fresh—we hadn't practiced yet. For another, it was almost all downhill. The run back up the mountain to the campus following practice was something else again. Like sheer torture.

First there was the steep grade from Five Points up Highland Avenue—nearly a mile! Then for about another mile, Highland Avenue gently curved around the mountain at approximately the same elevation. It afforded some relief to weary runners, but not much.

Then came the final, grueling section—it seemed like ten miles, but actually stretched for less than a mile—up the nearly 30 percent grade of Pawnee Avenue. This was the point where every one of us was tempted, at every step, to quit. In fact, the first few times I made the run, I was convinced I would fall dead somewhere on the sloping sidewalk beside Pawnee Avenue.

But within a week my endurance, and that of the rest of our team, had been developed to the point where we could actually voice complaints while on the final laps. The adversity of running long distances up hill under pressure produced endurance.

This in turn led to the quality of experience or proven character. (The word Paul uses is the Greek term for proof.) And this in turn leads to the final link in the chain reaction— hope itself, that quality of positive expectation that does not disappoint, but remains confident that, no matter the circumstances, God is still in control.

From adversity to steadfastness to proven character to hope that doesn't disappoint. If ever there was a *positive* chain reaction, Paul had identified it!

From my conversations with both Cleon Rogers and Kit Marple, I'm confident that had things gone differently in their respective bouts with cancer, they would have had just as much joy, confidence, and hope in the Lord.

Veda's Story

One reason I'm convinced of this is my experience with Veda. I met Veda shortly after she had been diagnosed with, as she put it, "terminal cancer—but I'm not ready for the terminal yet." I was a young pastor, fresh out of Bible college. One day I called on Veda.

She and her husband owned a nursing home. On my first visit I learned two things about Veda. She suffered a great deal—and she was incredibly cheerful. I learned very quickly what others had warned me of in advance: "You'll think you're going to Veda's to minister to her, to cheer her up. But if you don't watch out, that's what she'll do to you."

Many times I left Veda's home marveling at her courage in facing the lung cancer which would eventually take her life. I was amazed at her concern for her husband, her children, the older men and women that populated their nursing home—they're called convalescent centers today—and her persistent interest in other people and their needs.

Soon after I met her, Veda shared with me what she considered her most important goal. She wanted to live to raise her young son until he entered high school—"If I can get him to that point, I'll feel I've raised him."

Time after time Veda would take a turn for the worse—then recover.

Then one morning I received a call in my office saying that Veda had been taken to the hospital again—probably for the last time. When I saw her at the hospital, all she could say was, "It's in His hands." Soon Veda was in the presence of the Lord.

Veda's son had only recently turned thirteen.

God had seen fit to allow her son to have his mother beyond the years of young childhood, although not quite as long as she had hoped.

But it was at Veda's funeral that we began to see the amazing impact of Veda's life. Three people—including Veda's brother—trusted Christ immediately following her burial. Veda's persistent cheerful spirit, her witness through the years to her ultimate hope in the Lord, the character God had developed in her life through adversity, her experience as a "veteran" in suffering—all this God had used to point others to Veda's hope. As one of her friends put it to me following the funeral, "She was a person who lived with one foot inside heaven's door. To visit her was to get a small sample of what heaven surely must be like."

Like the apostle Paul, Veda rejoiced in the face of her adversities, recognizing that when she was weak she was strong. In this way the power of Christ rested on her—and reached out through her to others, motivating them to hope.

Hope, Suffering, and Scripture

So tell us, Paul—how do we develop this hope? If we could have visited the apostle in the Mammertine Prison around the time he wrote 2 Timothy, just before he died, and posed that question to him, he probably would have given us a simple, two-piece answer: *suffering* and *Scripture*.

Because that's exactly what he wrote to tell his friends in Rome. Near the end of his letter to them, he reminded the Roman Christians, "Whatever things have been written in earlier times were written for our learning, that we through steadfastness and encouragement of the Scriptures might have hope" (Romans 15:4).

For Paul, the steadfastness developed through adversity, plus the encouraging words of such individuals as Abraham and David—to whom he had referred in detail earlier in the letter—provided ample insight and encouragement for facing the adversities of life.

No wonder Paul can pray, "Now the God of hope fill you with all joy and peace in believing, that you may abound in hope through the power of the Holy Spirit" (Romans 15:13). For Paul, hope was produced supernaturally. It was not a product to be harvested by earthly means, but developed as the supernatural Spirit within used the adversities of life to produce godly character and fruit. As we walk in faith, we will be able, with Paul, to "abound in hope."

THE HOPE UP AHEAD

For Paul, not only was hope a character quality to be forged to maturity in the flames of adversity. Hope was also a future objective, a specific event which would transcend human possibility. This is the final goal toward which all creation moves, the concept we Christians have come to refer to as "the hope."

Ironically, this concept of hope in Paul's mind was nourished in the soil of Pharisaism. It actually sprang into view following his arrest in Jerusalem. At a hearing before the Sanhedrin, the apostle sensed the division between the Sadducees, the more liberal party, and the Pharisees. The Pharisees believed in the resurrection and other supernatural elements of divine revelation, such as angels, while the Sadducees believed in neither.

Paul's cry, "Of the hope and resurrection of the dead am I called in question" (Acts 23:6), was accurate—because the resurrection of Jesus Christ lay at the heart of his message. Later Paul repeats this theme of hope and resurrection before Felix the governor (24:15), before Herod Agrippa (26:6, 7), and to the leaders of the Jewish community in Rome (28:20).

For Paul, the hope of Israel was wrapped up in the promises of Messiah; and the apostle now possessed firsthand evidence that Messiah had come. As predicted in the Old Testament, He had overcome death. Paul knew this because he found out the hard way that the Messiah was none other than Jesus of Nazareth, the One whose followers he was attempting to obliterate from the face of the earth.

Paul peppers his letters with references to "the hope," the "hope of his calling," the "hope of righteousness," and "the hope of glory." But it is in 1 Corinthians 15 that he most carefully explains the fundamental connection between the resurrection of Christ and the Christian hope.

Hope And Resurrection

In this great chapter, Paul addresses the single most crucial doctrinal issue he must explain—the resurrection. He makes it clear that the resurrection is just as essential to the gospel as the substitutionary death of Christ (vss. 3, 4). He maintains that over 500 eye witnesses can testify to having seen the Lord after His death and burial. The last in this parade of witnesses is Paul himself.

Yet the apostle makes it clear that the issue of Christ's resurrection is not simply a matter for apologetic discussion. Some within the church at Corinth—like the Sadducees Paul encountered earlier—denied the resurrection of the dead. Using careful logic, the apostle draws a clear connection from the evidence for Christ's resurrection to that of Christians, and the ultimate credibility not only of Christian witnesses but of God himself. He concludes with a simple, yet profound statement: "If in this life only we have hope in Christ, we are of all men most miserable" (vs. 19).

Paul's logic is irrefutable. What separates Jesus Christ from every religious leader—and Christianity from every religious system—is the resurrection, of Christ as first-fruits, then His followers at His coming. This ultimate distinctive of the Christian faith is an empty tomb!

The greatest enemy of hope is death—the final enemy to be destroyed, Paul says. This is why he was more than willing to face wild animals in the arena at Ephesus, rather than take the "eat, drink, and be merry" approach of those who find hope only in this life. For Paul, like John (1 John 3:1-3), the hope of the resurrection was a purifying truth, motivating Christians to avoid the corruption of an evil society.

And even though he only uses the word hope once in 1 Corinthians 15—in his climactic statement in verse 19—hope is the concept which permeates this chapter. This is evident from Paul's concluding and encouraging quote from Isaiah— "Death is swallowed up in victory" (Isaiah 25:8).

Spiking the Ball

Paul is so moved at the climax of his extended discussion on the nature of the resurrection and how it will occur that he literally cries out, like a winner in a sporting event, taunting death and the grave (the losers): "Thanks be to God, who gives us the victory through our Lord Jesus Christ" (vs. 57).

Imagine Paul as an all-pro wide receiver in the NFL. He had just caught a pass more difficult, more unlikely, than the so-called "Hail Mary" reception that vaulted the Pittsburgh Steelers over the Dallas Cowboys to the championship of the

NFL. Against all odds, where there appeared to be no hope, God had thrown the pass—and Paul had been allowed the privilege of catching it!

Now the verbal camera of Scripture zooms in for a close-up of his emotion, no less intense than that of a championship receiver who has just made the game-winning catch. In effect, Paul spikes the ball in the face of Satan's chief defensive cornerback—death—calling out, "Where is your sting? Where is your victory?" Then, reflectively, he acknowledges there is a sting to death—sin and its strength is the condemning flaw.

Finally, like a player kneeling with bowed head in the corner of the end zone, Paul voices his thanks to God for the victory he has been given. Then the final shot. The camera shows him trotting over to the bench to encourage his beloved brothers to be firm in faith, unshaken in hope, and always abounding in the difficult task before them—a task which, because of the resurrection, will not be in vain!

Preacher on Horseback

When I first met him, I learned quickly that Seth was a member of a dying breed, in more ways than one. A missionary to south Louisiana, he began his ministry by planting churches; and during his early years as a circuit rider he made his rounds to the churches he had planted on horseback. The church I was privileged to pastor was one of more than a score he'd had a hand in starting.

A rugged outdoorsman, Seth preached, performed weddings and funerals, found the time to start a Christian camp ministry and a church planting and conference mission, and even tended to a herd of Brahma cattle on the side—for the express purpose of providing both food and support for the camp he had established.

A man from one church Seth had founded said of Seth, "He's just as heavenly when he's out there rounding up his cows as he is when he's rounding up church members." Here was a modern-day Paul who spread the gospel far and wide, planting churches and strengthening saints, but who wasn't afraid to get his hands dirty with honest work.

When Seth suffered a massive heart attack, his doctor made it plain that all the work—the traveling, the preaching, the hauling hay, the building fences, the rigorous physical labor, plus the emotional trauma of ministry—all had to stop. "Keep up your pace, Seth, and you'll soon be a dead man," the doctor warned.

To which Seth replied, "I'll be here as long as the Lord wants me here—in fact, I'll probably bury you!"

Though he never claimed the gift of prophecy, I found it ironic about six years later when Seth, still going strong, conducted the funeral of the very doctor who had predicted that Seth wouldn't last more than a few months at his pace.

The last time I saw Seth, I had brought a group of young people from a church I was pastoring in another part of the country to visit the camp he had founded. We drove to his modest home, out in the country several miles from the camp. As was still his custom, he had been out tending his cows—and his sheep, since he still had a pastor's heart.

Pick Up the Mantle!

Our urban teenagers were mystified. Only in history books had most of them read of men who actually crossed a river on the back of a swimming horse, or who could brand a Brahma cow. But Seth wasn't interested in impressing these young men and young women with his exploits as a cowboy. He was concerned about encouraging them to pick up the spiritual mantle he would soon be forced to lay down.

It was like the apostle Paul using the twilight of his career to challenge young Timothy to preach the word in season and out of season. Seth made it clear that, from his perspective, there was no more important mission, no greater challenge, no more rewarding purpose in life, than to invest it in serving the God who not only takes care of us in this life, but who has given us life eternal.

In the manner of an apostle, Seth spoke of some of his goals for young ministers and young churches—like Paul who "hoped to send Timothy" to the Philippians, or to receive an encouraging report from Titus regarding the Corinthians.

But above all, Seth's hope was centered in Christ. This was evident from the content of his speech—and from the twinkle in his eye and the energy in his voice. The prospect of death for Seth wasn't a nightmare. It was an eagerly-anticipated event—one which would reunite him with his beloved wife, and bring him face to face with the Person he loved most—his Savior.

The Difference Faith Makes

Not surprisingly, when Seth died just a few months later, the funeral, as had been the case when his wife had died, was far more celebration than dirge.

That's the difference Christian faith makes. It's that abiding hope, the hope of eternal life which, as Paul reminded another of his protégés, Titus, was promised before the world began by the God who cannot lie. It was this hope that Paul had been duly commissioned to preach, following the instructions of his Savior (Titus 1:2, 3).

For Paul, the blessed hope was the ultimate focus of a godly life. To summarize the essence of his message to Titus, Paul explains that salvation is by grace, and that it produces godly character. And salvation prompts us to focus on "that blessed hope . . . the glorious appearing of our great God and Savior, Jesus Christ" (Titus 2:11-13).

It was that hope, that firm focus not on the things seen, but the things unseen, things that are eternal (2 Corinthians 4:15, 16) that motivated Paul, when he faced life's adversities, never to give up. How appropriate that we label him the apostle of hope.

Yes, the Berlin Wall has been breached. Cleon and Kit both survived their cancer. Veda and Seth went on to meet their Savior, having completed their tasks in this world. And they all shared in common the perspective lived out by the great apostle of hope. It's a perspective that provides character and strength in adversity today, and is firmly fixed on that grand and glorious tomorrow when we will ever be with the Lord Jesus Christ—who is Himself our hope (1 Timothy 1:1).

Peter, the Soviet Union, Aunt Dorothy the atheist—
if hope can leap over their defenses, think
how it could change your life as well!

15
Peter: The Power
Of a Living Hope

*W*hile there's life, there's hope," I thought as I looked out the aircraft window. A few puffy clouds were interspersed across the green Mississippi landscape.

While there's life, there's hope—but Dorothy didn't have much longer to live.

I was on my way home to Birmingham, where I had been born and raised. It was Mother's Day weekend, and I was looking forward to seeing my mother—who was also getting on in years. But a special part of my weekend would be set aside to talk to Dorothy—Aunt Dorothy the atheist.

Dorothy's subtle physical resemblance to atheist leader Madalyn Murray O'Hare was ironic—because Dorothy had just about the same attitude about God for which Ms. O'Hare was famous. Dorothy had never married, and never had time for church. Not only had she never been interested in spiritual things, she was openly hostile to them and actually seemed to take delight in ridiculing them.

Dorothy had taken a special interest in me from the time I was a young lad. My dad's older sister, she had frequently challenged me with her love of classical music and opera—areas of interest we came to share. Dorothy loved reading, and one of my prized possessions is a book on astronomy she gave me when I was about nine. Not surprisingly, the book presented an evolutionary perspective on the universe. None-theless, we shared an interest in the heavens which, from my perspective, gave evidence to the reality of God.

Although Dorothy had no interest in God, she was strongly disposed toward helping people. Several months earlier, when I had been in the Birmingham area for a speaking engagement, Dorothy had taken me to the community library where she had served many hours as a volunteer. She was pleased that I was involved in helping people, although she just couldn't understand why I had to cling to what she considered to be those silly notions about God and Christ.

As the plane banked low over the Birmingham skyline in preparation for landing, I could see Red Mountain—the back-drop against which the city was spread out. I had not only been born and raised here; this was the city where I had ministered, where I had conducted funerals—a number of them for family members.

A Tough Marine Believes

Less than a year earlier I had returned to Birmingham to conduct a funeral for the uncle for whom I was named—a tough old Marine named Don Hawkins, my dad's younger brother, who had built a successful automotive parts business. I was aware that a spiritual interest had been rekindled in my Uncle Don in the months preceding his death from cancer. But little did I realize the impact this had had on his older sister Dorothy.

My parents met me at the airport. We exchanged warm greetings, then went straight to the hospital to see Dorothy.

As I looked at her, lying in bed, hooked to the various machines that are so much a part of acute medical care today, I couldn't help wondering, Is there any hope that this wo-man, who has been so bitter against God, could ever become a Christian? She had only days—perhaps only hours—to live. What could I say?

PETER, HOPE, AND THE NEW BIRTH

It's often been said that Christ is the Living Hope. No one connected that living hope to the new birth quite like Peter:

Blessed be God the Father of our Lord Jesus Christ who according to His abundant mercy has begotten us again unto a living hope by the resurrection of Jesus Christ from the dead (1 Peter 1:3).

But then no one had an experience with Christ quite like Peter. Like my Aunt Dorothy, Peter was unique, an original. After him, they broke the mold.

One of a Kind

A natural leader, Peter was referred to as "the big fisherman," according to tradition. He responded to his brother Andrew's invitation to come see for himself the man who was the Messiah. From that point on, following Christ became more important to Peter than catching fish.

Peter quickly became the leader of Jesus' followers— whenever the disciples are listed, his name invariably appears first. Even Paul, in his letter to the Galatians, recognized Peter as premier among the "pillars of the church," and noted that, following the resurrection, Christ first "was seen of Peter, then of the twelve" (1 Corinthians 15:5).

This in itself was remarkable evidence of the grace of God —after all, while Jesus was on trial, Peter had denied even knowing Him. Then, after the crucifixion, he and the other disciples simply went home, leaving Christ to hang on the cross and suffer alone.

Yet, when Mary Magdalene shocked the disciples with the word that the tomb was open and Jesus' body was gone, Peter, along with John, immediately headed for the burial site to check out the story. John, apparently younger and faster, arrived first. But bold Peter was the first to rush into the open tomb.

Following the resurrection, Peter was the one who first expressed the sentiment, "We might as well go back to fishing." Following a night when they caught no fish, a mysterious figure on shore suggested a different approach—one that proved successful. Peter, recognizing the figure to be the Lord, jumped into the water and swam to shore to meet Him.

It was Peter who seemed to have had the greatest grasp of

who Jesus really was—"You are the Christ, the Son of the Living God" (Matthew 16:16). But it was also Peter who steadfastly resisted Jesus' prediction about his death—and to whom Jesus said sternly, "Get behind me Satan, you are an offense to me. You do not savor the things that are of God" (Matthew 16:23).

We don't know just when Peter experienced the new birth of which he wrote in the opening words of his letter. We do know that he professed to believe in Jesus as the Messiah early on. Following the resurrection, Peter's life took on renewed stability, vision, and commitment. Although he wasn't perfect—Paul confronts him for hypocrisy in Galatians 2—the first twelve chapters of Acts nonetheless show Peter playing a key role in the spread of the early church. And on that remarkable day of Pentecost, it is Peter who delivers the initial message of hope, based on the resurrection of Christ.

A Remarkable Day in Jerusalem

Picture yourself gathered with hundreds of thousands of visitors from across the Roman Empire—Jewish proselytes from every conceivable nation, gathered in Jerusalem to celebrate the feast of Pentecost.

Suddenly, passing through the crowd are men who are obviously from Jerusalem but are somehow able to communicate in the native languages of these foreigners, including yours! The crowd begins to buzz. Then, near the steps of the Temple, you join the throng pressing foward to focus on eleven men. Were these the followers of the man Jesus who so recently was crucified? The largest of the group, this man Peter, begins to speak in a loud voice.

"Some of you think these men are drunk. That's not the case—it's too early in the day! What's happening is, Scripture is being fulfilled before your eyes! It's the day of which the prophet Joel spoke—a day in which whoever shall call on the name of the Lord shall be saved!"

Looking around, you notice the people pressing forward and listening intently. It's amazing that such a huge crowd of people can hear one man—without an electronic PA system!

Peter's next words confirm what you suspected. This *is* about Jesus, the man from Nazareth who did the miracles, and who was ultimately crucified by the Jewish leaders. You cringe a bit as you listen to Peter and his outspoken message—not exactly taken from the pages of *How to Win Friends and Influence People*: "You took Him and by wicked hands, murdered Him!"

Then you hear the shocking affirmation, "But God raised Him from the dead, just as David predicted—'I saw the Lord always before my face. He is on my right hand that I should not be moved. Therefore my heart rejoiced. My tongue was glad. Furthermore my flesh also shall rest in hope.'" Looking around, you notice bearded heads nodding throughout the crowd. Obviously these people are familiar with the words of David—you recall that they are from Psalm 16.

As Peter continues, you reflect on the words *"My flesh shall rest in hope."*

Then Peter's voice again penetrates your consciousness. "This Jesus has God raised up. Of this we are all witnesses ... Therefore, let all the family of Israel know of a certainty that God has declared this Jesus, whom you crucified, both Lord and Messiah."

On this pointed note, Peter pauses to let his words sink in. You understand his message clearly. It's not the religious system of Israel—nor any other religion for that matter—that gives a person the hope of life beyond death. It's all wrapped up in this person—Jesus. And you, along with every other individual, must choose. You must either reject Him, as the religious leaders of Israel have done, the men who had him put to death; or you must choose to respond to Him in faith. You note the urgency in Peter's voice. And you just can't get those words from David out of your mind. "My flesh also shall rest in hope." How can a person have this kind of an attitude when facing death?

Suddenly a voice interrupts Peter with an urgent question: "Men, brothers, what shall we do?" Without hesitation, Peter responds, "You must repent—there must be a change of mind about Christ. You need to publicly acknowledge your faith by being baptized in the name of Jesus Christ. You will receive the gift of the Holy Spirit!"

Peter continues to speak to the crowd, encouraging them. You notice the response. First a trickle, then a stream. Later, you learn that over 3,000 people have acknowledged their faith in the man who died and arose—the one Peter proclaims to be divine.

Good Question

How *can* a person affirm confidently that "my flesh shall rest in hope"? That's the question raised by an ancient Greek writer named Aristeides. Observing this unique attitude toward death on the part of followers of the new religion, Christianity, he observed,

> If any righteous man among the Christians passes from this world, they rejoice and offer thanks to God, and they escort his body with songs and thanksgiving as if he were setting out from one place to another nearby.[1]

This is the attitude reflected in the early part of this century by the famous English preacher, D. L. Moody. His understanding of the hope of which David wrote was reflected in the words he wrote to a friend near the end of his days:

> Some day you will read in the papers that D. L. Moody of Northfield is dead. Don't you believe a word of it! At that moment, I shall be more alive than I am now. I shall have gone higher, that is all. Out of this old clay tenement, into a house that is immortal. A body that sin cannot touch, that sin cannot taint. A body fashioned into His glorious body. I was born in the flesh in 1837. I was born of the Spirit in 1856. That which is born of the flesh may die. That which is born of the Spirit will live forever.[2]

Moody's perspective—like that of the apostle Paul in 2 Corinthians 5:6—was that to be absent from the body is to be present with the Lord!

Back to Aunt Dorothy

But of course this perspective—the whole idea of the divine power of Christ to give life after death—is a stumbling block for many people. It has been for Dorothy, I reflect, for over eighty years. I stand beside her hospital bed and we talk. But whenever I seek to turn the conversation to spiritual things, she's alert enough to deflect it. "I just don't want to talk about that right now."

At the close of our conversation, I simply say, "Dorothy, I hope you're thinking about these things." I'm a bit surprised when she agrees to my praying with her. My prayer is simple—that God will ease her physical suffering, and help her make a decision based on the things she has heard, one that will prepare her for what lies ahead. I try to avoid "preaching" in my prayer, knowing that she has heard from my parents and others of us in the family who have witnessed to her time after time. After all we plant, we water—God must give the increase.

FAITH AND HOPE

Peter's letter to suffering, scattered Christians begins almost as a reflection of the message he preached on the day of Pentecost. This man of contrast draws a strong contrast—between people who were considered foreigners, scattered throughout the provinces of the Roman Empire, yet lovingly chosen by God, set apart by His Spirit and reborn to a living hope through Jesus Christ, who arose from the dead.

That's where hope ultimately begins—at the point of trusting Christ, at the new birth.

Remarkably, the flight attendant who had taken my boarding pass at the Dallas-Fort Worth International Airport as we were departing for Birmingham, had recognized me. "Didn't you speak at Frazer Memorial Church in Montgomery last year?" When I acknowledged that I had, she said, "That's our church. My husband and I attend there regularly!"

During a break in her responsibilities, we had the opportunity to talk further. Just a couple of years before, Mindy had come to personal faith in Christ. She and her husband were growing in the Savior. Mindy shared how she had discovered a new peace, plus the strength to cope with life's pressures like she had never experienced before. I asked her to pray for my Aunt Dorothy, and she agreed to do so.

Trusting after Betrayal

I thought of another flight attendant with whom I had talked a few months before, on a flight between Dallas and Minneapolis. It turned out that Melanie had heard my radio call-in program over a station in Denver. She told me how for years she had been bitter and deeply hurt because of physical, emotional, and sexual abuse she had suffered for many years as a child. The scars of those experiences had left her closed toward God. Her attitude was understandable—after all, if people you should be able to trust hurt you so badly, how can you trust God?

That's a question I've heard over and over again in my years of ministry—especially in recent years as I've been involved with counseling organizations and Christian radio call-in programs dealing with emotional and spiritual issues.

So many victims of abuse feel that life is totally hopeless —in fact, that's why there's such a high suicide rate among victims of abuse. One beautiful young lady—a close friend of my two daughters—put it to me like this: "How can God love me—when the people who first told me about God did these terrible things to me? What possible use could God have for me? Now I'm just damaged goods. There's no hope."

Tragically, this young lady eventually took her life. Yet for many others, usually slowly, a more positive perspective has dawned. God is different. He's not like the parent who abused me, the authority figure who took advantage of me. He really is good, loving, and kind. He can be trusted. And I can understand this because He was willing to sacrifice His own Son—because He loved me so much.

But beyond that, He had the power to raise from the dead the Son who gave His life for me. That's why whatever I face in life—or even in the face of death—I can have confidence, experience hope, and know that I am secure in Christ.

Hope and Inheritance

This living hope of which Peter speaks is what assures us of the prospect of an inheritance, one that cannot be corrupted or polluted, one that is specifically reserved for us—

who are ourselves kept by the power of the God we have trusted for that ultimate salvation (1 Peter 1:4-5).

How many times have we thought, or even voiced, a sentiment something like this: "If only I had a rich uncle who would die and leave me enough money so I'd be fixed for the rest of my life! I'd be happy from now on. All my worries would be over."

That's exactly what happened to Phil, a factory worker who struggled financially for years. He learned that an uncle —a man he had hardly known—had died, leaving him a fortune in Texas oil and real estate holdings. Phil was ecstatic. His troubles were over! The inheritance was his.

Then, a few months later, the bottom dropped out of the oil market, and Texas real estate came crashing down through the Savings and Loan scandal. Phil ultimately saw his inheritance dwindle to a few thousand dollars—and this was soon gone as a result of his recently adopted lavish life-style.

Bitter, hurt, and angry, Phil found himself worse off than before. His inheritance had simply been a cruel illusion of the security he thought it would provide.

The apostle Peter makes it clear that the inheritance of those who have placed their trust in the Savior can never be corrupted. It doesn't need to be insured by an agency of the federal government—in fact, it's far more secure than the FDIC, the FSLIC or the SIPC! Not only is there a guarantee that there can be no loss of the principle—but the interest itself will continue to grow, compounding and multiplying exponentially, until the time God has designated for this all to be revealed—that time of the appearing of Jesus Christ.

So hope begins with trust in Christ. That was the lesson John Wesley had to learn. He had come to America, served as a missionary among the Indians, preached the gospel. Yet, returning to England from a missionary stint in Georgia, Wesley voiced a crucial question: "I went to America to convert the Indians, but oh, who shall convert me?"

Not long afterward, in 1738, both John Wesley and his brother Charles came to authentic faith. A small group had gathered in Aldersgate Street in London, Wesley among them. From his journal, Wesley describes what happened:

> I felt my heart strangely warmed. I felt I did trust in Christ, Christ alone, for salvation; and an assurance was given to me that He had taken away my sins, even mine, and saved me from the law of sin and death.[3]

For Wesley, it wasn't enough being a religious leader, being good, or even being active in worship—it all boiled down to a matter of trust in Jesus Christ.

For me it happened at the age of seven as I listened to a clear presentation of the simple facts of the gospel by my pastor's brother, who was conducting what we called "revival services." I realized this was what I needed if I were to have any hope of everlasting life.

Responding to the invitation, I sat in the front pew after that service at Westwood Baptist Church near Birmingham, and prayed a simple prayer in which I expressed my faith in Jesus Christ. It wasn't the prayer that saved me. It wasn't coming forward at the close of the service. Those were simply the means by which I expressed my inner commitment to trust Jesus Christ, and Him alone, as my hope of salvation.

Saying 'I Do' To Christ

So what makes this point so special? Many people pray at different times, often asking Christ to come into their lives, asking Him to save them, asking Him to forgive their sins—especially, in many instances, some particular sin.

I like to illustrate the difference this way. As a pastor, I performed numerous weddings. When a couple marries, they stand before God and man and exchange vows. The two most familiar words in the wedding ceremony are the simple words, *"I do."*

Now most couples who marry have used the words "I do" many times in their lives. Perhaps they've even voiced those words to each other in some way. For example, during the courtship he may have said to her, "Do you want to go out to eat tonight?" and she replied, "I do." Or she may have said,

"Do you like this dress?" To which he replied, "I do." Furthermore, either or both of them may have actually participated in some kind of a "pretend wedding" as a child, in which they used those same words.

But there's a difference when a couple says those words in a real wedding. Both of them are of age, both of them understand the implications of what's happening as they voluntarily entrust themselves and the rest of their lives to that special person they are taking as husband or wife. At that point—before God and the company of human witnesses—the words "I do" take on a special significance.

So it is with the believer. Whether alone in the middle of the night at the close of a worship service in Aldersgate, England, or in Westwood, Alabama, or even lying in a hospital bed—when a person simply says "I do" to the Lord Jesus Christ, the transaction is settled. The new birth occurs, the inheritance is ours by designation, and we are reserved to be kept by the power of God!

WHAT ABOUT DOROTHY?

But what about Dorothy? Was she beyond the point of trust? When I left the hospital that Friday evening, May 11, 1990, I frankly felt there was no human hope. A part of me recognized that God was sovereign. Certainly He was capable of pulling off a miracle. But, to be honest, I didn't expect it to happen. I hadn't given up—but I was close.

Through a weekend filled with family gatherings and ministry meetings I kept thinking "What can I do? Is there anything else?" Finally I decided to write Dorothy a letter when I returned to Dallas. If she was so quick to deflect the conversation to another topic when we were talking face to face, perhaps she would "hear me out" on paper.

Finally, that Sunday afternoon, I was sitting in the living room of the home I had grown up in, preparing to speak at 7 o'clock that evening in the church where I had trusted Christ as Savior as a lad of seven so many years before. As time passed, I began feeling more and more an awareness—a constraint—to go back and see Dorothy once more.

I kept putting that feeling out of my mind until Dad came into the living room. In his quiet but persistent way he suggested, "What do you think about you and I going back by to see Dorothy?"

Now no one would confuse my dad with a preacher—but he's a man with a heart for God and for people, nonetheless. He and Mother have carried such a burden for Dorothy through the years; loving her, befriending her, putting up with her hostile, atheistic remarks as she so often ridiculed their faith, reaching out to her when she had first been diagnosed with cancer.

We Devise a Plan

As Dad and I drove the familiar streets of Birmingham to Montclair Medical Center, neither of us said very much. We parked in the garage, then took the elevator to the tenth floor. We had devised a plan. Together we would chat with Dorothy briefly. Then Dad would slip out, "to get the car."

When we entered the room we found that Aunt Dorothy had been turned on her stomach. She was obviously in pain, but was clear-headed. During our conversation she called for some pain medicine. In a few moments the nurse brought it in, and helped her take it. Almost immediately, Dad excused himself, according to plan. Dorothy and I chatted for a moment. Then she looked at me with those sharp eyes. "I'm really hurting. Why don't you do something for me?"

To which I replied, "Dorothy, all I can do is pray for you."

Quietly, she said, "Okay."

So I began praying, "Lord, You love Dorothy more than anybody. You've never stopped loving her all these years. Your Son died in her place. He paid for her sins. You continued to love Dorothy even though she hasn't been interested in spiritual things . . . ."

I was startled when Dorothy interrupted. "But I am. I am," she said.

Hardly daring to believe what was taking place, I simply said, "Well, why don't we do something about it?"

And we did.

So just before 5 o'clock on that Sunday afternoon, the Lord's day, Mother's Day, May 13, 1990, Dorothy, who had never been a mother or a wife, after eighty-two-plus years, most of which were lived in bitterness toward God, experienced the peace and forgiveness of that living hope of which Peter had written. She simply trusted Christ.

When I asked her several questions to determine her level of understanding, she simply nodded and smiled. "I think I feel better, even though I still hurt," she said. It was about all she could say. The pain medication had begun to take effect.

The next day I learned from my aunt, the widow of the uncle for whom I was named, that Uncle Don's faith and willingness to talk about it during the final months of his bout with cancer had made a profound impact on Dorothy. I also learned that a number of painful things that had occurred early in her life had left her bitter toward God—a bitterness she hadn't given up until that Sunday in May so many years later. From my aunt I also learned of the remarkable difference in Dorothy's attitude after she trusted Christ there in her hospital room—the peace she now had, and how the bitterness had seemed to melt away.

Less than seventy-two hours later, Dorothy passed into the presence of the Lord, where, because of this living hope, she will spend all eternity. For most of her more than eight decades, she had lived a life of angry defiance toward God. By word and deed she sought to exclude Him from her life. But ultimately His love had reached out to include her.

Friend, it doesn't matter what you've done, how angry or bitter you've been toward God, or how deeply you've been hurt or how many sins you've committed or what kind, or how hopeless you feel things to be. God's grace can still give you new life and a living hope—if you will, as Dorothy did, simply trust Him.

And what if you have a loved one for whom you've prayed and to whom you've witnessed, who hasn't trusted Christ?

As I walked out of the hospital that Sunday afternoon, I

thought about the people for whom I'd prayed. I thought about a fellow worker whose father for years had declined to trust Christ . . . about a widow who cheerfully witnessed to a husband who simply had no interest in spiritual things . . . about a man who cried out to God regularly for the salvation of an older brother he deeply admired—but who had no use for his faith.

Where there's life there's hope, I thought. Truly we should never give up.

HOPE IN ADVERSITY

But there's more to Peter's message about hope than just its perspective on the future. He also tells his readers, "In this, you greatly rejoice, even though at the present time you are facing great difficulty because of a variety of trials" (1 Peter 1:6).

When psychiatrist Scott Peck began his book *The Road Less Traveled* with that simple, yet profound statement, "Life is difficult," he didn't tell us anything we didn't know. The people to whom the apostle Peter was writing were well acquainted with just how tough life can be. In fact, these early Christians probably could have written extensively on the subject of suffering. Many had encountered economic reverses, the loss of family and friends, being forced to relocate, physical suffering, the death of close relatives—and undoubedtly a number of them eventually gave their own lives because of their faith.

Some of them probably felt like giving up. Knowing the difficulty they faced and the temptation to throw in the towel, Peter shifts from simple statements of fact about our salvation and hope to a series of strong imperatives designed to motivate his readers not to give up under pressure.

In essence, what he tells them is that hope persists, even in the face of what seems like hopeless adversity. The wording in the literal King James translation, "gird up the loins of your mind" (1:13), paints a picture in the mind's eye. We see a man wearing a long robe who gathers up its folds, then tucks them into his belt in order to be able to move quickly.

Perhaps Peter had girded up his own robe as he and John raced to the tomb, after Mary Magdalene told them that Jesus was no longer in it. One commentator translates Peter's phrase here in 1:13, "Pull yourselves together," as a comparable English idiom.[4] "Prepare your minds for action," he warns his readers. "Stay sober—not only unintoxicated, but self-disciplined, using discretion and sound judgement."

The final component of Peter's program of mental exercise involves "setting your hope fully on the grace to be bestowed at the appearance of Jesus Christ" (13b). In short, Peter's instruction to believers under the gun is to *live with heaven in view.* Like Paul's reminder to live one day at a time while focusing on eternity (2 Corinthians 4:15-16), Peter's warning underscores the importance of proper focus.

Perhaps the experience that taught him most about that is something most of us can't relate to. After all, unless we know where the stumps are, we've never walked on water!

Walking Above the Storm

It happened late one stormy night, when the disciples were in the middle of a terrible storm on the lake of Galilee. Things seemed hopeless, when suddenly they spotted Jesus coming toward them across the water. Their first terse response was "It's a ghost!" Then they recognized the familiar face of their master, their Rabbi. Peter's response was both impulsive and immediate. "Lord if it's really you, let me come to you on the water!"

When the Lord agreed, Peter stepped over the side of the boat and onto the water—which supported his weight completely. Now most of us have walked on many different surfaces—concrete, asphalt, grass, perhaps a rope ladder suspended over a stream, or a trampoline. Some are firmer than others, some pretty unstable. Unlike water, all will support your weight. But for Peter, in this one incredible moment, the water actually supported his weight.

Now this happened just a few hours after Jesus had miraculously fed more than 5,000 men, plus women and children, with five cakes of bread and two small fish. Peter knew

Jesus' power—and at first he was utilizing that power, focusing on the Lord, walking toward his Savior. But when he took his eyes off the Lord and began to examine his circumstances—the storm, and the violence of the wind and waves—he became fearful and started to sink (Matthew 14:30). At this point, again impulsively—but with the right impulse—he cried, "Lord, save me!" Immediately Jesus reached out, caught him, then shared a pointed lesson, *"Oh you of little faith. Why did you doubt?"* (vs. 31).

Perhaps Peter had this remarkable experience in mind when he wrote, "Fix your hope completely on Christ." Don't look at the surrounding winds of adversity. Don't let the waves of trouble overwhelm you. Sure, life is tough. Things seem hopeless. But fix your hope completely, discipline your minds, focus on the ultimate outcome—claim the grace to live in light of the return of Jesus Christ!

When Jesus and Peter stepped into the boat, two things happened. One was totally abnormal, the other should be the norm. Immediately the storm ceased—that rarely happens, particularly not with the kind of timing the disciples witnessed. They knew this was no coincidence.

Yet their response was precisely what we need today. *They worshipped.* And their worship was directed toward Jesus, as they confessed, "You are truly who You claim to be, the Son of God!"

At times, even those of us who have fixed our hope on the risen Christ for salvation can lose sight of this truth, especially when we face impossible circumstances. Peter warns us not to lose sight of the awesome power that is ours— power we can apply for holy living, godly conduct, in every area of life ... power to see the Father answer prayer in an awesome manner ... power to maintain a solid doctrinal foundation, based on a hunger for and application of the Word where we find unfolded the details of our "faith in hope" that rest in Him (1 Peter 1:21, 23) ... power for effective witness, an appropriate response to everyone who asks, "a reason of the hope that is in you" (3:15) . . . power to respond in meekness toward men and fear toward God, with a clear conscience . . . power that leads to an authentic love for brothers and sisters in the Body of Christ.

HOPE FOR THE U.S.S.R.

For years I had carried the burden—as had others among my family and friends—to see Dorothy come to Christ. Yet I realized just how small that burden was some time ago, when I was introduced to a man who for years had carried a burden for an entire nation—one that was officially atheistic, and had been for many decades. It was a nation larger than our own, stretching across eleven time zones, a nation where anywhere from 10 to 20 million people—Aleksandr Solzhenitsyn, in his *Gulag Archipelago*, estimates between 60 and 70 million— died under the oppressive atheistic Soviet Russian state.

The man to whom I was introduced in a hotel in Washington, D.C., was a stout, rugged-looking man with a wrinkled face, thinning gray hair, and a pleasant look. For almost fifty years, Alex Leonovich, a native of Russia who came to the United States at the age of seven, had given his life to producing Christian radio programs and broadcasting them back into the Soviet Union.

I was amazed to hear what had happened to Alex and several other Christians just a few months earlier. Even Alex admitted that at times he had given up hope that the gospel would ever penetrate his homeland. Sure, the Berlin Wall had come down. But to see the might of the Soviet Bear toppled also seemed impossible. Even with *glasnost* and *perestroika*, many still had questions—were the reforms simply superficial, a camouflage preceding even more intense persecution of anything or anyone Christian? It could still happen.

Yet a sovereign God, according to the prophet Daniel of old, controls history, raising up kings and putting others down (Daniel 2:21). But of all the developments in recent history, perhaps even more shocking that the breaching of the Berlin Wall the previous year, was the collapse of the Soviet government during the fall of 1990. In October, 1990, the still-existing Union of Soviet Socialist Republics adopted a freedom of conscience law which formally abolished restrictions on religious faith and outlawed government sponsorship of campaigns to promote atheism. A short time later, the Union itself collapsed, to be replaced by a Commonwealth of Independent States.

The most amazing thing I heard from Alex Leonovich was the story of a man whose pleasant face I had encountered the day before on the elevator in the hotel. I had seen him on the platform at one of the sessions of the National Religious Broadcasters. He was Konstantine Lubenchenko, former chairman of the Supreme Soviet.

A Mere Coincidence?

Within the preceding year, dramatic changes were occurring throughout the Soviet Union, moving that formerly totalitarian state toward democratic reforms. So Lubenchenko decided to come to the United States to see democracy up close. Humanly it seemed a coincidence—although we know it wasn't—that he wound up staying at the Sheraton Washington Hotel the very week of the National Religious Broadcasters convention!

Alex chuckled as he reminisced over how he had met Lubenchenko. His wife, also attending the convention, happened to overhear Lubenchenko speaking Russian in the lobby. She and her husband introduced themselves, and, by the next day, had arranged for Lubenchenko to attend the presidential prayer breakfast, where the Soviet leader actually met President George Bush!

Later I picked up the details on how that seemingly chance contact led to Project Christian Bridge. Alex Leonovich, author Philip Yancey, pastor John Acre—a former U.S. intelligence agent—and other evangelical Christian leaders were invited to Russia to meet with the highest officials of the then Soviet Union, including Mikhail Gorbachev.[5]

Remarkably, this group of men wound up in a meeting in Lubyanka, the headquarters of the KGB—the Russian secret police! Lubyanka's basement housed the most notorious of Russia's numerous prisons. Yet in that very building this small group of Christians met with General Nikolai Stolyarov, vice chairman of the KGB in charge of personnel. It was a meeting that no fiction writer would ever have dared put into a book, for the subject raised by Stolyarov was not *détente,* but national and individual *repentance.*

The meeting concluded as Alex Leonovich, president of Slavic Missionary Service, whose uncle had died in the gulag, expressed forgiveness in the spirit of Christ. Then the KGB leader and the Russian Christian embraced in what must surely have been one of the strongest Russian bear hugs in history! Finally, in that room in the Lubyanka Prison, home of the KGB, in the heart of the capital of what for decades had been an atheistic state, the meeting was closed in prayer to the God of Heaven!

Opening Closed Doors

To Alex it was the capstone in a remarkable opening of seemingly hopelessly-closed doors. For now hundreds of millions of citizens of the former Soviet Union, who had never before had the opportunity, could hear and respond to the hope available through Jesus Christ.

Shortly after that historic meeting, Alex Leonovich would reminisce, "I have seen the promised land. I am ready for glory!"[6] Although he chided himself, then and since, for his own lack of persistence in faith, who among us could have thought such incredible events could occur? And even if the door were to swing shut—if repression were to return to the former Soviet Union as a way of life—who can deny the incredible opportunities—Christian broadcasts, Bibles, evangelistic efforts, which began to spread the hope of Jesus Christ across that vast land?

With government cooperation even beyond what can be seen in the United States, the good news continues to be rapidly spread to the diverse peoples of the Russian republics. For hundreds of millions of people for whom spiritual hope seemed nonexistent, hope is now a present reality with a future perspective! These changes in the former stronghold of unbelief illustrate the power of the living hope that is ours in Jesus Christ. They call us to hope to the end.

Atheists are coming to the Savior—both here and abroad!

There is hope!

HOW SHOULD WE THEN LIVE?

The evidence is clear: We must not quit.

No one gave the 1980 U.S. Hockey Team a chance at Lake Placid, New York. Everyone knew the Russians were as superior to the young, fuzzy-cheeked Americans as the Super Bowl champions of the NFL would be compared to a small-college football squad. But those American Olympic hockey players, against all odds, never gave up. We still refer to their victory as "The Miracle on Ice."

'It Ain't Over 'til Its Over!'

At the beginning of the 1991 baseball season, not every sports authority agreed who the best teams in major league baseball were. But most people agreed that there were few teams less likely to wind up in the World Series than the Atlanta Braves and the Minnesota Twins. After all, both had finished last in their division the previous year. No one in his right mind would have predicted that these two teams would persist through the ups and downs of a 162-game season to wind up winning their respective divisions, defeating the other two division winners, then facing each other in a dramatic seven-game World Series. But as the immortal baseball philosopher and famed catcher Yogi Berra once put it, "It ain't over till it's over."

On this point Paul and Peter strongly agree. The final word from the apostle to the Gentiles is, "We must never give up." And from the big fisherman the last word is, "Hope to the end."

We must live in light of the hope that is ours in Christ, not giving up in adversity, not giving in to the temptation of the flesh or of an evil society, not giving up in persistent prayer or faithful witness—even when it seems the prayers bring no answer other than Wait, when the witness seems to fall on deaf ears, when the temptations intensify.

Don't Give Up!

To the exhausted housewife I plead, Don't give up. Don't let the drudgery of the daily grind rob you of the joy of your steadfast hope!

To the burned out business executive I encourage, Don't give up. Your job may be on the line, your future insecure, your performance slipping, your exhaustion quotient rising. But wait on the Lord. Renew your strength. Don't throw in the towel!

To the weary pastor, missionary, or vocational Christian worker I say, Please don't give up. We're in a war! It's exhausting. But there's greater danger to the one who slows down. Sure, you're unappreciated. No doubt about it. It seems at times that God is sending all the blessings the other direction, and the problems toward you. You're not sure how much more you can stand. But you've found God faithful in the past. You remember the sense of His calling you experienced earlier. And although that memory may be faint—blunted by the blows of circumstance and the winds of adversity—open your eyes, catch sight of the banner of hope fluttering in the breeze. Don't give up!

To the lonely, perplexed single parent I plead, Don't give up. Don't walk away from the priority of your relationship with Christ—even though you've been deeply hurt, perhaps to the point of disillusionment, perhaps in the tragedy of divorce. Don't turn away from God—even though some of God's people may have turned away from you! They may have trouble accepting you. He doesn't. He never shames us, even when our performance doesn't measure up to His standards. He accepts us in His beloved Son—and He gives us strength to handle the multitude of incredible demands faced by you and thousands like you.

Christ can even meet those deepest of needs—and meet them far better than the temptations that sometimes present themselves as the best way out. He can give you grace, not simply for the rest of life, but for one day at a time, one moment at a time, one difficulty at a time. So please, please—don't give up.

To the frustrated teenager, trying to overcome conflicts at home, sorely tempted to give in to the temptations of life, confused over many issues, struggling with questions about your faith . . .

To the frightened, lonely senior citizen feeling abandoned, rejected, not knowing what the future holds, trying to somehow stretch a retirement income to cover rising medical and food costs, wondering if life has lost its meaning . . .

To the victim of childhood abuse, struggling with suicidal thoughts, feeling like a totally worthless reject, but unable to share those feelings with others, battling the performance traps of life . . .

To all these I urge, Don't give up.

And to the person on the brink of despair, feeling there's no hope of salvation for you—that somehow you've committed the unpardonable sin—I say, Don't give up.

Dorothy and Sir Winston

What a tragedy! Sir Winston Churchill—the man whose encouraging words, "Never give in, never, never give in" galvanized and motivated a nation—lay on his deathbed. As he thought about the conditions in the world in which he had played such an heroic role, he sighed, "There is no hope."[6]

And with that he died.

What a contrast to Dorothy, who passed from decades of looking at a hopeless end, to a life that ended with an endless hope.

I've had to learn it the hard way. Perhaps you have as well. But let's not forget the lesson. God has provided strength for today. And our hope for tomorrow—and for eternity—is bright indeed.

So let's never give up. Never.

Chapter 1

1. Michael P. Green, ed., *Illustrations for Biblical Preaching* (Grand Rapids: Baker Book House, 1982), p. 194.

2. Karl Menninger, *The Vital Balance* (New York: Viking Press, 1963), p. 276—citing the futility of what he termed "hopeless physicians presiding over hopeless patients."

3. Ibid., pp. 384-85.

4. Gary R. Collins, *Beyond Easy Believism* (Waco, TX: Word Books, 1982).

5. Ibid., p. 171.

6. *The Funk & Wagnells Standard Desk Dictionary,* Vol. I (New York: Harper & Row, 1986), p. 309.

7. Menninger, op. cit., p. 384.

8. Ibid., p. 384.

9. Collins, op. cit., p. 168.

10. Gerhard Kittle, ed., *Theological Word Dictionary of the New Testament* (Grand Rapids: Wm. B. Eerdmans, 1964), Vol. II, p. 527.

11. Nigel Turner, *Christian Words* (Nashville: Thomas Nelson, 1981), p. 215.

12. Zig Ziglar, *Dear Family* (Gretna, LA: Pelican Publishing Co., 1984, pp. 194-95.

Chapter 2

1. *International Standard Bible Encyclopedia,* James Orr, ed., (Grand Rapids: Wm. B. Eerdmans, 1939), Vol. III, p. 1419.

2. R. Laird Harris, Gleason L. Archer, Jr., and Bruce K. Waltke, *Theological Word Book of the Old Testament* (Chicago: Moody Press, 1981), Vol. I, p. 102.

3. Ibid., p. 859.

4. Turner, *Christian Words*, p. 213.

5. Plato, *Laws* (from about 664 B.C.).

6. Sophocles, *Antigone* (p. 615ff.)

7. Plato, op. cit., p. 898.

8. Kittel, op. cit., p. 527.

9. Turner, op. cit., p. 214.

10. W. E. Vine, *Expository Dictionary of New Testament Words* (Old Tappan, NJ: Flueman-Revelle, 1940).

Chapter 3

1. Vine, op. cit., p. 69.

2. W. F. Arndt and F. W. Gingrich, trans. *A Greek-English Lexicon of the New Testament* by W. Bauer (Chicago: University of Chicago Press, 1957).

3. A. T. Robertson, *Word Pictures in the New Testament*, (Nashville: The Broadman Press, 1930), Vol. II, p. 231.

Chapter 5

1. Funk & Wagnells, op. cit.

2. N. Kline, "Practical Management of Depression," *Journal of the American Medical Association,* Vol. 198, pp. 732-40.

3. Harold Wolff, "What Hope Does for Man," *Saturday Review,* Jan 5, 1957), cited by Menninger, *The Vital Balance,* p. 390.

4. Frans M. J. Brandt, *Victory Over Depression* (Grand Rapids: Baker Book House, 1968), p. 19.

5. Harold Kaplan, M.D. and Benjamin Sadock, M.D., *Synopsis of Psychiatry*, 5th ed. (Baltimore: Williams & Wilkins, 1988).

6. Loc. cit.

7. Timothy Bright, *A Treatise of Melancholia*, cited in Kaplan and Sadock, op. cit., p. 3.

8. Charles Swindoll, *Growing Strong in the Seasons of Life* (Portland: Multnomah Press), p. 45.

9. *Diagnostic and Statistical Manual of Mental Disorders,* 3rd ed., revised. (Washington, D.C.: American Psychiatric Association, 1987).

10. Kaplan and Sadock, p. 291.

11. Gary R. Collins, *Christian Counseling: A Comprehensive Guide* (Waco, TX: Word Publishing, 1980), p. 85.

12. Francis Brown, S. R. Driver, and C. A. Briggs, *Hebrew and English Lexicon of the Old Testament* (London: The Oxford Press, 1907), p. 588.

13. G. Abbott-Smith, *Manual Greek Lexicon of the New Testament*, 3rd ed. (Edinburgh: T. & T. Clark, 1937), p. 159.

Chapter 6

1. Alden Gannett, *How to Keep Your Eyes on God When They're Full of Tears* (Birmingham, AL: Gannett Ministries, n.d.), p. 5.

2. Roy B. Zuck, "Job," *The Bible Knowledge Commentary* (Chicago: Victor Books, 1983, Vol. I, p. 721.

Chapter 7

1. Elizabeth Kübler-Ross, *On Death and Dying* (New York, MacMillan Company, 1969).

2. James Dobson, "The Tribute," in *Straight Talk to Men and Their Wives* (Waco, TX: Word Publishing, 1980).

3. C. Everett Koop and Elizabeth Koop, *Sometimes Mountains Move* (Wheaton: Tyndale House, 1979), p. 40.

4. *Christian Counseling,* p. 351.

5. C. S. Lewis, *A Grief Observed* (New York: Seabury Press, 1961).

Chapter 8

1. Lehman Strauss, *In God's Waiting Room* (Grand Rapids: Radio Bible Class, 1984), p. 7.

2. Catherine Marshall, *Beyond Ourselves* (New York: McGraw-Hill, 1961), p. 39.

3. Walter Hendrichsen, *After the Sacrifice* (Grand Rapids: Zondervan Publishing House, 1979), p. 83.

Chapter 9

1. Charles Colson, *Kingdoms in Conflict* (Grand Rapids: Morrow & Zondervan, 1987), p. 272.

2. Ibid., p. 270.

3. Joel Freeman, *God Is Not Fair* (San Bernardino, CA: Here's Life Publishers, 1987), p. 68.

Chapter 10

1. Colson, op. cit., pp. 273-74.

Chapter 11

1. Jim Hedlund, *The Gospel Message*, Vol. 100, No. 1, 1992, p. 4.

Chapter 12

1. *Here I Stand: The Life of Martin Luther* (Nashville: Abingdon Press, 1950), p. 144.

2. Mark Bubeck, *Overcoming the Adversary* (Chicago: Moody Press, 1984), pp. 82-83.

3. Frank E. Peretti, *This Present Darkness* (Westchester, IL: Crossway Books, 1986).

Chapter 13

1. Walter C. Kaiser, Jr., *A Biblical Approach to Suffering* (Chicago: Moody Press, 1982), p. 79.

2. *Theological Word Book of the Old Testament,* p. 305.

3. Katherine D. Sakenfeld, "The Meaning of Hesed in the Hebrew Bible, a New Inquiry," loc. cit.

4. Robert McGee, *The Search for Significance* (Houston: Rapha Publishing, 1987), p. 73.

5. John Woodbridge, ed. *Great Leaders of the Christian Church* (Chicago: Moody Press, 1988), p. 322.

6. C. W. E. Nagelsbach, "The Lamentations of Jeremiah," *Lange's Commentary* (New York: Scribner-Armstrong, 1870), p. 117.

Chapter 14

1. Vaclav Havel, in *The Readers Digest,* February 1991, p. 179.

2. Vine, op. cit., p. 572.

3. Ibid.

Chapter 15

1. Paul Lee Tan, *Encyclopedia of 7700 Illustrations* (Rockville, MD: Assurance Publishers, 1979), p. 308.

2. Ibid.

3. John Woodbridge, ed., *Great Leaders of the Christian Church* (Chicago: Moody Press, 1988), p. 291.

4. E. G. Selwyn, quoted in *The Expositor's Bible Commentary,* Frank Gaebelein, ed., (Grand Rapids: Zondervan Publishing House, 1981), Vol. 12, p. 223.

5. See the fascinating details of this meeting in Philip Yancey, *Praying with the KGB* (Portland: Multnomah Press, 1992).

6. Yancey, op. cit., p. 37.

7. Colson, op. cit., p. 369.